Way to Liberation

Mokṣa-Mārga

An Itinerary in Indian Philosophy

Way to Liberation
Mokṣa-Mārga
An Itinerary in Indian Philosophy

T.K. Sribhashyam
Alamelu Sheshadri

D.K. Printworld (P) Ltd.
Publishers of Indian Traditions

Cataloging in Publication Data — DK

[Courtesy: D.K. Agencies (P) Ltd. <docinfo@dkagencies.com>]

Sribhashyam, T. K.

Way to liberation : mokṣa-mārga : an itinerary in Indian philosophy / T.K. Sribhashyam, Alamelu Sheshadri.

p. cm.

Includes bibliographical references (p.) and index.

ISBN 13: 9788124605981 (Hb)

1. Mokṣa. 2. Philosophy, Indic. I. Sheshadri, Alamelu, joint author. II. Title.

DDC 181.483 22

ISBN 13: 978-81-246-0598-1 (Hb) ISBN 10: 81-246-0598-X
ISBN 13: 978-81-246-0599-8 (Pb) ISBN 10: 81-246-0599-8

First published in India in 2011

Published and printed by:
D.K. Printworld (P) Ltd.
Regd. Office: '*Vedaśrī*', F-395, Sudarshan Park
(Metro Station: Ramesh Nagar)
New Delhi - 110 015
Phones: (011) 2545 3975; 2546 6019; *Fax*: (011) 2546 5926
E-mail: indology@dkprintworld.com
Website: www.dkprintworld.com

To the revered memory of our Parents

Mucchukunte Sri T. Krishnamacharya

and

Srimati Namagiriammal,

with profound respects and gratitude

Life Sketch of Sri T. Krishnamacharya

Sri T. Krishnamacharya, also called Muchukunte Krishnamacharya, was born in Muchukunte, Karnataka, south India in 1888. Sri T. Krishnamacharya belonged to a family of philosophers and spiritual Masters. He was the eldest of five children.

The majority of his studies were done in Varanasi (Benares) and Calcutta (Kolkata), strongholds of traditional Hindu philosophy where he quickly obtained the highest distinction in all the branches of Hindu philosophy. He mastered Hindu *yoga* in the Himalayas and Buddhist *yoga* in Burma, then part of India. Later, he went to Cashmere (Kashmir) to study Sūfīsm. He taught Hindu philosophy at the Banaras Hindu University and Calcutta University before accepting the king of Mysore's invitation to teach Hindu philosophy at Mysore Sanskrit College. Like his forefathers, he taught the king and was appointed a philosopher of the Royal Court.

As a Master of Philosophy, Sri T. Krishnamacharya was invited by many Indian Royal Courts and Monasteries to participate in the Philosophical Debates, characteristic of Indian Culture since time immemorial. He emerged victorious, not only in his arguments, but in his ability to explain the application of Hindu philosophy, to the general public in a simple and convincing way. In addition, he had mastered 15 Indian languages, was an astrologer, musician, sportsman and refined cook.

In the 1920s, Sri T. Krishnamacharya began teaching *yoga* to the Royal Family and residents of Mysore. With time, he gave increasing importance to the teaching of *yoga*. He always integrated the philosophical aspects of *yoga* when practising or teaching. Around 1935, Sri T. Krishnamacharya taught his first non-Indian students. These were Europeans, and as their numbers increased, he taught himself English in order to teach them in English. He lived in Mysore till 1954 when he moved to Madras (Chennai) where he lived until his death in 1989.

Sri T. Krishnamacharya had six children, three sons and three daughters. His wife, Srimati Namagiriammal as well as his children were taught by him. Sri T. Krishnamacharya continued to teach his family until his death.

Sri T. Krishnamacharya never abused his position. He refused the rewards offered by the king and the Royal Courts and lived on the modest income earned as an inspector of a coffee plantation, carrying sand and stones for construction projects and practising Indian Medicine (Āyurveda). He even conceded his rich inheritance to his brother and sisters in order to remain true to his philosophical principles.

Sri T. Krishnamacharya taught *yoga* to his wife's brother, Sri B.K.S. Iyengar. Following the ancient tradition, Sri B.K.S. Iyengar, born in 1918, lived in his master's house and started teaching *yoga* at the age of 15. Apart from both the authors, Sri T. Krishnamacharya taught his eldest son, Sri T.K. Srinivasan, who was born in 1936, Indian philosophy and *yoga* right from his childhood. The gained insights made Sri T.K. Srinivasan, also called Muchukunte Anna, become an outstanding scholar in Mīmāṁsā and Tarka philosophies. He lectures in Sanskrit in traditional Vedānta monasteries, Sanskrit institutions as well as to PhD students in some universities in India. Furthermore, Sri T.K. Srinivasan holds a university degree in law. Sri T.K.V. Desikachar, born in 1938, the second son of Sri T. Krishnamacharya, first completed his university degree before studying under his father in the 1960s.

He refused distinguished positions offered by courts and monasteries in order to maintain his liberty and freedom in teaching. His wife, Srimathi Namagiriammal followed his example and shared his simple life. For Sri T. Krishnamacharya and his children she represented a living philosophy.

While Sri T. Krishnamacharya was a strict practising Hindu, he had great respect for all religious, traditional or contemporary thoughts.

His open-mindedness brought him to meet many spiritual heads of other faiths. Many religious chiefs, head of states, *yoga* masters and philosophers came to learn under him. He respected their need for confidentiality and never used these relations for his own personal benefit or advantage.

Genealogy

EVER since the ninth century the philosophy of Viśiṣṭādvaita Vedānta has been transmitted from generation to generation by the authors' ancestors. This traditional teaching has been bestowed upon both the authors of this book.

Srimathi Alamelu Sheshadri and Sri T.K. Sribhashyam are two of the six children of Srimathi Namagiriammal and Sri T. Krishnamacharya.

Paternal Genealogy:

Īśvaramuni also called Īśvara Bhaṭṭa (ninth century)

Nātha Muni (son of Īśvaramuni) (ninth century)

Īśvaramuni (son of Nātha Muni) (tenth century)

Āḷavaṇḍār also called Yāmunācārya (son of Īśvaramuni) (917-1042)

Devarāja (son of Āḷavaṇḍār) (949-)

Mahāpūrṇa Perianambi (son of Devarāja) (973-)

Śrī Kurukeśa (son of Mahāpūrṇa Perianambi) (1062)

Thirumalai Śrīnivāsācārya (fifteenth century)

Śrīnivāsā Tātācāriyar (sixteenth century)

Śrī Śrīnivāsā Brahma Tantra Parakāla Swamy (Spiritual Head of Śrī Parakala Maṭha, Mysore (1790-1860?)

Appaiah Dīkṣitar (son of Śrī Śrīnivāsā Brahma Tantra Parakāla Swamy (1800-69)

Śeṣa Dīkṣitar (son of Appaiah Dīkṣitar 1820-70?)

Śrīnivāsā Tātācāriyar (son of Śeṣa Dīkṣitar).

Śrī T. Krishnamacharya also called Sri Muchukunte Krishnamacharya (son of Śrīnivāsā Tātācāriyar) (1888-1989).

Maternal Genealogy (by courtesy of Sri B.K.S. Iyengar, the authors' maternal uncle).

Śrī Mudambi Varadācārya (brother of Śrī Rāmānuja, founder of Viśiṣṭādvaita Vedānta) — fourteenth century.

Śrī Mudambi Antācārya

Śrī Hastagiri Annan, disciple of Śrī Vedānta Deśika (a disciple of Śrī Rāmānuja). He conquered Śrī Narasiṁha Mishra, a great master of Advaita Vedānta, in a philosophical debate.

Śrī Antācārya — honoured by the king of Bangalore for his knowledge of Viśiṣṭādvaita — received the land of Vellur (at present Bellur, 50 km to the east of Bangalore) as a gift.

Śrī Vallur Alagiya Manavaḷa Perumāḷ

Śrī Vallur Govindācār

Śrī Vallur Anantācār

Śrī Vallur Aṣṭa Putra Śrīnivāsācār

Śrī Vallur Govindācār

Śrī Vallur Śrīnivasācār

Śrī Bellur (ex-Vallur) Rāmānujācār

Śrī Bellur Govindācār

Śrī Bellur Śrīnivasācār who propagated Viśiṣṭādvaita in Gujarat and Rajasthan

Śrī Bellur Kṛṣṇamācār

Śrīmati Bellur Namagiriammal (daughter of Bellur Kṛṣṇamācār) (1912-86)

Benediction by Sri B.K.S. Iyengar

I AM delighted to hear that my nephew, Sri T.K. Sribhashyam, and my niece, Alamelu Sheshadri, have undertaken to kindle the spirit of *bhakti* in order to experience the pure, unalloyed and untainted blissful state, which springs out from the path of love without the tinge of lust.

Patañjali deals with *bhakti-mārga* at the very beginning of the text with *Īśvara Praṇidhāna* (*Yogasūtra*, I.23). This is sufficient proof to trace that *aṣṭāṅga yoga* begins with *bhakti-mārga* as its practice takes the practitioner towards the realisation of God.

Actually, it is Patañjali who defines God as a Supreme Being, totally free from conflicts, unaffected by actions, untouched by cause and effect. *Kleśa karma vipāka aśayaiḥ aparāmṛṣṭaḥ puruṣaviśeṣaḥ īśvaraḥ* (*Yogasūtra*, I.24).

While concluding the text Patañjali explains that when one is freed from the fourfold aims of life (*puruṣārtha*), he transcends the qualities of nature (*guṇa*) and establishes in its purity of the self — the *puruṣa*.

In this foundation of pristine purity in the consciousness he automatically gets transformed to become a true *bhakta* (devotee) of God.

It means that one reaches God after self-realisation. Or it means self-realisation is the springboard to leap towards experiencing God. In order to achieve this quality of pure consciousness, one has to make an effortful effort to sublimate *prakṛti śakti* (power of body), earn *yukti* (skilful intelligence or ripe intelligence) which definitely leads the *bhakta* towards *bhakti* and qualifies him to the noblest part of total surrender towards God — *śaraṇāgati yoga*.

When *jñāna* reaches that ripe state, the quality of surrender develops in *bhakti* and gets established in him. The *bhakti sādhaka* surrenders all his thoughts and works to the Lord.

For an average individual, this approach to devotion consistently depends upon the way of developing *śārīrika śakti* and earning *jñāna* in order to attain the skilfulness or *yukti* for *bhakti* to grow.

The way to liberation (*mokṣa*) needs perfect knowledge, perfect action and perfect surrender to the Lord. The *bhakta* becomes a *bhāgavata* in every aspect; he not only knows and sees but lives as a true servant of God and thus uses his words (*yukti*), work (*śakti*) and wisdom (*bhakti*) as if it is from the grace of God, and leads a spiritual happy life with contentment (*anuttama sukha*) as if it is the words of God.

I pray to the Lord to grace the authors for their efforts in treading the path of *bhakti*. May their works of action and words of wisdom touch the hearts of all readers so that they too reach this destination of total surrender commonly known as *śaraṇāgati yoga*.

Pune, India
8 September 2006

Preface

> We meditate upon that Supreme One, who has the neck and face of a horse, who has a radiant, blemish-free crystal body, who is the embodiment of Divine Knowledge and Bliss, and who is the support of all branches of learning.
>
> — An invocation to Lord Hayagrīva, the God of knowledge and wisdom

MIND is like the wandering moon. There are always fluctuations in the emotional conditions. This is natural in all living beings. However, man is capable of stabilising his emotional agitations by personal efforts through various methods. The easiest and successful way is to make sincere appeal to God with love. This type of emotional loving approach to God is *bhakti* (devotion). *Bhakti* is supreme love to God. Love springs from God and enters into the human heart. The abundant treasure of God's love is hidden in the human heart. That is to say, the human heart is overflowing with God's love. Man has only to realise this wealth of God's love in him and feel its richness. God shelters man from the scorching miseries of life, when man clings to God. Loving shelter from God is the reward of *bhakti* practice.

Showering a brilliant light amid gloomy darkness, radiating the sweet fragrance of life, bringing reconciliation to all contradictions are (some of) the gifts of *bhakti*, in spite of innumerable contradicting views. *Bhakti* is the golden bridge which links man on earth to the divine paradise. To train the mind for divinity, there is no road equal to devotion, *bhakti*. Words fail to bring out the pleasure of devotional practices (*bhakti sādhanā*).

Complete trust in God is capable of making man remain unconcerned to the problems of life, as they just pass off by themselves by God's grace.

Only a man who knows the place can tell the right direction to reach it. Our father, Sri T. Krishnamacharya of Mysore, infused *bhakti* in his children and in his disciples right from the beginning. God's blessings and our father's sailing grace helped us to move on in this writing.

In the name of God, this work is dedicated to our father — our *guru*, with profound respect and gratitude.

In a work on *bhakti*, it is unavoidable to use Sanskrit terms. The use of such terms is minimised and the nearest English equivalent is provided. An exhaustive glossary is appended. This work does fall short of the degree of excellence that might be attained.

We offer our deep gratitude to Cornelia Heyde from Germany for the sincere interest she has taken in our writings, going through the major part of this work, offering useful and valuable comments and thus helping in the completion of the work.

We owe our sincere thanks to all our well-wishers who helped us in one way or the other to make this book come to light.

Above all, there is the grace of God.

O! Almighty, lead us from darkness to light.
— *Bṛhadāraṇyka Upaniṣad*, I.3.28

Presentation

THOUGH man acquires and enjoys the material life to his satisfaction, he still feels dissatisfied and he fails to understand the reason. This is because he is in need of peace and real happiness. He takes this as a major suffering in his life. Man suffers, because he identifies his soul with the conglomeration of body and mind. He wants a sort of freedom that he is unable to explain for himself. This state of freedom so badly needed, freedom from suffering and freedom from the sensation of bondage is liberation (*mokṣa*). It is obtained when this identification ceases and consciousness too ceases with it. Through devotion, the hook that binds the soul to the created world (*prakṛti*) with its modes is released and the bondage does not reappear. Man finds his ultimate joy through this liberation.

Mokṣa is the direct path to perfection. It leads to the very heart of the Self-consciousness. It is the final approach to the purity and the perfection of the soul.

Happiness is the universal aim of life. True happiness of human beings does not lie in the possession of external things, but in the attainment of the higher mind and spirit, that is to say, in the development of what is the innermost part in us. It may mean pain and restraint, but it will lead us to joy and freedom.

Our mind has a tremendous power. Every individual mind is the master of its destiny and the maker of its body and circumstances. It is the mind that gives us our desired objects. It can create its own body; it can change the form of the body by its own intense and repeated imagination. It can create physical disorders and its own disorder too. In other words, whatever the mind determines to experience, no other agency can withstand. Bondage and freedom are states of mind too and are determined by it. Bondage is due to our wrong belief that we are finite beings. Freedom from ignorance, wrong knowledge and the firm conviction of being one with the Absolute Reality constitute *mokṣa*. Realising the absolute is to know the truth and live accordingly. Our knowledge of the truth should go beyond a mere belief; it should become a living experience.

The subject is vast and every effort will be made to clarify the points to enable the reader to feel at ease and to suit the present- day life.

All the presentations in the write-ups are taken from the great teachers of the past, who served the individuals as torchbearers to achieve the goal of spiritual realisation. We owe all our knowledge to these souls of the past, who invested much effort in making man reach his higher planes of consciousness, thereby helping him to develop his soul together with physical developments in the process of evolution of his life. We owe our gratitude to our father and *guru* who repeatedly quoted them in all his "classes" as he used to call his lessons.

> The lotus-plan of wisdom that has seen the sun of Consciousness and is bearing the blossoms of virtue, blooms with a pure and superior lustre, beautiful like the sky at dawn.
>
> — *Vāsiṣṭha Darśana*, III.7.11

List of Tables and Figures

Contents

1

Hinduism

A Brief Perspective

> May we ever unswervingly follow the path of duty as do the sun and the moon!
> May we always serve humanity without demanding the price of our service!
> May we ever be benevolent, kind, self-sacrificing, detached and adjustable!
> May we surrender all and serve humanity like the sun and the moon!
> —*Ṛgveda*, 5.51.15

HINDUISM is perhaps the oldest of all the living religions even though it is more a philosophy of life than a religious doctrine. It has neither any definite date of its origin nor has it any definite founder associated with it. It is called Sanātana Dharma meaning laws coming down from eternity. Nearly every religion of the world is associated with a definite personality claimed to be its founder and has a definite text which is regarded as its basic reference. But Hinduism has none. It is a spontaneous growth coming out of people. Even if a number of sages and saints are associated with Hinduism, they do not claim to be its founder. Similarly, an enormous corpus of sacred literature is also associated with Hinduism, but none can claim exclusive authority. Some of the important texts of Hinduism are the Vedas, the Upaniṣads, the Purāṇas, the Dharmasūtras, the *Rāmāyaṇa*, the *Mahā-Bhāgavata* and the *Bhagavad-Gītā*. Of these, the Vedas are the oldest and they are considered not only as beginningless but also as the highest authority.

Varying beliefs and practices can be found in Hinduism. A polytheist is as much a Hindu as a monotheist or a monist or even an atheist. There is only one basic reality underlying everything which is differently named in different religions. Everyone has the right to follow his own path and approach God in his own way.

The two ethnic groups were present in India before the Aryans introduced their marks on the Hindu beliefs and convictions: the Draviḍians and the aborigines. The Aryans assimilated their beliefs and practices to a great extent with those of the Draviḍians and the aborigines. So the overall culture, philosophy and religion which is now known as Hinduism is a fusion and synthesis of beliefs and practices of various strands.

Hinduism believes in an overall supremacy of the spiritual over the profane and the material. It is a general belief that behind and beneath the mundane world order, there is a spiritual order which is the basic, the essential and the eternal. In his inner and essential being, man is a soul which is immortal. Hinduism believes in the transmigration of soul from one body to another popularly known as the doctrine of rebirth. The death of a body simply means soul's casting off one body in order to put on another one and so on. This transmigration is a sign of soul's bondage. Liberation from this cycle of birth and rebirth is the real goal of man. Hinduism calls the attainment of this state as liberation (*mokṣa*).

A Hindu[1] (one who believes in the principles of Hinduism) is a firm believer in God in either one God or in several gods and goddesses. Even if Hindus believe and worship various gods and goddesses, they have an inherent faith that in reality there is only one god and that the various gods and goddesses are simply His manifestations.

1. A Hindu is one who believes and applies the principles of Hinduism while an Indian is a national of India. Consequently, not all Indians are Hindus.

God is the inward dweller (*antaryāmī*), and the inner soul of the entire universe. He is infinite, eternal and all-pervading. He is the creator, preserver and destroyer of the world. He is endowed with infinite auspicious qualities such as truthfulness, knowledge, bliss, tenderness, compassion, etc.

In Hinduism, man has been given a very high status. Although outwardly he is a psychophysical being, in the inner core of his being, he has a soul which is a ray of the Divine within him. Despite this divine gift, man is a victim of ignorance and is in bondage. His greatness is overshadowed by his attachment with the material and sensuous life. Yet, he has the possibility of getting over this ignorance through right knowledge that is not intellectual knowledge but wisdom of what is real and what is unreal.

According to Hinduism, the soul after the death of the present body has to enter some other new body which is caused by the deeds of the past life. The idea of rebirth is essentially bound up with the idea of *karma*. As one sows, so he reaps. One has essentially to undergo the consequences of whatever actions one performs. No action goes waste or undone. It does produce its fruit eventually and the performer has to reap the fruits without fail. If one does not undergo the consequences of his actions in this life, he will have to undergo them in a life after death. Rebirth is, therefore, a necessary consequence of the actions done in one's previous life. So long as one does not exhaust the fruits of his actions, he has to be bound in a continuous chain of birth and rebirth. One's actions done without attachment do not generate this vicious circle of births and rebirths. It is these actions without desire for results that help one to attain liberation. Liberation is the attainment of a purely spiritual status which is beyond the limitations of space and time, a status of perfect peace, tranquillity and equanimity. Liberation means freedom from all sorts of worldly bonds, but it does not imply immediate cessation of the physical body.

Hinduism lays great stress on ethical and moral virtues and duties. Duties are well defined according to the social class to which one belongs as also according to the life stages. If self-control, austerity, purity, forbearance, uprightness, wisdom, etc. are the duties of one social class, heroism, vigour, steadiness, resourcefulness, generosity, etc. are that of another social class.

Irrespective of the social class and the stage of life to which one belongs, a Hindu should respect some general duties. Some of them are steadfastness, forgiveness, non-stealing, cleanliness, restraint of senses, wisdom, learning, truth, freedom from anger, non-violence, faith, etc.

Hinduism does not impose hard and fast rules on worship and prayer. Each one adopts a method that suits him best. Prayers and worships are mostly individual. Mostly Hindu worship consists in sitting or standing before some idol of a God after taking a shower and offering sacred water, flowers, some food (fruits, cooked food which is neither tasted nor eaten), lamps, etc. to the God with utmost love and devotion. After the worship, a Hindu takes back his offerings to partake with family members and friends who are present. These offerings are received with utmost sense of sacredness. The worship is done either at home or in a temple. Temple worship is not an obligatory duty and is conducted by a temple priest. Hindu temple worship is not congregational nor does it contain any sermons.

Hindu prayers mostly consist of the silent recitation of *mantras* that are repeated for long hours. Singing songs in praise of God is also considered as a prayer, just like reading passages of sacred books. Listening to religious discourses conducted in the temple premises is also considered a sort of silent prayer.

Hinduism does not preach enmity or hatred against other thoughts or other religions. Nor does it teach excessive attachment to worldly objects. Hinduism lays great stress on tolerance and non-violence.

2

Introduction

> The bright dawn heralds a new day,
> Its rosy lances have opened the golden gates of the Sun
> And lit up the path of action.
> Awake, O man, the slumber and darkness of the night are over.
> May each dawn lead us from triumph to triumph in the long journey of life!
> — *Ṛgveda*, I.113.16

What is Love for Man?

LOVE for man is the feeling of oneness that awakens the soul. This love is not a sense of duty towards any one person or thing. Where there is love, there should be no thought of duty. Duty is bondage, while love is freedom. When one person falls in love with another person, he loses all feelings of duty towards friends, relatives, partners, society, etc. Love in the true sense annihilates all consciousness of other duties and brings freedom to the soul. If we are bound by duties, we are slaves. Duty refers to the actions done by the dictates of one's conscience. If duties are not done, they become a form of bondage. Wherever bondage exists, the sense of slavery is sure to take over. The pre-condition for rising above the level of bondage is non-attachment to the actions done, and not hankering for the results of all actions. Non-attachment to actions means actions are to be done for actions' sake, not with a motive of benefit or gain. This is possible when true love dominates the mind.

Duty is rarely pleasant when it is not accompanied by love. Suppose a wife has to perform her duties towards her husband; if there is no love between them, it will not be pleasant. Or if the husband does his duty towards his wife, not from love but simply because they are bound together, there will be no happiness in it. Where there is love, there is joy and peace. This joy and peace will flow in abundance if the partners expect no results from their love. Their desires should not be one-sided with selfish motives. They should each have respect for the desires of the other. They should protect one another. The love between husband and wife is expected to be mutual. In India, the Vedas uphold the ideal of domestic life. The marriage vow has united the couples in India for thousands of years. The ideal wife is addressed as the mistress of the home. The wife's place in the household is an exalted one.

According to the Veda, domestic life occupies a central place in life. It is established in love and marriage, the conjugal bond and the family ties. The romantic conception of life is maintained by mutual love. We find in the Vedas a demonstration of the wonderful continuity of married bliss. The bride is addressed as the "bringer of good fortunes":

> Bringer of good fortune in this bride,
> come all of you and look at her,
> wish her full happiness
> and then return home.[1]

Again,

> Be a queen to thy father-in-law
> a queen to thy mother-in-law
> queen to thy sister-in-law
> and a queen to thy brother-in-law[2]

The idea is that a queen protects her subjects. So the bride is addressed this way, to ensure she protects her family with love. Because, "A wife, verily, is home".[3]

---

1. *Ṛgveda*, I.85.33.
2. Ibid., X.85.46.
3. Ibid., III.53.4.

If the partners understand the knowledge of true love, then the fulfilment of the highest duty brings freedom. Love should not be the cause of mental agitation. It should bring joy to the mind and the soul. Love is to be given freely. There should never be the feeling of possessiveness in love. When there is the feeling of love towards every living being (including lifeless objects), love reaches the state of divinity. With the awakening of love, all knowledge comes to man. Unless man masters all kinds of knowledge, he cannot develop the sense of true love towards all things. Once he has attained knowledge, his love reaches the state of divinity. When his love reaches the state of divinity, what he has already learned, pours down to him without fail.

But the body-mind combination creates in man the "I-sense" or the sense of "mine". As long as this feeling of "I am" is in him, it is difficult for him to give true love to anyone, be it a partner, a pet, a child or an inanimate object of some importance. To love is to give. This is to transfer one's own goodwill to another. As long as his partner, friend or pet animal obeys him, man loves them. But if he senses a lack of obedience, he feels anxious about losing them. This anxiety is transformed into anger that makes him withdraw his love towards them. On the human plane, everyone requires protection. So any sense of lack of protection brings changes in man's attitudes.

Moreover, the human being by his nature is power-conscious. He becomes mad if he is dominated. This is another reason for changing the human attitude of love. If the mind is not purified through the proper methods, the sense of ego will continue to grow.

True love towards any one person or object is possible when man emerges from his ego-consciousness. *Prakṛti* is the lower nature of God and *jīva* or (the life principle) is His higher nature. Ego is the mistaken conception of "I" applied to the working of *prakṛti*, which is not "I". In the process of evolution, the three *guṇa*s of *prakṛti* perform all activities appropriate to them. The constituents of *prakṛti* mingle with each of its transformations. Ego is one of the constituents of *prakṛti*. It acts under the three modes of *sattva*, *rajas* and *tamas*. Creation of the material world started with the interaction of *tamas* on the ego, while the cognitive and connotative senses come from *sattva*. The action of *rajas* on the ego produces a movement that leads to the disturbance of the equilibrium. *Sattva*, acting on any of the constituents of *prakṛti*, induces the awareness of one's self. *Sattva* is considered as a spiritual substance on which experience is superimposed. On the other hand, the *tamas* brings ignorance in *prakṛti*. It makes man's mind assert itself as having an independent existence and makes the individual tend to be self-centred. Egoism does not belong to the soul. Pleasure and pain, which do not belong to the self, are wrongly attributed to the self.

When man's ego is under the influence of *tamas*, he identifies himself with his body-mind and suffers because he cannot attain peace. When all types of wrong understandings about the soul and the body-mind combination are removed through proper knowledge, man emerges from his ego sense. When this happens, spiritual evolution begins within him and he understands the difference between the Self and *prakṛti*.

On the human plane, love is maintained in the sense of protection only. This is difficult for all because it should be unconditional. Unconditional love is also difficult to maintain for normal human beings, because their minds are always wavering.[4] It is the nature of the mind to remain unstable. But if a person tries to control his mind, he will experience the joy of divine bliss in his attitude of love. "When a person does not crave for sense objects and attain total self-control, remaining unperturbed, all the worldly bounties accrue to him."[5]

4. The normal human mind is generally tempted towards the sense of attachment to all of its actions. Man performs actions with a purpose for himself. But if he tries to go beyond the normal human mind, gradually he can perform actions without hankering for personal benefits.

5. *Bhagavad-Gītā*, II.71. "All the worldly bounties accrue to him", means, "he attains peace". A peaceful mind is always satisfied as if it has acquired the "worldly bounties".

If a man truly loves another person without expecting something in return, he will be showered with nectar from divine.[6]

What is Love that can Never be Measured?

Love is a deep and tender feeling of affection for a person or a principle or an object. It implies intense fondness towards these things. Love is the continuous and unconditional giving of goodwill. It usually means man's dedication to God. Love sprouts from God. The spring of love that can never be measured is God's love. This immeasurable love must be that of God, because *bhakti* is the highest love towards God alone. If a man does not belong to any religion or does not believe in God, his object of love can be anything that gives him joy. If it is of a higher nature, it will be of spiritual value to him and will bring him the joy of peace. If it is of a lower nature, it will be of material value and will create mental disturbance.

Just as God is self-luminous, His love that sprouts in man is also self-luminous. It is kept in dark in men, due to lack of understanding of its virtue.[7] Love is self-luminous because man in the correct sense does not understand the virtue in it. In every man's heart, there is the spring of this love which when released to share with others gives tremendous joy. This light of love transforms the agitated mind to a calm stillness. Man has forgotten this real nature in him due to circumstances.[8] If he comes out from the dark side of his nature, his rush of love towards the goal of wisdom flows spontaneously like the rivers rushing eagerly

6. Nectar from Divine is Divine bliss — *Ānanda Rasa* — Essence of pure love.

7. In Vedānta philosophy, the reason for this *ajñāna* is *karma*.

8. Man forgets his real nature due to: (1) Ignorance, (2) He has to work hard to carry out the responsibilities that must be fulfilled, and (3) Among his many responsibilities, he has to work hard to satisfy his own hunger.

towards the sea. Love is the special quality of the soul and so is always spontaneous.[9]

As said earlier, love is the supreme attachment to an object, a person or a principle, and is selfless and pleasure giving. It is not possible to derive happiness or pleasure without a feeling of affection towards an object. The mental feeling of joy that unites the person and the object is love. "Because, affection is what dwells in pleasure."[10] The affection of love is of a supreme nature. The soul in bondage loses its direct source of joy within. It gropes after joy in the external world. If one is attracted to any person, object or principle that attraction is due to some kind of joy — physical, mental or emotional. The joy that arises due to attraction is love.

But if a man is dedicated to a particular pursuit, because it gives him intellectual satisfaction, that feeling of pleasure is also love. Supreme love is devoid of all lower attributes and free from the characteristic tendencies towards selfish actions. It is a homogeneous and completely subjective experience. It is subtler than the subtle and manifests itself automatically, if only one wishes for it.

Intense love is the complete surrender to the object of dedication. This is the highest manifestation of love. If one attains this state of love, one sees, hears, talks and thinks only of love.

Man realises the perfection and divinity in him and becomes thoroughly contented. This highest manifestation of love in man is selfless spiritual love. It is divine love. In its intrinsic nature, divine love is no less than the immortal freedom of liberation (*mukti*). When divine love emerges, it purifies the environment and permeates everywhere. This divine love in man is beyond measure and comparison.

---

9. "Soul is unconscious in itself and acquires consciousness as a result of suitable collections." *A History of Hindu Philosophy* by S.N. Gupta vol. I, Chap. Nyāya-Vaiśeṣika Philosophy.

10. *Pātañjala Yogasūtra*, II.7.

Mukti is the state of final liberation from bondage or release from bondage due to one's *karma*. This is a sort of spiritual rescue. This may also be a mental attitude of man when he is alive. *Mukti* means salvation, liberation, that is, to be free from bondage. *Yoga-Vāsiṣṭha* mentions that liberation can be attained in the lifetime of a person or after death. *Mukti* attained in one's lifetime is called *sadeha mukti* or *jīvan mukta*. In this state, all desires of the devotee cease. He has true philosophic knowledge of the essence and nature of all phenomena.

Liberation is a mental attitude. Total detachment is never possible. It is the attachment to God that provides liberation. One can renounce the lower grades of attachment. This helps to enter into the higher grades of spiritual attachment. Even contact with God is a form of attachment, as is the desire to realise this state. Higher degrees of attachment are of a spiritual nature. A spiritual aspirant finds it difficult to remain detached from his spiritual goal unless his *jīva* becomes like that of a parched seed. One should develop detachment towards lower degrees of attachment and should renounce them. Here again, what one considers the lowest attachment may become the highest attachment to another person, as some poisons react like very favourable medicine to some people.

The Impermanency of Human Love

Love is the expression of a feeling of oneness. Normally man loves his self, that is, himself. Anything he does is for his own sake. He does not recognise the need of others nor does he consider their thoughts. At this stage of his development, he has no other thought than to seek his own pleasure or gratification. When moral nature begins to unfold, the same individual learns to consider others, that is, those with whom he is constantly associated. When man finds another person who cares for his needs and gives him some pleasure, he loves the other person. He feels that the other person loves him and protects him.

This kind of love is motivated by selfishness. Man does not realise that the other person is also in need of love and protection. His love is only for his own care and protection. So the love that is considered as a divine quality in man is reduced to a form of duty. As we are bound by duties, we are slaves to one another. This slavery becomes a form of bondage that naturally upsets the mental attitude and breaks the original feeling of love. Wherever there is true love, there is freedom and no vestige of duty can remain. Duty binds us, while love brings us freedom.

As long as there is the "I-sense" in man, he will never experience permanent love. The ever-changing *guṇa*s[11] of *prakṛti*,[12] that is, *sattva*, *rajas* and *tamas*, perform activities appropriate to them. *Prakṛti* is the lower nature of God, and the life principle by which this universe is sustained is His higher nature. *Prakṛti* is God's own primordial nature that has existed since time immemorial. *Guṇa*s are characteristics or constituents of *prakṛti*. The three *guṇa*s, (*sattva*, *rajas* and *tamas*), are inherent in the essential nature of *prakṛti* and are its particular expressions. *Sattva* (goodness) is of the nature of pleasure; *rajas* (passion) is of the nature of pain, and *tamas* (dullness or darkness) is of the nature of indifference. *Sattva* is buoyant and illuminating, *rajas* is stimulating and mobile, while *tamas* is heavy and enveloping. They function for the goal of the spirit and their action is like that of a lamp.[13] In a lamp, the wick, the oil and the flame are substances that are opposed in nature (*guṇa*). Yet, they co-operate in the lamp by giving light.[14]

---

11. *Guṇa* — Quality, attribute, characteristics, constituent, rope.

12. *Prakṛti* — Primal Nature, Primal Matter. According to Sāṁkhya philosophy, it is one of the two categories basic to its system, the second one being *puruṣa*. *Prakṛti* is fundamentally active, but non-conscious. It is imperceptible, inferred from the effects. It is a composite of three constituents called *sattva*, *rajas* and *tamas*.

13. *Sāṁkhya Kārikā* of Īśvara Kṛṣṇa, 13.

14. Ibid.

These *guṇa*s are constantly changing. The nature of man depends upon the domination of one of these *guṇa*s in him. Sāṁkhya philosophy says that one is born with a preponderance of one of the *guṇa*s. So human beings are classified into three categories according to the domination of *sattva, rajas* and *tamas* modes in them.

These three constituents of *prakṛti* (Primal or Primordial Nature) are said to co-operate for the *summum bonum* of the spirit. Like the brightness of the action of a lamp, the *guṇa*s can be known only through their effects. They are not apparent in the un-evolved state of *prakṛti* but become apparent in its transformations as different principles, until the total transformation as matter is reached. The *guṇa*s bind the Self by virtue of the limitations of living in the body. But the Self is immutable. *Sattva* being pure is bereft of qualities which veil light and it gives enlightenment about a thing as it really is. *Rajas* is of the nature of passion and springs from thirst and attachment. It binds the embodied self through attachment to actions. *Tamas* is the cause of erroneous knowledge. Knowledge means the right perception of things. False knowledge, which is contrary to the knowledge obtained through right perception, veils the true nature of things. It deludes all embodied selves.

Since the human being is in a state of evolution towards perfection, varying classes of human beings exist according to their degrees of evolution. Consequently, the attitude of love differs from the lowest to the highest grades.

In the human plane, some individuals are born with an animal nature, and are usually said to have an animal's soul. Of course, they are in the human form. These people love others only for the fulfilment of their personal desires. If their desires are not satisfied, they do not hesitate to destroy the other whom they consider themselves to love. This is the lowest grade of love of *tāmasika* nature. It is not possible for an ordinary man to maintain a permanent love relationship with these types of people.

Then there are those with a *rājasika* nature. Their love is of moderate intensity and they too belong to the human plane. Mutual love is possible, but permanent love is difficult. Man always expects something from the other. It is his nature. But at the same time, he is willing to give something in return. Here the love may be out of a form of duty, or in the form of a barter system — a mutual exchange of love. So love becomes bondage. This bondage creates ego-conflicts. The love falls into a lower grade. In this plane, man can distinguish between right and wrong, but an attitude of permanent love is not possible. Man's mental faculties are limited to a certain extent in this plane. Unless there is a psychological progress, permanent love in this human plane is not possible.

But there are some who are fortunate enough to have full control over their attitude of love. They may be said to have permanent love that can also be termed as divine love. These people are of higher grades and possess the higher quality of love. They love others for the sake of love without any thought of gaining something in return. They cease to think of the results of their love. True love makes one love for love's sake and the sense of duty disappears. This results in full freedom without bondage.

But ordinary people who are between human and divine planes do not easily attain this true love. Their love is constantly oscillating between lower and higher grades, and they are unable to realise permanent love.

Two Ultimate Aims in Man

Man usually thinks that comfort, pleasure and wealth are the highest goals. He undertakes a mad struggle to fulfil his ambitions in life. He runs after power, wealth and fame, and believes only in the physical nature of the world. Like a hungry man, he thinks of satisfying his personal appetite. He seldom realises that the main purpose of life is not the pursuit of material happiness. He has little understanding that this is going to misfire as he approaches the end of his life due to old age or infirmity.

When wealth escapes him even after repeated efforts, he gets restless. Burdened by responsibilities, dogged by misfortunes and facing failures in all his efforts, he becomes dazed and pitiable. He sighs in despair being incapable of supporting anyone, or even himself. He is neglected by all, just like a heartless farmer with his aged animals. He is surrounded by an all-encompassing misery. Thus, a man who lives his life entirely for the pleasure of material success is subject to suffering. He finally becomes the victim of death. When he thinks of this final stage, he trembles with fear. Why should he feel afraid of death? Because man by nature loves the comforts of life and works hard to acquire the wealth that brings comfort. However, when he fails to achieve that to which he has aspired, despite many hardships, he becomes sad. He generally grows old and weak and the feeling that he has to die leaving everything behind comes automatically to his mind. He erroneously thinks that death is total annihilation, and he wants to have eternal life. So the idea of death frightens him. The idea of death enters his mind after seeing something that was alive once, but is no longer so. His fear is due to his attachment to live in the world and enjoy life.

The strong attachment to life is universal. It is well ingrained in all men, whether he suffers in life or enjoys life. The attachment to life is sustained by its own inherent force or potency. This desire to live is not the result of some accidental development in the cause of evolution. This force is rooted in every living being and comes into play the moment the consciousness comes in contact with matter and the evolutionary cycle begins.

Clinging to life is the sentiment that causes its own potency to flow equally in all. The desire to live forever would not have manifested itself in living beings if they had not experienced death in previous lives.[15] This is an affliction suffered by all beings, and man is no exception because the habitual potency caused by the experience of the fear and pain of death is same in all.

Death may destroy the body, but not the soul. When a man sees someone, whom he loves dearly, dying, why should he become miserable? The true man is not dead. It is only the flesh that is left behind at death. The real person is still alive, for he always remembers the dead person; he talks about him with other people. This shows that the subtle body of the dead man is always alive. This subtle body[16] is supported by the soul. Man has little understanding of the subtle body.[17] So he suffers, because he has lost the consciousness of his soul. Moreover, falsely identifying the soul with the physical body makes man suffer. Misery overcomes him.

The soul resides in the subtle body in its pristine pure state. The subtle body is not eternal like the soul, for it is created. In seeking to gain the knowledge of the soul, there is no need to denounce or neglect the material aspect of life. One should simply place proper values upon both. One must cherish the soul, as the soul should be cherished, and consider the material aspect of life according to their merits.

---

15. The desire to live forever points out the existence of previous lives.

16. Sāṁkhya philosophy postulates two bodies: *sūkṣma śarīra* and *sthūla śarīra*. The subtle body or *sūkṣma śarīra*, also called *liṅga śarīra*, comprises the mind, the intellect, the ego, the five sense-elements of sound, touch, colour or form, taste and odour, and their sensory functions. The whole body or *sthūla śarīra* is the material physical body. The Vedānta philosophy, particularly Advaita, postulates a third body — the *kāraṇa śarīra* or causal body — because it is the cause of the two other bodies. The causal body comprises the soul and nescience or ignorance.

17. Man has an ordinary intellect provided to some extent by nature. Unless he develops his intellect by proper methods, it is difficult for him to understand what the subtle body is because he cannot see the subtle body with his naked eyes. He has to feel it within himself.

This body so fondly nourished will fall to death as hundreds of other bodies have done. But the one who understands the undying nature of the soul is not afraid of death. He understands how to face death. It is the attachment to the body that brings suffering and fear. When man cultivates an attitude of detachment to the physical body and its material pleasures, and understands the constant existence of his soul, it does not matter much to him where he lives — whether in the world or out of it, in the midst of activity or in the calm of solitude. Everywhere, he carries his mighty soul. St. Paul said, "The last enemy that shall be destroyed is death." This means that man should overcome his ignorance of what dies and what is undying. It does not mean that he should save the body from dying. Death is certain. Man should realise that there is no death for the soul that which is "real" in man. This, as most religions put it, is the part of God that cannot die.

The *Bhagavad-Gītā* says,

> As the waters of different rivers enter the ocean, which though full on all sides remains unperturbed, likewise we in whom all enjoyments merge themselves attain peace, not who hankers for such enjoyments.[18]

The volume of the sea does not visibly increase or decrease, whether the waters of the rivers enter it or not. In the same way, when all objects of desire enter into one who is self-controlled, they produce no reaction in him except sensorial impressions. Such a person will attain peace because peace is the nature of the soul.

Human life is a series of limitations. These limitations influence the soul and make it hanker for something real, something permanent that is beyond the poles of pleasure and pain. Pleasure and pain are both obstacles to mental peace. Though man does not know how and where he should experience "real" life, he feels its existence. He feels this through an in-born conviction. He

---

18. *Bhagavad-Gītā*, II.70.

longs for this "real" life, because immortality is the soul's very nature.

Man feels that he is always pulled between two paths, the lower and the higher paths. The lower one drags him towards worldly desires and the higher one draws him towards the purity of life. He finds the outcome of worldly desires unsatisfactory. He remains discontent. The fight for contentment takes place every moment in man's mind. He needs a balance between the opposite conflicts of his life pleasure and pain, joy and sorrow, failure and success, and so forth. Naturally, he searches for an approach that gives him mental strength and poise.

The complexities of modern life have made man's life miserable. He has all the material comforts, but his mental suffering has increased. Man has become more refined and more sensitive. He tries to offer solutions for existing problems, but these create new problems. Man in despair does not know where to turn in order to get respite and relaxation. He feels like a hunted hare trapped within closed walls, and which in a mad attempt to escape, dashes its head against the hard stone.

Desires lie buried within the mind of every individual. They constantly try to force themselves up to the conscious plane. Man often tries to push the desires that are not good to the lower level of the mind. But still they rise up again on their own, due to natural impulses of the mind and due to the changes in the activities of *sattva, rajas* and *tamas*.

Normally, the subconscious works in collaboration with the conscious and man does not even suspect its presence. But if traced back to the original instigative pattern, the full force of the subconscious will be realised. Unless the individual has complete self-awareness, he cannot become the master of himself. The lack of knowledge about himself brings conflict in his mind. Because of this conflict, he suffers mentally as well as physically. The subconscious can be ignored for a short period, but not for a long time. Man is helpless in the clutches of his subconscious. It is his nature. Man cannot go against nature by disobeying it. Because of his very intense suffering, man earnestly tries to find a remedy. The remedy should be brought out slowly and smoothly. Any solution man chooses will bring a sense of disappointment in the beginning. The solution may be like helping a needy person, educating the uneducated, etc. These acts not only divert the mind from the clutches of the subconscious, but also gradually bring peace to the mind. The happiness of those helped and supported, brings resolve to do increasingly more good actions.

According to Sāṁkhya philosophy,[19] all these disturbances and weaknesses are due to the injuries[20] of the intellect.

According to Indian psychology, good and evil come from the depths of the subconscious. The subconscious is said to be the repository of the past tendencies of previous lives. They leave their impression on the mind. When the opportunity arises, these good or evil impressions take form and shape in the mind. This is the reason why man can sometimes be full of hope and at other times feel hopeless. He can find a solution to his problems if he tries to act on the good impulses. As long as he continues to strive for a state of mental tranquillity, there is the hope that he will achieve it. Dawn must come after the night.

Body-Soul Relation

Man is a combination of body and soul. The body is essential because the soul resides in it. The soul is essential to the body, because without the soul the body is nothing. All actions need the body as well as the soul. "Indeed! Body is the only agent for

19. One of the six philosophical systems of Hindu philosophy, and the oldest.

20. Injuries of the intellect or defects of the intellect (*buddhi vadha*). The primary function of the intellect is to provide the knowledge of the Real, but it is also capable of providing the knowledge of the non-Real. When it functions to provide the latter, it is called a defect or an injury.

performing one's *dharma*."[21] Whether the soul owns the body or the body owns the soul does not make any difference while performing actions. Man knows only part of his being, the outward appearance of his mind.[22] He has no knowledge of the layers of the mind beneath this outward layer. This is because the process of evolution of the life principle is not yet complete.

Ordinarily it is understood that higher forms of life gradually arise from the lower forms of life. The lowermost plane of life manifests itself in the vegetable form; it goes then to the higher animal plane and then becomes an intelligent human being. According to this doctrine, human life is not the end of evolution. It is only an intermediate step to a still higher form of perfect human life.

According to Indian psychology, the individualised souls transmigrate from one body to another, from the vegetable kingdom to the animal kingdom, and finally to the perfect human plane. These bodies serve as vehicles for the souls in their upward journey. The total number of these different kinds of vehicles is said to be 840,000.[23]

Indian scriptures say that the different species of animal life are the direct results of the rays of the sun on earth. And the life-giving rays of the sun are said to total 100,000 (100×1000) and are

---

21. *Kumārasambhavam* by Kālidāsa (V.38) "Indeed! Body is the only agent for performing one's *dharma* (*dharma* = actions that are to be performed for the good of the world)." *Śarīra* or body is that form which has different limbs like hands, feet, etc. in living beings and is animated by *ātmā* (soul). Here *śarīra* is referred to human body.

22. Indian psychology introduces two concepts of mind: *manas* and *citta*. The inner faculty which is directly related to the sense organs and to the organs of voluntary and involuntary action and which rules over them is *manas*. *Citta* is the seat of all conceptual and perceptual ideas and their latencies. *Citta* and *manas* are used indiscriminately in many texts.

23. 12 months of the year × 7 days of the week × 100 × 100 = 840,000.

radiated all year round. The Vedas describe the sun as having thousands of rays, with each ray playing its role in 100 ways.[24]

The human being is the best-evolved life form. Only in the human form can man develop the faculties required for the march towards the final goal of his perfection. He goes on developing his faculties from one birth to another. Man's thinking power should reach perfection. Unless the individual has complete self-awareness, it is difficult for him to decide whether the soul dominates the body or the body dominates the soul. Whatever may be the ideology, as one progresses spiritually one develops equanimity of mind.[25] This helps a person to accept the vagaries of life with poise. A person with a spiritual outlook is better equipped to face life in general, although a spiritual outlook is in opposition to a material outlook.

The soul is usually defined as life with relation to intellect and mind. The spirit is the illuminating life principle that animates both the mind and the body. Through learning and high thinking, the mind can be trained to flow in the desired channels of right understanding, thereby arriving at a correct judgement. At this stage, one finds greater pleasure in intellectual pursuits alone and attains the ability to transform the pursuits. Spiritual quest opens the way to a higher domain.

Attachment to and Detachment from the Body

Hindu philosophy considers that the body is the vehicle for the soul in its journey through life, regardless of which body the soul

---

24. The correct meaning of *sahasra* is varied. For example, the temperature of the larva coming out of the sun is 100 000°.

25. Equanimity of mind is that state of mind which does not yield to the restless desire for change and which is not at the mercy of emotional ups and downs. When equanimity of mind is developed, man accepts the work assigned to him without minding loss and gain, pleasure and pain, victory and defeat. This means that he remains unaffected by the outcome of his actions, considering all actions as his duty.

occupies. The *jīva*, embodied soul,[26] carries the body and maintains it. It remains clinging to it by ego or self-sense (*ahaṁkāra*).[27] This self-sense makes man cling to his body in the beginning. The

---

26. Embodied soul refers to the identity of one's own person as distinct from all others. It is not mentioned in the spiritual sense because *jīva* tends towards egoism the moment it enters into the body.

27. *Ahaṁkāra* means "ego". This aspect is conceived in the individual mind. In the process of the evolution of *prakṛti* "the primal nature" the first principle to emerge is *mahat* or "the great one", otherwise known as the intellect from which intellect emerges. *Ahaṁkāra* or egoism is the process of individuation. The egoistic aspect of mind is the cause of man's miseries. *Ahaṁkāra* can be controlled through the practice of detachment.

    Asmitā means almost the same as *ahaṁkāra*. *Asmitā* is derived from the Sanskrit root *asmi* meaning, "I am". The meaning may be considered as the identification of consciousness with the mental vehicle through which it is expressed. "I am" represents the pure awareness of self-existence. It is an expression (*bhāva*) of pure consciousness. (Pure consciousness is termed as *Puruṣa* in Sāṁkhya.) When pure consciousness gets involved in matter, due to illusion, real nature is lost and "I am" » changes into "I am this", where this is the subtlest or most sensual vehicle (the physical body), through which consciousness is working.

    The moment consciousness identifies itself with its vehicle it falls from a pure state and puts limitations on itself. This is due to the veil of *avidyā* (nescience) falling on the consciousness. The mind is compared to a mirror. The reflection of consciousness in it is the soul (*jīva*) which undergoes the worldly conditions. When the mirror (the said mind) is removed, the reflection reverts to its original state. *Jīva* is the transmigratory soul (till it is finally released from all the *karmas*). This transmigratory condition of *jīva* is due to the effect of past *karma* remaining in a subtle form. This past *karma* puts limitations on *jīva* which in turn forms the veil of *avidyā*. These past *karmas* may be compared to the debt to be repaid with due interest as per the conditions.

    The sense of "I am this", "I think", "I walk", "I write", "I see", "I approve", etc. are produced (due to this reason) in the mind.

    Asmitā is manifested through the physical body in the sensual form of *kleśa* (afflictions). There are levels of consciousness even beyond that of intellect. In all these, *asmitā* is present, though it becomes more and more refined in each ascending layer of vehicles.

physical body is the source of energy. So on the physical plane, man cannot act without his body. There must be the presence of his ego-sense as the doer of all actions. It is the impulse of this "I"-consciousness that makes man function. The body provides the instruments of the eyes, ears, nose, tongue and the sense of touch, together with the hands and feet. The mind, with all its faculties, is also in the body. For all physical actions, one needs the sense organs. The self-conscious actor is also present when the body is functioning.

Generally, it is considered that the Self is the same as the body. When the body is born, the Self comes with it into the world. What is born must die some day. Death does not mean total extinction of the being. The body stops functioning. Death is only the assumption of a new condition of existence. The fundamental Self[28] passes through various conditions of existence. This self is not dependent on the body for its existence. But the body, insentient by nature, is subject to change and its birth and death are natural. The fundamental Self enters the body and leaves it.

The body will appear to be real as long as it is not overcome by death. But the great time[29] limits human life. Attachment to

28. Usually Self, Being, Spirit, etc. are different names mentioned in books for the "life principle" that animates the physical body. Sometimes these words are also used when the sense of ego is present in them. Ego is also pure and unallied when referred in the sense "I". It becomes impure when used in the "I-am" sense (just as *ātman* is used to refer to *Paramātmā*, the universal soul, the source of all individual souls). *Ātman* is also used to refer to *jīvatmā*, the individual soul. It is also used to refer to pure ego.

29. "Great time" *kāla* in Sanskrit, is referred to as such because time is under the control of God and man failed to bring it under his control. "Great time" is a word of appreciation used by man (for its special powers of not yielding to man). "Time, nature, low, chance, matter, energy, intelligence neither these nor a combination of these, can bear examination because of their own birth, identity and the existence of the self. The self is also not a free agent, being under the sway of happiness and misery." *Śvetāśvatara Upaniṣad*, I.2.

the body will persist since the body appears to be real, as long as ignorance persists in man.

When the right knowledge dawns and man understands that the body is not permanent and is sure to perish, then he changes his attitude. The body changes during childhood, youth and old age and is afflicted by all types of diseases until it is overcome by death. After observing all these changes, man understands that attachment to the body brings only misery. Once man realises this he begins to develop an attitude of detachment to the body. Man understands that the body will ultimately perish.

Whatever is enjoyed for the pleasure of the body due to its attachment is like the dream experiences of the enjoyment. When one comes to the waking state, one realises that the dream experiences are false. But in the dream state, one does not consider the experiences of joy as false.

As long as man is ignorant of the knowledge that the body is sure to perish, he will be attached to the body. When he views the faults with the right knowledge, he becomes detached from the body.

When the mind identifies with any of its concepts, it appears to become that concept. The iron ball in the fire becomes itself like the fire. When it is taken out of the fire, it assumes its original state.

It is the mind that is the cause for both attachment and detachment towards the body. It is the mind that functions as an agent of these types of feelings and not the body, as the body is dead without the soul. The mind is also the agent that brings knowledge of the soul to the man.

What is Devotion?

Devotion is a relationship of trust and unquestioned love for an object of worship. It is the sincere dedication to the object of worship, the complete absorption with firm love in one's ideals.

It is the constant flow of mind brimming with love towards the Supreme, without any selfish motives. Devotion gives a warm emotional contentment. Devotion is the absorbed state of mind, when one's own natural state of affection for one's chosen ideal matures into extreme love. Devotion is an emotion. It takes the form of emotional love towards the object — which may be a person, a principle, or even an inanimate object. Devotion is the special quality of the soul, of its nature of selflessness. When one completely renounces one's self, this renunciation liberates man from the feeling of the sense of bondage.

The soul is unconscious. It acquires consciousness as a result of forging the suitable links. The mind is the intermediate link that connects the soul with the senses, and thereby produces different qualities in the soul. Intelligence functions on the reflections of the soul on the mind. Liberation from bondage is a mental attitude.

There exists a difference between ordinary love and devotion. Devotion is the transcendental experience of bliss that can never be expressed adequately in words. This is supreme love and as such is liberation. Devotional love is the bliss of the divine to man. Again, the spirit of love itself is devotion. The devotee enjoys all knowledge in the light of kindling love. He alone understands it. This joy melts his heart, subsides the dominant ego in him and thereby purifies the mind. The process of taming the mind with love and care to bring the mind to tranquillity is a step towards devotion. It is a mental process that leads man to reach the highest perfection possible in his life.

The true joy of the devotee is expressed in the form of a story:

Once the great sage Nārada, considered in India as a true example of a perfect devotee, was on his way to heaven to meet the Supreme Lord. On his way, he happened to meet a devout sage who was living in severe austerity in the hope of attaining heaven. The sage asked Nārada to obtain an answer from God to his question. His question was: How long would it take him (the sage) to reach heaven? Nārada promised to oblige him and continued his journey. After travelling some distance, another man who seemed to be an ordinary but devout man asked Nārada to ask the Lord the same question. On his way back, Nārada met the sage, who was still living in austerity and told him that it would take seven more births for him to reach heaven. On hearing this, the sage became very depressed because it seemed to him that his efforts were not properly rewarded. To the ordinary man, Nārada said that it would take many births for him to reach heaven. But this man jumped with joy on the assurance that he would attain heavenly abode, forgetting about the passages of time. This joy is the joy of a true devotee and this ordinary man immediately attained *mukti* because of his contentment. He was not disappointed by the idea of repeated births. His main interest was devotion.

The emotion of love replaces all other emotions and frees the mind of all desires. It concentrates the mind and keeps it in *sattva guṇa* (illumination), suppressing both *rajas* (activity) and *tamas* (inertia). Therefore, intense love for God should be cultivated. God is to be loved but not feared. The love for God should be for the sake of love only, not with a desire for some reward in return. This is because action is lost in reaction.

Man thinks of God or prays to God for different reasons, very often to obtain something better in this world. Most people think that God sends misery and misfortune, and His wrath therefore should be appeased. Such people worship Him through the fear of His wrath. Others invoke His blessings for temporal gifts, for the fulfilment of their desires for gaining secular objects like wealth, prosperity, progeny, or even worship him for a reward after death. Many people pray to God for His assistance but only when they are overcome by some calamity. No doubt, the merciful God understands the mental limits of the human plane and all these types of prayers receive a response. Moreover, on the human plane, there is often a cause that turns man's mind towards God and develops the attitude of devotion to Him. Liberation is the cause. But this is not the real meaning of devotion (*bhakti*). It is taintless love. This love itself is strength and its potential increases as long as it remains charged. One-sided love without the slightest desire for a result is devotion (*bhakti*). The constant uninterrupted contact with God is the benefit in the action of devotion. The constant contact with other goals cannot be considered as devotion. The desire for results in devotion (*bhakti*) should not be for personal rewards. The results should be offered to the Supreme.

It is only pure love that loves to suffer. Kuntī, mother of the virtuous Pāṇḍavas, prays to Lord Kṛṣṇa: "O! Guide of the universe, let hardships and sorrows come always, if during the course we are blessed with Thy vision that puts an end to birth and death."[30] Such is the meaning of devotion, the highest form of which is pure love.

Madame Guyon, a 17th century Christian mystic saints, says in her "Acquiescence of Pure Love":

> *To me it is equal whether love or ordain,*
> *My life or death, appoint me pain or ease,*
> *My soul perceives no real ill in pain,*
> *In case of health no real good she sees,*
> *One good she covets, and that good alone,*
> *To choose thy will, from selfish bias free,*
> *And to prefer a cottage to a throne.*
> *And grief to comfort, if it pleases Thee.*

True devotion in man is ready to accept God even if it means trouble and tribulation. Devotion is the direct pathway to perfection and it leads to the very heart of religious consciousness. Misery and difficulties come at times to strengthen our character. They are very good for the formation of character. The more we meet with difficulties, the more we remember God for protection. Generally, we forget the Lord when we find everything easy and

30. *Śrīmad Bhāgavata*, I.8.24.

enjoyable. So it is a blessing when this *guru* (the spiritual teacher)[31] in the form of misery comes and reminds us of our duties.[32]

It is through love and adoration that we feel the nearness or presence of divinity. Love unites God and man. When wholehearted and fully focused devotion for the Ideal awakens, it comes like a flood and washes away everything else — ignorance, narrow-mindedness, fear, doubt and selfishness — leaving only the Ideal. This alone is left shining in the heart. Everything that is earthly will be renounced by one who keeps the value of devotion to God, for he understands that He is the effulgent spirit and everything else is perishable matter. He is the eternal, the permanent, the unchanging, while all other things are transitory and changing. In this blessed state, one realises His ultimate goal, the true vision of God in devotion.

What is Religion?

Any system of faith and worship is religion. Religion is an integral part of society. It has a firm hold on the human masses. A man by instinct is a religious being.[33] There is a natural yearning in him for something that is beyond his sensual or intellectual pleasure.

Usually religion is a means by which one's heart can realise the God within. Man offers prayers to God daily in order to

31. In India, many regard God as Guru or teacher because "presiding in one's heart as "*guru*", he guides the spiritual aspirant." So he is considered as the "Great Guru". Of course, He is not considered as human except in the case of incarnation.

32. Even in India, many people inflict physical injuries on themselves and on others as an offering to God. But the *Bhagavad-Gītā* (XVII.19) considers this as *tamas*-type of penance.

33. A religious being is one who adheres to a religion by following the principles laid down in that particular religious system with faith and with respect for the principles. In general, religion means any system of faith and worship. Religion also means a belief in a divine or super human being, or super human power. Any object of conscientious respect and pursuit also comes under the category of religion because the person concerned follows certain principles that are essential for seeking the object being pursued.

receive His benediction and achieve this end. God can be felt only in the innermost recess of one's heart, not in temples, churches or mosques, though they exist for this goal. Rites and ceremonies are mere accessories, but they lead to the purification of the heart. Man has to purify his heart of all evils, because God resides in the holy temple of the heart.

A comparative study of all religious systems would show that despite wide differences in their rites and ceremonies, they are united in essence.

Religion is mostly a personal concern. It comprises the practice of certain principles prescribed to develop man's uprightness, thereby bringing the highest possible evolution in his lifetime. Religion is a means for the dual development of an individual — mental and spiritual. Each particular religion defines principles in its own way in terms of its doctrines and dogmas. The religion and culture of Hindus are rooted in the Vedas and one can note the distinct imprint of tolerance that the Vedas inspired in the Hindu religion. Buddhism arrived with a mission of compassion. The Zoroastrian advocated the virtue of patience and kindness. Christianity proclaimed that all men were created in the image of God and established a relationship of brotherhood among mankind. Islam taught respect and care. All the religions made a unique contribution to upholding the spiritual aspect of man's life. The doctrines of these religions are similar in their final essence, although there are so many variations in the methods of teaching, that it is difficult to define each religion accurately.

As said earlier, religion is the outcome of man's inner urge for freedom. It is the outward manifestation of his great need for the Infinite, although it is the study of his inner world. The whole of humanity is moving towards this goal. Different religions represent different aspects of this struggle.

No one is satisfied in this life. Man longs for many things, expecting happiness and joy from them. But the moment he has achieved happiness, he sees the emptiness and desires either more things or something else. Thus, he continues to acquire while remaining discontented and dissatisfied. He constantly struggles to obtain something that he is not aware of. This nature of dissatisfaction indicates that man wants infinite freedom. Man usually seeks the Infinite in this finite world, which is impossible. So he is dissatisfied and eventually suffers.

True religion is a science that teaches man how to lead a life of unity and bliss, while still remaining in the world of diversity. Religion consists of realisation. It is the innate, spontaneous urge of each individual towards ultimate freedom. Religious feelings and approaches of men may differ, but the goal is the same, the ultimate freedom.

In the pursuit of man's inner urge, he found a way to reach the goal of peace and bliss which later was named religion. Man created religion by adhering to the principles he adopted to find peace. He preached these principles to others who were in need of peace and bliss. This way religion became an integral part of man's very being. Saint Paul said: "the God thou unconsciously worshippest, the same I preach unto thee." The Upaniṣads[34] say: "From the Great joy the world has come into being; through that Great joy, the world lives and to that Great joy the world enters in the long run."

So everyone in the end obtains that "Great" bliss. Every man is sustained in his daily existence through that bliss. The role of religion is to make man realise the truth that the enjoyment he derives from worldly pleasure and objects is only a minute reflection of the infinite bliss, which comes from within his own self. Reasoned thinking reveals that happiness and unhappiness are only limitations of the mind. It is the mind that makes one feel happy or unhappy. Man identifies himself with his body and his mind. As the body and the mind are unstable factors, man suffers. The condition of the mind varies every moment and the body

34. Indian authoritative texts, next in importance to the Vedas.

may also go to pieces any time. As long as one depends on the mind for one's happiness, one is bound to suffer.[35] So if one wants to obtain lasting peace, one must transcend the limits of the mind.[36]

Whatever may be the state beyond the mind, whether it is a state of annihilation or something else, Indian sages experienced that superconscious state and found real and permanent peace therein. According to the *Māṇḍūkya Upaniṣad*, "this self within (*ātman*) is *Brahman*." The self has four quarters or four states of mind:

> The waking state (*jāgrata avasthā*) whose consciousness relates to the external world (things) and who enjoys sensual things; the dream state (*svapna avasthā*) whose consciousness is internal and who enjoys subtle objects; deep sleep (*suṣupta avasthā*) where there is not even the sensations of dreams; and the transcendental state (*turīya avasthā*). This fourth state is known as the real state of the mind where the soul, the *ātman*, can be known. This state is the reality behind all phenomenal experience.

The Indian sages experienced and described this fourth transcendental state. *Turīya* is described as existence, knowledge and bliss.[37] Actually, this state of consciousness is not a state at all. It is identical to existence itself, and it is this that appears as having the three previous states. The principles that lead to this state belong to all religions, even if they are named differently.

The mind can be compared to a pendulum. The emotions swing from one extreme to another: from joy to grief, from liking to disliking, from love to hate, from belief to disbelief, from

---

35. If one is able to feel properly what happens in the physical body, one finds that everything, including happiness, pain or bliss will be noticed in the mind. Without the presence of mind, nothing can be perceived physically or mentally.

36. It is the view in all scriptures that the soul pervades the body through consciousness, and consciousness is limited to each body, depending upon the modes of *sattva, rajas* and *tamas*. Past *karma* is the cause for this.

37. *Sat, cit* and *ānanda*, the characteristics of the Absolute *Brahman*.

conviction to doubt, and so on. It is only by stopping this incessant movement of the mind that one can obtain harmony within oneself. This state of perfect stillness is the essence of life.

Religion makes man alert, like a bird sitting on a small twig that may fall down any moment with the slightest breeze. Religion teaches man to understand that this precious life is not only to nourish his body, but also to evolve to the state of perfection. Religious principles give man the strength and courage to face problems of any type with a calm and balanced mind. They teach him to serve, forgive, endure and interact with all, with love and compassion. Religion is something to be lived.

The Cultivation of Devotion without Religion

Seen from outside, religion and devotion seem to go hand in hand. But in reality, they can either go together, or devotion can be separated from religion. There is no need for devotion to be always attached to religion. Devotion is man's mental relation with any object that he likes immensely. Devotion is offering oneself with love to some purpose, setting one's mental action apart for a special use like duty, longing for knowledge of higher aims or purpose, etc. Devotion is the elevation of the value of one's principles, ideals, duties, knowledge and so on, to a higher moral plane. Religion is not always required in these matters. Man can attempt to achieve perfection in his life without depending on religion. The views depend upon the persons concerned. The pursuit of any objective can be achieved with pure devotion. Devotion applies to the inner and outer worlds of man.

Religion believes in a divine or superhuman being. It speaks of and studies the inner world of man. It follows certain principles with faith to understand the inner being within man. Many people think that only religious knowledge can save them. But religious knowledge is distinct from religious experience. It is possible to learn the techniques of Vedānta philosophy[38] without having

38. One of the six systems of Indian philosophy.

the sense of spirituality. It is also possible to explain the secrets of the kingdom of God. But if man's heart has never been visited by a "divine" person, he is not a "loyal one".

When we look at science, we can observe that it deals with the objects and phenomena of the external world, that is, external nature. There is no talk of religion in it. But science and religion are not rivals. They are parallel and may never meet. But unless a scientist has a deep love for knowledge, he cannot reveal any knowledge of science. He is devoted to science, without cultivating any interest in religion. He is totally absorbed in his knowledge of science that it is bliss to him. Because of man's devotion to science, it is always at the forefront of his mind. The discoveries of science are spectacular and clear. Science is the fundamental necessity of life.

In religion, discoveries are to be felt, rather than demonstrated. They cannot be shown objectively to an audience. Yet religious discoveries are as true as scientific ones. Politics is an abstract science. When put into practice, it assumes a shape. Politics can also be taken to perfection without attaching religious values to it. A politician becomes perfect while practising politics at its best. The degree of elevation of the knowledge of political science depends on the politician's devotion to politics. Similarly, there are astronomers, astrologers, medical doctors, psychologists and others who are devoted to their duties and knowledge, with or without being religious. It is the true devotion to the Ideal that is important. Devotion is to put love in what one does. It helps in maintaining concentration and achieving an outcome from one's pursuit.

Devotion helps a non-religious man to adjust himself to the problems he has to face in achieving his goal in life. It ensures the balance of mind and freedom from entanglements that man needs for the steady pursuit of his objective. Moreover, it brings the kind of health and harmony to the mind that is required for man to achieve any greater goal in life.

Whatever may be man's aim in life, he has to work hard and against great odds. The results of his efforts may take a long time to bear fruits. Usually, man's lower nature craves only for success. Very often, the results may not be satisfactory. Only an extraordinary concentration on his purpose can enable him to keep on course in the face of difficulties and obstacles. Devotion helps in overcoming obstacles and in developing concentration that is free from emotions.

For cultivating devotion, one has to keep in mind three important points:

The object or the aim,
The efforts for its achievement, and
The means for attaining it.

The characteristic of the ordinary mind is that it is constantly and completely turned outwards. It is used to taking a strong interest only in the objects of the outside world. This disturbs[39] the mind and therefore a strong effort is required to reverse the direction of the consciousness and redirect it to the required goal. By developing a strong longing for the aim in hand, one finds it easier to concentrate on the required means for achieving it. This strong longing is devotion. Through devotion, an artist perfects his skill for painting and drawing. A musician writes emotionally expressive compositions. In this approach, religion is not a necessity. But it is devotion that is at work and that brings joy to all those people who come in contact with the artist or musician.

Devotion is essential to maintain harmony between knowledge

---

39. Various objects of attraction are found in the outside world. So the mind, although used to being interested in the outside world and the items and objects found there, finds difficulty in choosing the required object. The selection of the right object creates a struggle in the mind, thereby disturbing it. As the mind has the tendency to oscillate between what is outward and what is inward, a strong effort is needed to divert the mind towards the required goal.

and actions.[40] It is the sense of devotion that brings these two things to absolute perfection, enabling the person concerned to understand the inner essence in action as well as in knowledge. Through action, knowledge is gained.[41]

Man always remains in action whether he is religious or not. Cessation from thought, deed or work is mentally impossible. For no man, even for a moment, rests without doing work. Everyone acts in spite of himself by the *guṇa* born of *prakṛti*.[42] But during liberation, there will not be the union of *puruṣa*[43] and *prakṛti* and as such it would be possible to stop actions gradually. Man performs actions because of his practical reasons and his moral consciousness that includes reasoning and will-power. The cultivation of devotion concerns action as well as knowledge, for without the experience gained from actions, knowledge cannot be obtained. Through cultivating such devotion, one can halt the outward tendency of the mind and direct it towards one's goal. When a man concentrates with devotion on his aim, he automatically conquers himself. It is said that not even God can conquer such a man, because he performs actions for actions' sake and strives hard for knowledge for the sake of knowledge, without

---

40. To bring knowledge and action means to unite knowledge and action. This is *jñāna karma samuccaya*, that is, joining knowledge and action.

41. Experience gained through action provides knowledge. *Karma-yoga* has two aspects — knowledge and material ingredients. Of these two, the component of knowledge is superior to the component of material ingredients. Knowledge is provided through the experience gained via actions and it is the culmination of all actions. When this knowledge is practised regularly with devotion, the person concerned reaches the height of perfection, understanding the inner essence in action and knowledge. This height of perfection is the point for attaining the vision of the "self".

42. *Bhagavad-Gītā*, III.5.

43. *Puruṣa* — Spirit or individual soul; one of the two basic categories of Sāṁkhya philosophy. It is pure consciousness, unattached and unrelated to anything. It is non-active, unchanging, eternal and pure. There are an infinite number of individual souls.

caring about the results. Even though non-religious, his highest moral good consists of his unconditional duty that must be done.

Like a religious man's penance for his spiritual goal, a non-religious man's penance is his devoted efforts to achieve his aim to perfection. Devotion to his actions and knowledge are for duty's sake, not an end in themselves. His devotion fills his heart with love that spreads to his whole surroundings. This is spirituality without religion. One should try to give one's best, to seek to develop familiarity with affection and to cultivate devotion.

The *Bhagavad-Gītā* describes the divine aspects:[44]

> Indissoluble is the Absolute *Brahman* (the Supreme Being), and His Self-aspect (*svabhāva*, nature) is called the *adhyātma*. *Karma* (or His work) is the creative (dynamic) aspect of *bhūta bhāva*. *Visarga*, the creation, is His work, the outcome.

Bhūta bhāva and *visarga bhāva* have been used here as separate terms to denote the causal and the created aspects. The four aspects of God are:

> *Parama bhāva, the absolute aspect called Brahman*
> *Ādhyātmika bhāva, the Self-aspect,*
> *Bhūta bhāva, the creative aspect, and*
> *Visarga bhāva, the creation.*

The unmanifested (*avyakta*) form is absolute; the second and the third forms are respectively the subjective and objective sides of His manifestation. The subjective aspect shines as his own Self and is static, while the objective aspect creates and as such is dynamic.[45]

It is said that God's will is his *visarga bhāva*, the dynamic Self that is manifest in the form of creation. It (His will) is the seed of creation, or the creative energy in its potential state. From this

---

44. *Bhagavad-Gītā*, VIII.3.

45. *Avyakta*, Unmanifested energy. Higher than this is another *avyakta*, the unmanifested *Brahman*, the ever eternal.

will comes action, followed by the knowledge of what it accomplishes. Will, action and knowledge are three aspects of one dynamic Self. When a person wills a thing, he sets his will to action and progressively the accomplishment follows. So, it is will that governs work and its details.

Individual will is a ray of creation's will. Will is the faculty by which a person decides upon and initiates action. By exercising his will, man can cultivate devotion to any of his higher goals. Have a strong will and nature shall yield to it. The nature must unreservedly permit man to step into the threshold of the nature's immense treasure of knowledge. Strong will can move mountains. So it is not a problem for a non-religious man to cultivate devotion to achieve his ideals and feel oneness with them.

The Three Yogas

Man does not live by bread alone. Our ancient sages have classified the aim and objective of human life into four categories of *dharma, artha, kāma* and *mokṣa*.[46] Among these four, the first three are of a transient nature and only the last, the *mokṣa*, is eternal. It has to be sought after. All branches of Hindu religion agree that liberation from cycles of birth and death is the *summum bonum* of mankind, although the form and nature of liberation vary from one religion to another. *Karma-yoga, jñāna-yoga* and *bhakti-yoga* lead to liberation and the details are given in the scriptures. Moral discipline is the process of self-purification elaborated in *karma-yoga. Karma-yoga* emphasises the disinterested performance of action (*karma*), such as sacrifice (*yajña*), charity (*dāna*) and austerity (*tapas*) as divine services without any expectation of rewards. Spiritual culture is the method of self-realisation prescribed in *jñāna-yoga*. It signifies constant meditation on *ātmā*, the individual self, with the control

46. *Dharma* is righteousness. *Artha* is wealth. *Kāma* is desire. *Mokṣa* is the same as *mukti*. *Mokṣa* means the awakening of the soul into divine life. *Mokṣa* is the final state of spiritual illumination.

of the mind and senses. *Bhakti-yoga* (devotion) is the realisation of God as the completion of the moral and spiritual disciplines.

These three *yoga*s are the tripartite ways of Vedānta culture that lead to the knowledge of *Brahman*. The main steps in the path of perfection consist of the moral discipline or self-purification brought about by the performance of duty, or *karma-yoga*, the spiritual illumination of *jñāna-yoga* and the loving meditation on *Brahman*, or *bhakti-yoga*. *Karma-yoga* and *jñāna-yoga* are interrelated and the aim of these is self-realisation.[47] Both these are subsidiary means to *bhakti-yoga*, which is the direct means to realising God.

In the Advaita philosophy, it is said that *jñāna-yoga* leads to liberation, while the Viśiṣṭādvaita[48] says that *karma-yoga* and *jñāna-yoga* lead to *bhakti-yoga*, which in turn leads to liberation.

Advaita, which means "not two", hence non-dualism, is a well-known system of Hindu philosophy based on the principles of Gauḍapāda and Śaṅkara.[49] Advaita means non-dual, one without having a second. It recognises *Brahman* (the absolute) as the only Reality, and denies permanent reality to the world as well as individual souls. The teaching is based on the statement, "Dear Śvetaketu, in the beginning (before creation) Reality (*Brahman*) alone existed, the one without a second."[50]

The concept of "*Brahman* without a second", appears as a world of multiple names and forms. Advaita philosophy claims that it is because of erroneous cognition. The example of perceiving a rope as a snake in insufficient light is often used. The basic cause of this erroneous perception is wrong knowledge (*avidyā*), ignorance (*ajñāna*) which is endowed with two powers: veiling power (*āvaraṇa śakti*) and transforming power (*vikṣepa śakti*). According to the Advaita philosophy, it is ignorance that causes

47. *Ātmāvalokana*.

48. Dvaita, Advaita and Viśiṣṭādvaita are three main schools of Vedānta.

49. Seventh-eighth century CE.

50. *Chāndogya Upaniṣad*, VI.2.1.

the one *ātman* (the self) to appear as many, and it is illusion (*māyā*) that causes the world of phenomena.

Brahman associated with *māyā* is *Brahman* with attributes (*Saguṇa Brahman*), the Lord of Creation, God (*Īśvara*). It is this aspect of *Brahman* that is responsible for the creation, preservation and destruction of the world.

Brahman with attributes, which is *sat* (eternal reality), *cit* (pure consciousness) and *ānanda* (perfect bliss), is involved in the body-mind complex due to *avidyā*. The involved *ātman* is designated as *jīva*. This *jīva* in bondage performs actions motivated by desires, experiences pleasure and pain due to *karma*, and undergoes transmigration until liberation. Liberation from transmigration is not the achievement of a new state, but the recognition of the existing, original state.

Śaṅkara declares that this *jīva*, when shorn of its limiting adjuncts like the body and the mind, is identical to *Brahman* since its essential nature also is *sat-cit-ānanda*.

According to the Viśiṣṭādvaita (special or qualified non-dualism) school of Vedānta philosophy, the world which is a transformation of *Brahman* is real and not illusory.[51] It postulates three entities: *Brahman* or *Īśvara*, *cit* or *jīva* and *acit* or *prakṛti* as the ultimate realities. Of these, *Brahman* is the absolute, independent Reality, and the other two are dependent realities. It is for this reason that this philosophy is known as Viśiṣṭādvaita.[52] This philosophy accepts one Reality, but with attributes or modes.

Brahman is both the Absolute of philosophy and the God of religion. Truth (*satya*), knowledge (*jñāna*), infinity (*anantatva*) and bliss (*ānandatva*) are his attributes. He is the master of Śrī, his wealth.

*Jīva*s are innumerable but of identical form and nature. Even though essentially free, they become bound in *saṁsāra*[53] by the

51. As against the assertions of Advaita.
52. Viśiṣṭa specialised, Advaita non-duality.
53. Life cycles of births and deaths.

influence of *prakṛti* — ignorance, activities of the sense and motor organs, of the mind and the ordinate desire.

These bondages are destroyed through *bhakti* and *prapatti*, self-surrender to God and the consequent grace of God.

The liberated soul has a direct vision of *Brahman* and is absorbed in the eternal bliss of union with him (*sāyujya*). The distinction between him and *Brahman* remains and there is no loss of personality. He will continue forever to enjoy this state of bliss by serving *Brahman*. Viśiṣṭādvaita guarantees the vision of God and salvation to all finite beings — human, sub-human or celestial.

3

Concept of Liberation (Mokṣa)

That alone is real faculty of speech which is used for reciting the Lord's attributes and His glories;

Those alone are real hands which are used for the service of the Lord;

That alone is the real mind which contemplates on the Lord as dwelling in everything; and

That alone is the real power of hearing which is utilised for listening to the description of the Supreme Being.

Again, that alone is the real head which bows down before the two symbols of the Lord, His image and His devotees;

They alone are the real eyes which see them both (the images and the devotees);

They alone are the real limbs which become purified by the waters with which the feet of holy images and holy men are washed. — *Śrīmad Bhāgavata*, II.80.3-4

MOKṢA is the liberation of the soul from bondage or union with the Absolute. It also means attainment of the state of *Brahman* and release from the life cycle which is a bondage due to *karma*. It is also called *mukti* or *kaivalya*.

A study of the theory of evolution, involution and transmigration of souls helps in understanding the need for liberation.

Every evolution presupposes a previous involution. Involution is the first half of the life cycle and evolution is the other half. When it is said that nature evolves consciousness, it is on the assumption that the evolved consciousness was lying involved in nature. Different schools of thought bring out different tables of evolution.

The process of involution and evolution is like burnt fuel. When fuel is burnt, heat is evolved and the fuel turns into ashes. This shows that heat is stored up in the form of the fuel. This accumulation is a process of involution. Through combustion, the heat takes the evolutionary course. Evolution is the reverse transformation of an effect into its cause. Every cause coming across modification undergoes involution to take on the form of an effect. Cause and effect are connected with each other in a chain of different forms. During the course of involution, the life principle gets involved in the folds of physical creation. During the course of evolution, the life principle begins to evolve in different phases, psychic as well as spiritual.

In the process of germination, a seed becomes a tree which will bear crude form of seeds. These seeds will produce multiple trees of the same species under suitable conditions. The unfolding of a seed into a tree is evolution and the transformation into the crude form of seed is involution again.

In the process of involution, life descends through the causal and subtle stages to the gross form of a crude state. In the process of evolution, life ascends from the raw state of matter and living forms through their subconscious state. This is the unfolding of the crude nature through evolution.

In the process of evolution, higher forms of life gradually arise out of the lower, just like vegetative life progresses towards animal life and so forth, until the intelligent human being is formed. According to this theory, the perfect form of human life is yet to come. The existing human life is just a transitory step in evolution.

According to the Hindu doctrine, in their passage of evolution, the individual souls (*jīva*) transmigrate from one body to another after death. The transmigration is from the vegetative plane to the animal kingdom and finally to the human plane, with a human body. All these bodies serve the souls as vehicles in their upward journey.

It is said that the rays of the sun are the life-giving source for these different species. "The Sun verily is *prāṇa*".[1]

In Vedas, the number of life-giving rays of the sun is defined as 1000 × 100 rays. They awake *prāṇa* in all beings. The number 8,400,000 is arrived at as follows: 12 zodiac months of the year × 7 weekdays × 100,000 rays of sun = 8,400,000.

All the forms of the vegetative, animal and human life are made up of two parts — physical and metaphysical. These two parts are connected by *prāṇa* (the life force). *Prāṇa* shines in them. It provides life to vegetative, animal and human species. The first part is formed of gross, physical elements and is called physical body (*sthūla śarīra*). The second part is called subtle body (*sūkṣma śarīra*). The subtle body is formed of finer principles. On the one hand, *prāṇa* takes the form of mind, intelligence and so forth, and on the other hand, it becomes physical electrons, atoms, etc.

The vegetable kingdom possesses one or two of the five powers and senses and the power of absorbing the nourishment, but it has no mental faculty. Animals express joy and fear. All animals do have intelligence to some extent. They understand the affectionate and angry mood of others. They have memory and do have fear of death. But their thinking power is not perfect.

Transmigration is that process which causes psychological development in living beings.

Man's spiritual part is called soul (*jīva*) which has to progress through psychological development. As human being is the best evolved in form, he is capable of thinking, feeling, desiring, etc. This is the combined effect of the life principle, mind and intellect.

Soul is defined as life principle with relation to mind and

---

1. *Praśna Upaniṣad*, I.5

intellect. The spirit is defined as the illuminating, pure life principle that animates both the body and the mind.

This pure life principle never undergoes any change; there is neither development (because it is perfect) nor deterioration (because it is not attached to bondage). It is the mind and everything concerned to mind that changes but is capable of development too.

Hindu philosophers classified mind as the product of nature and one of the created principles.

The process of the passing of the soul (*jīva*) from one body to another after death is called transmigration. According to Hindu doctrines, after death the soul takes on a fresh body that is physiologically best fitted for further psychological development.

Bhagavad-Gītā says,

> Just as a man leaves the worn-out clothes and takes new ones, the embodied soul also casts off the worn-out bodies and enters new bodies.[2]

The life principle seems to evolve higher and higher degrees of intelligence. Memory of the past, even though it looks forgotten, merges into subconscious. However, this process is not called evolution. This is just a psychological growth from the lower to the higher form of life.

In reality, in the course of evolution the involute *prāṇa* is reversed. In Vedic literature, *prāṇa* is a dynamic life energy and is referred to as the first emanation of the cosmic life radiation (*adhyātma bhāva*). This is also known as *bhūta bhāva*.

Push a cart and let it go. It moves on for some time. While pushing the cart, a force is imparted to it by a person. This force comes from the soul, and in the cart, it takes on the form of physical force. Likewise, Prajāpati's force of will to create automatically

2. *Bhagavad-Gītā*, V.2.

sends the radiation, and creation begins. With the cessation of Prajāpati's desire, the radiation would also stop and creation reverts to its cause.

During creation, the radiating dynamic energy (*bhūta bhāva*) begins to manifest and becomes the cause as *prāṇa* itself. It also becomes the material cause and manifests both as animate and inanimate beings in the created world.[3]

Prāṇa is radiated by the *adhyātma bhāva* of Prajāpati; universal *prāṇa* controls the whole universe. The individual soul (*jīvātman*) is a spark of the universal *prāṇa*. The soul enters the body, identifying itself with the body and the mind. Therefore, it is an aspect of the individualised *adhyātma bhāva* of God.

Thus, creation is a cycle of involution and evolution of the creative aspect of the soul (*jīvātmā*). There are cycles of involutions and evolutions at different planes. They are classified as *prāṇa* coming from the absolute to the physical plane and returning back again. The return of *prāṇa* to the Absolute is the real evolution. It is the merging of the individual soul (*jīva*) with the universal *prāṇa* (Hiraṇyagarbha)[4] and finally with the Absolute (*parama bhāva*).

There is another cycle, namely the cycle of transmigration of the souls of individual species from the whole body organism into the seed form and then the evolution of the body from the seed. Every seed possesses the potentiality of evolving into a corresponding living body in all its details; and everybody recedes its whole Self into innumerable seeds of its species over and over again (like that of a tree). The physical and psychic body of a person (that belong to the category of *bhūta bhāva*) reflect life. This is the work of *prāṇa* radiating from the individualised *adhyātma bhāva*.

---

3. In Veda, the word *prāṇinaha* is often used to indicate that they are possessed of *prāṇa* (the life energy).
4. The Golden Egg. See Chapter 5 on "The Universal Spiritual Entity".

The *Bhagavad-Gītā* describes four divine aspects:[5]

1. The Absolute aspect called *Brahman, parama bhāva* (also termed *akṣara*),
2. The Absolute's material nature dwelling in the creation[6] *adhyātma bhāva,*
3. The creative aspect, *bhūta bhāva,* and
4. The creation, *visarga bhāva.*

The *Bhagavad-Gītā* continues:

> All the manifested things arise out of the non-manifest at approach of the day (of Brahmā); and at the approach of (his) night they are absorbed into that same thing which is called the non-manifest.[7]

The Absolute is the Supreme not only because the next two aspects (*adhyātma bhāva* and *bhūta bhāva*) are correlated to each other but also because they form respectively the subjective and the objective sides of *Brahman*. While the subjective aspect (*adhyātma*) shines as his own Self and is imperishable and immutable, the objective aspect (*bhūta bhāva*) creates and as such is dynamic. From the creative aspect (*bhūta bhāva*) of *Brahman* emanates the cosmic energy, which before manifestation takes up different forms both on the psychic and physical planes.

For instance, a person in deep meditation loses (as it were) consciousness of his own self and that of his surroundings. He is conscious of his action, that is, deep meditation, but when he comes out of his deep meditation, he would not only be conscious of his personal existence but also cognisant of his actions. In deep meditation, his consciousness merges into his absolute Self, while at work both his subjective consciousness and his objective consciousness of his capability to work revive simultaneously.

---

5. *Bhagavad-Gītā*, VIII.3.
6. Śaṅkara defines *adhyātma* as "He who dwells in the body".
7. *Bhagavad-Gītā*, VIII.18.

Life exists in two aspects: the Self-aspect (*adhyātma bhāva*) and the consciousness which is the reflection of *prāṇa*. As the self-aspect, it is soul and as *prāṇa*, it is *Brahman*'s radiation which shines in all living beings as consciousness or life.

That is to say, *Brahman* is the absolute. The self-aspect is the nucleus (*adhyātma*); the creative aspect (*bhūta bhāva*) is its emanation; and the creation (*visarga bhāva*) is its physical and psychical creations. The latter reflects life as *prāṇa* which is a radiation of *adhyātma bhāva* (usually called the universal *prāṇa* or Hiraṇyagarbha), controls the whole universe and individual *prāṇa* enters the body identifying itself with the body and mind giving an individualised appearance. At death, individual *prāṇa* leaves the physical body and the components of this physical body dissolve into their respective elementary forms.

But death does not separate *prāṇa*[8] from the subtle body. During life, the rays of *prāṇa* radiate from the Self and they stop their flux at death. They revert to their centre in the sub-consciousness of the causal body.[9] Along with the subtle body, this causal body migrates to assume a new physical body. *Prāṇa* does not leave the body immediately when the mortal body is cast off.

Commenting on *Brahma-Sūtra*, Śaṅkarācārya says that, at the time of death, a soul having cast off the old body departs to enter a new one. This psychic body is clothed in a substance formed out of the past subtle impressions (*bhūta sūkṣma*, subtle matter).

The subtle body is beyond normal perception. It is fireproof and transparent, in the sense that it does not burn at the burning of the physical body, and it is not visible to the eyes. A soul without a subtle body has no individual existence, so there would be no movement. Moving from one body to another the subtle body serves the soul as a vehicle. This movement is called transmigration.

---

8. The rays of life that animate the initial body are here spoken of as rays of *prāṇa*.

9. *Kāraṇa śarīra*.

According to Hindu psychology, mind and intellect survive the body after death, in the form of impressions (*vāsanā*) because they have an independent existence. They transmigrate with the soul to a new life. These impressions are made up of a very fine substance, finer than ether. They are the main constituents of subtle matter, *bhūta sūkṣma*. The past impressions (*vāsanā*) accompany the soul on death to its future destination.

The fine substance of which mind (*citta*) is formed, has the capacity to store up the impressions of everything a man perceives, does and thinks. Ancient Hindu psychologists used the term *citta* for all different mental functions like perceptions, passions, emotions, sentiments and so forth.

Impressions imprinted in *cidākāśa*[10] are never erased or worn away. A person can revive them again and again as memory. But at the time of death, *cidākāśa* undergoes a change, bringing all impressions gained during the whole lifespan in a nutshell no bigger than a seed. This seed-body composed of *vāsanā*[11] is called the causal body. It is the cause of the next change.

The causal body (*kāraṇa śarīra*) has the capacity to cocoon itself in a new body of mental and intellectual powers, that is, a subtle body, *sūkṣma śarīra* and evolve into the next life and body, which exactly meets its needs, with improved mental and intellectual powers achieved from previous births. Thus, man goes on developing his faculties from one birth to another in his march towards the final goal of perfection.

In this way, the past impressions survive death and transmigrate to a future life or birth. These impressions can be

10. *Brahman* in Its aspect as limitless knowledge; unbounded intelligence. This is a familiar concept of the Upaniṣads. It is not meant that the physical ether is consciousness. The Pure Consciousness (*cit*) is like the ether (*ākāśa*), an all-pervading continuum.

11. Past impressions.

revived by special exertion.[12] But they are not needed, because when a person keeps to his goal on ascending a higher rung on the ladder of mental stages, he need not look back to previous stages to get involved in bondage. The mind that cannot put the needed effort is the greatest obstacle. It is this weak mind that feels like looking at previous stages, as it does not like to renounce anything. The fall in reacting to any aim is due to the lack of intensity in efforts. Unless the effort is strong and the mind is firm, success is not assured. So not only the efforts should be strong, but the firmness in reaching the goal should also be intense. A weak mind makes the person fall down on his efforts to reach the goal. One should not mind the number of births one has to take to reach the goal, just because success in this approach is not assured in one single life. It should be considered as a test of patience. *Bhagavad-Gītā* speaks of innumerable auspicious births to reach the goal and how hard it is to find such fortunate persons.

A person who concentrates on his goal intensely will never waste his exertion to revive the past impressions, because he need not have to depend on them in his forward movement to reach the goal. For example, before ascending a ladder, the climber fixes the ladder on the ground and assures himself of its stability. Then he starts climbing, without turning his head to any direction lest he loses his balance. He thinks of the next higher step only. He does not bend back to see the lower rungs. Turning back retards his progress. This is an obstacle to reach the goal. In the same way, when the mental firmness to reach the goal develops in the mind, the person desires to reach the goal through ascending stages only.

Past impressions are always present in the mind. One has to unearth them by intensely focusing the mind on them and bring them up to the level of consciousness, recollecting them from

12. The cases of recollection of the past life are of extraordinary nature. One can revive them to memory by deep meditation. The special exertion is the efforts put to master deep meditation and the ability to bring to the memory the impressions of the past life.

memory without reviving their values. Impressions of the past life are said to be similar to that of the present life and they can be revived through intense concentration on the mind itself. "By the realisation of latent impressions, knowledge of previous birth is acquired."[13]

But this is possible under certain conditions. In a human form, only the impressions of human births will revive in the memory. The other forms of previous lives like those of animals, insects and others will not be revived. In a celestial form, only the impressions of the celestials will be revived. The other impressions will remain in the form of a seed. A favourable condition is a prerequisite for reviving the past. "From these only those tendencies are manifested for which the conditions are favourable."[14] Different kinds of impressions require different kinds of conditions and surroundings. They also need different births for their manifestations. They cannot be expressed in a causal way nor can they find expression by chance. They must follow a certain sequence, according to different types of environments and conditions. Only a limited number of past impressions (*vāsanā*) can find expression in a particular birth. This is because of the limited time accorded in each lifespan.

Success in reviving the desired impressions without invoking the emotions is difficult. If a person has inherited a weak and diseased body, his desire to become a great athletic may not be fulfilled in that life. Likewise, a weak-minded person cannot revive the past impressions in his life. It takes a long period to train the mind and make it strong. For example: An intelligent student by birth can read his lessons once to grasp the subject. But a mentally weak student is not fit for this quickness. He needs repeated readings for understanding depending upon the degree of his mental weakness. The duration of time he needs to master the

---

13. *Pātañjala Yoga-Sūtra*, III.18.

14. Ibid., IV.8.

subject may be long. So there is no certainty of success to him in that particular life. If the lifespan is short and limited while the time required is too long, he cannot accomplish his tasks in this life. So, the conditions should be favourable. "There is no discontinuity in them in spite of lapse of life, surroundings and time, because of the oneness of memory and impressions."[15]

His memory is confined only to the particular experiences gone through in this life.[16] In the same way, the contact of the higher consciousness with the impressions (*saṁskāra*) in the higher vehicles of the soul (*jīvātman*) reproduces memories corresponding to the impressions. This vehicle with the repository of the *saṁskāra* is also called causal body (*kāraṇa śarīra*).

As long as the past impressions (*vāsanā*) are present, so long would be man's transmigration. The creation rolls on from one body to another. When all the impressions are eliminated, mind becomes like a parched seed, the transmigration of the soul comes to an end. At this stage, the soul (*jīva*) realises *Īśvara;* and this state is liberation (*mokṣa, mukti, kaivalya*).

The feeling of freedom from the sense of bondage is liberation, Final Bliss. Every man aspires after liberation, a state which is free from all types of sufferings he undergoes throughout his life.

Views on Soul and Liberation

To put an end to the transmigration of the soul (cycle of rebirths), the mind should be trained intensely, to remain unaffected (just like the water droplets on a lotus leaf) to all happenings in the world. Different schools of thought bring out different views regarding liberation, but a proper look into these confirms that all the views lead to one goal — Eternal Joy.

Buddhism, without admitting the existence of soul, says that liberation comes as a result of the destruction of the process of

---

15. *Pātañjala Yoga-Sūtra*, IV.9.

16. Memory of the person who is keen on practice.

knowledge through continued meditation. Jainism views that the state of liberation is the state of the soul in Pure Happiness. Caraka[17] and Kapila[18] describe liberation "as a state in which there is complete cessation of pleasure and pain arising through the association of the Self with the mind (*manas*), the sense and the sense objects, attainable only when the mind is steady." According to *Yoga-Vāsiṣṭha*,[19] liberation is realised when knowledge is absolutely and ultimately dissociated from all objects and remains in its transcendent purity, having neither an object nor a subject. Bondage remains so long as a person's knowledge has an object associated with it. *Sāṁkhya Kārikā* holds that even after the true knowledge is attained, the body still continues to remain as it was simply by inertia or ignorance (*avidyā*), just as even after the potter has ceased to operate the potter's wheel, it would continue to move as a result of the momentum which it has acquired. According to *Bhagavad-Gītā*, liberation means freedom from the ties of *karma* associated with man through the bonds of attachment, desires, etc. It does not come by itself as a result of philosophic knowledge or devotion to God. But God as the liberator, grants it to those wise men who set their hearts on Him through devotion. The south Indian saint, Nammāḻvār, says that the true definition of liberation is to attain the position of God's servant. Upaniṣads define liberation as a means to realise the bliss, the knowledge of the Ultimate Truth.

Only when man shall roll up the sky like a skin, will there be an end of misery for him without realising God.

Liberation is every man's goal. To the religious minded, it is the realisation of God, who is above births and deaths. This is the highest stage of development.

So long as the impressions of the past and the present continue

17. Author of *Caraka Saṁhitā*, one of the fundamental texts on Āyurveda.

18. Author of *Sāṁkhya-Sūtra*.

19. The teaching of Sage Vasiṣṭha to Rāma, which has a great inclination towards Advaita Vedānta.

to be active, there would be scope for rebirth. So, to obtain liberation, past impressions have to be erased and the imprints of new impressions have to be stopped. Then only it is possible to break the chain of rebirths.

According to Sāṁkhya philosophy, when the three *guṇas* (*sattva*, *rajas* and *tamas*) attain equilibrium, the transmigration of soul comes to an end. Rebirth is a law of nature. "Like a corn a mortal ripens, and like a corn is he born again."[20] Until the cosmic process ends, the multiplicity of each species (individuals) with their special quality persists, because this universe is filled with multiplicity.

The scriptures also say that the creation is the will of God and with the cessation of His will, creation reverts to its cause.

Therefore, to put an end to the transmigration of soul is a hard task. It is better to adopt a suitable method, which consists in training the mind intensively, to remain unaffected to all the happenings just like a lotus leaf on water. For this, a necessary condition must be created with our own efforts.

Liberation is achieved with the eradication of ignorance. Liberation is the result of perfection which can be attained by training one's emotions in achieving a state of steadiness. The more we concentrate on an object, the steadier the mind will be on it. The more we give values to the object, the more the mind would be disturbed. If the mind acquires the habit of indifference towards likes and dislikes, ups and downs in life, attachment and hatred and such other opposites, it will remain unsoiled by them. This act of indifference helps the mind to acquire a steady calmness and will lead to perfection. This in turn draws man towards the path of liberation.

When the mind is absorbed in deep concentration, a person loses the feeling of the self (or ego). Though the mind is extremely active in the state of concentration, it remains calm and quiet. During this time, man will not be affected by any disturbing

20. *Kaṭha Upaniṣad*, I.6.

elements coming from the different types of emotions, which he is accustomed to when he is not in concentration. He thus becomes immune to the influences of fear, happiness, misery, etc. The absorption in deep thinking (or in contemplation) helps man to acquire a habit of high stability and when the mind acquires it, man hardly tends to drop down to the state of disturbances caused by opposites. Fortunes or misfortunes do not affect him. So, a deep concentration has a more lasting effect on the mind. It renders all disturbing forces feeble, and so it takes one to the stage of liberation. A person, who remains free from the disturbing forces, is free from worldly bondage. He attains liberation when still alive. Freeing himself from the normal thoughts and actions, he becomes absorbed in the Universal Spirit.

At the time of liberation, the components of the psychic body undergo an evolution and one after the other evolve into *prāṇa*, which merges in the Self-aspect of God or Creator (*adhyātma bhāva*) and then in the Absolute aspect called *Brahman* (*parama bhāva*). This means the spiritual experience in the consciousness becomes so subtle that it pervades everywhere and becomes more expansive. The discriminating man should merge the (organ of) speech into mind, he should merge that mind into the intelligent self (*jñāna ātmā*); he should merge the intelligent self into the Great Soul (*mahat ātmā*)[21] and the Great Soul into the peaceful Self.[22]

To attain liberation, *mokṣa* is the end of human life. One can attain the end of human life, simply through prayer or meditation only upon the objective that is the self.

Lead me from evil to good,
Lead me from darkness to light,
Lead me from death to Immortality.
Immortality is liberation, mokṣa.[23]

---

21. Also called *Hiraṇyagarbha* (the Golden Egg).
22. *Kaṭha Upaniṣad*, I.3.13.
23. *Bṛhadāraṇyaka Upaniṣad*, I.3.28.

Means to Liberation

Knowledge is the only means to liberation. True knowledge is liberation, while ignorance is bondage. Liberation is the experience of all beings in the Self (*ātman*) and the experience of Self in all beings. The person who has acquired integral experience, remains in the highest condition of *Brahman*-hood. Integral experience consumes all merits and demerits, which are the causes of rebirth. It destroys grief, delusion and other afflictions, which obscure the knowledge of *ātman*. It can be acquired by meditation on *Brahman* with a concentrated mind free from all taints of attachment, aversion and other afflictions. Those who have extirpated all desires for enjoyment here and hereafter, acquire integral experience. They shake off false egoism, and do not identify themselves with the mind-body complex. They are suffused with universal goodwill, amity and compassion. They are freed from enmity to all, full of forgiveness and become indifferent to their own joys and sorrows. They renounce all desires and actions. They have the direct experience of *Brahman*.

The indispensable preparation to the knowledge of *Brahman* is the discrimination of the eternal and the non-eternal, detachment from enjoyments on earth and heaven, restraint of the internal organs, control of the external senses, withdrawal of the mind from external objects of enjoyment, endurance of heat and cold, concentration of the mind on *Brahman*, faith in the instructions of preceptors and desire for liberation.

These moral qualifications make a person fit for the study of Vedānta and enquiry into the nature of *Brahman* (*brahma-jijñāsā*).

Non-killing or non-injury, truthfulness, celibacy, non-acceptance of gifts, renunciation of all possessions, tranquillity, sense-control, withdrawal of the senses from their objects, study of scriptures, austerities, cleanliness or purity of body and mind, discrimination of the Self from the non-Self, fixation of mind, meditation and concentration of mind on *Brahman* with devotion are the auxiliaries to integral experience.

Truthfulness consists in eschewing falsehood, deceit, hypocrisy, pride and boastfulness. Non-deceit and non-crookedness in speech, body and mind constitute truthfulness. Celibacy destroys afflictions and purifies the mind.

Truthfulness and renunciation of desires lead to the attainment of the highest good. When the mind is purged of attachment, aversion, delusion and other afflictions, it can have pure knowledge and intuition of *Brahman*.

When purified by instructions of the scriptures and preceptors, tranquillity, sense control and the like become the organs of the intuiting of the Self.

Hearing the scriptural texts, reflection and meditation on them remove hindrances to higher knowledge and aid its manifestation.

The devotee should cultivate virtues like courage, penance, performance of sacrifices, spiritedness, fortitude, bodily and mental cleanliness, study of the scriptures, knowledge of *ātman* obtained from the scriptures, inactivity of the cognitive organs in the presence of their objects, inactivity of the motor organs, tranquillity of mind, purity of mind and concentration.

Likewise, he should cultivate social virtues like goodwill, love for all creatures, friendship, compassion for the distressed, forgiveness, selflessness, conquest of enmity, universal benevolence, equal treatment of all, charity and pursuit of the welfare of humanity.

There are other social virtues that should also be cultivated like charity, self-sacrifice, straightforwardness, non-killing, tenderness, non-malevolence, non-cavilling, pacification of anger, non-self-glorification, non-hypocrisy and modesty.

Social virtues purify the mind and aid Self-realisation.

Karma and Liberation

Liberation is the release from bondage to the cycle of rebirth by rendering the kārmic process inoperative. Yoga philosophy proposes *kriyā-yoga*[24] and meditation to attenuate the afflictions, *kleśa* and thereby rendering *karma* inoperative. Vedānta, particularly Advaita, proposes the discovery of one's own self which burns the seeds; because of the discovery of the self, one does not act at all and thus one does not create residues. Viśiṣṭādvaita declares that by abandoning oneself to the Supreme, automatically, all *karmas* are destroyed.

But the *karma* that has already started cannot be avoided. Once the soul (*jīva*) is liberated, even these will not leave residues.

Liberation as the Aim of Devotion

Though man acquires and enjoys the material life to his satisfaction, he still feels dissatisfied and he fails to understand the reason. This is because he is in need of peace and real happiness. He takes this as a major suffering in his life. Man suffers, because he identifies his soul with the conglomeration of body and mind. He wants a sort of freedom that he is unable to explain for himself. This state of freedom so badly needed, freedom from suffering and freedom from the sense of bondage is liberation (*mokṣa*). It is obtained when this identification ceases and consciousness too ceases with it. Through devotion, the hook that binds the soul to the created world (*prakṛti*) with its modes is released and the bondage does not reappear. Man finds his ultimate joy through this liberation.

Soul is of the nature of consciousness and is essentially identical with God. But the confusion between the soul and one's ego and its separation from God comes from its association with the intellect (*buddhi*). The consequent bondage of cycles of births and deaths (*saṁsāra*) is owing to the lack of knowledge of God because the real knowledge of the soul (*jīva*) is of the nature of God.

Though individual souls are actually identical with God, they appear to be many because of the multiplicity of intellects. It is

24. Austerity, self-study and devotion to *Īśvara*.

like the sun appearing as many being reflected in several mirrors. When all the mirrors are removed, all the reflections will merge again in the sun. That is why not all souls are liberated when one soul (*jīva*) is liberated, just like the reflections of the sun will continue in other mirrors, although one is removed.

Apart from the conscious entity which exists in a twofold form (God and individual soul), the only other reality that exists is the insentient primordial matter (*prakṛti*). It functions as the material cause for creation. Being the power of God, it is real. So, the whole creation, which is its product, is also real.

Devotion is the highest love for God. It is to be cultivated towards the one that is to be propitiated. While devotion leads to liberation, it does not provide the knowledge of God. The knowledge of God is in the soul.

The relation of the soul to the intellect creates bondage concealing the true nature of the soul. This bondage can only be removed by the removal of the association between soul and intellect, through devotion to God, the Supreme Lord. This devotion (*bhakti*) helps the aspirant to transcend the three *guṇas*.[25] He then is at the threshold of liberation.

The stage of liberation is the highest spiritual development of man in his transcendental evolution. It is the climax of his knowledge and existence. The scriptures say that liberation is the stage of final release. It is achieved through the cessation of ignorance. They recommend the path of action (*karma-yoga*) in the beginning to harness the mind. The desire for liberation attained through *karma* makes man tranquil in mind, with the senses restrained. "Having given up desires, resigned, patient and absorbed in abstract meditation, let the man see the Self in the Self."[26] These qualities release him from bondage. This form of abstract meditation is devotion (*bhakti*). Liberation is achieved

25. *Sattva, rajas* and *tamas*.

26. *Bṛhadāraṇyaka Upaniṣad*, IV.4.23.

through devotion. To a liberated person "that world obtained by *karma* indeed comes to an end".[27]

Only a liberated person can experience the bliss of *Brahman*. Hence, *Taittirīya Upaniṣad* says, "He who knows *Brahman* attains the highest."[28] After reaching the climax of man's knowledge, he will be released from bondage. On the other hand, *Śvetāśvatara Upaniṣad* says, "After knowing Him alone, one transcends death."[29] Transcending death is liberation. *Kaṭha Upaniṣad* expresses the same view in a different way. "Having perceived 'that', one is free from the jaws of death."[30]

Liberation, the final release, is the only solution for man's sufferings. Because "Just as the world obtained by works perishes here, so also there (in the other world as said in scriptures) the world obtained by merit perishes."[31] Man suffers, because whatever he earns through actions perishes ultimately. So, "when He, who is the highest, is seen, the knot of the heart is untied, doubts are shattered and the results of his actions (*karma*) perish".[32] Realisation of the highest as well as the lowest is the permanent achievement in life. This achievement alone brings liberation.

All the scriptures prescribe constant meditation on Him for attaining the final release. While *Chāndogya Upaniṣad* says, "He has to be sought after, He has to be specially desired and known",[33] *Bṛhadāraṇyaka Upaniṣad* brings out the point, "verily my dear one, the Self has to be seen, has to be heard, has to be reflected upon, has to be steadily meditated upon".[34]

---

27. *Bṛhadāraṇyaka Upaniṣad*, III.8.10.
28. *Taittirīya Upaniṣad*, I.1.1.
29. *Śvetāśvatara Upaniṣad*, III.8.
30. *Kaṭha Upaniṣad*, III.15.
31. *Chāndogya Upaniṣad*, VIII.1.6.
32. *Muṇḍaka Upaniṣad*, II.2.8.
33. *Chāndogya Upaniṣad* VIII.7.1.
34. *Bṛhadāraṇyaka Upaniṣad*, 4.5.

Constant meditation is the foundation of devotion. Devotion in turn brings liberation. This meditation is of the form of continuous memories. It is an unbroken remembrance. It is like a stream of oil. Stability of memory is considered as a means to final release, as said in *Chāndogya Upaniṣad*.[35] "The memory becomes firm, when such a memory is obtained; there is the loosening of all knots." The loosening of all knots is the road to liberation.

Lord Kṛṣṇa says,

> To those who are desirous of an eternal union with Me, and accordingly worship Me, I give with love, that faculty of understanding, by which they come to Me.[36]

He continues,

> It is not possible to see Me with the help of Vedas, through the practice of religious austerities, through the giving of gifts or through sacrifices, in the same manner in which you have seen Me (now). O Arjuna, destroyer of foes, it is possible really to know, to see, and to enter into Me, such as I am now, exclusively by means of devotion (*bhakti*).[37]

That Highest person is attainable exclusively by devotion (*bhakti*).[38]

Only the Supreme can bless man with liberation.

Liberation is only possible through a stable mind. Mind by nature is fickle. It cannot be easily fixed in one place by a person. It is hard to control on account of its agitated nature. But it can be controlled not without difficulties by cultivating a favourable attitude in the direction of the Self by repeated contemplation of its different attributes. This gives stability to the mind.

The process of bringing the mind to the stable state is devotion. This forms the basis of carrying all the senses to the point of

35. *Chāndogya Upaniṣad*, II.2.6.
36. *Bhagavad-Gītā*, X 10.
37. Ibid., XI 53.54.
38. Ibid., VIII.22.

liberation. The aim of devotion is liberation. When mind is stabilised, concentration develops. Concentration makes a man see that which his ordinary vision is unable to provide.

Liberation is realisable by winning God's love. Devotion is love of God (according to religious terms). But this love is not an escape from the harshness of life, but a dedication to the service of God. The only way to reach this ideal is pure love which is also termed as devotion. God's love can only be won by faith and devotion. Lord Kṛṣṇa says,

> Even if a man of most vile conduct worships Me with undistracted devotion, he must be reckoned as righteous, for he has rightly resolved.[39]

This means, if a person repents of having committed sins, he is freed from sin, if he resolves on never committing sin again, he will be purified. The evil of the past deeds cannot be washed away except by turning to God with an undivided heart. Thus, *Bhagavad-Gītā* brings out an assurance that Liberation is achievable even by the worst sinner by turning to God. But one has to offer his whole personality to God. This can only be possible through devotion.

Lord Buddha used an analogy in the *Dhammapada* (Puppavagga)

> The perfume of flowers cannot travel against the wind, be it the scent of sandal or that of jasmine, but the sweet odour of a good man travels against the wind. Like the sweet odour of a good man, devotion travelling against the wind reaches the abode of God. Those who walk on the path of devotion ascend to God's kingdom, the Highest.

Devotion is the sincere love of the Ideal. It brings total mental transformation. By drawing the presence of God within, man finds

39. *Bhagavad-Gītā*, IX.30.

tranquillity that removes all his sufferings. The Divine grace frees man from sorrow, blessing him with Liberation.

> The path of devotion is indeed excellent, because it contributes to well-being in every way and because it is free from fear of every kind.[40]

Happiness is the universal aim of life. True happiness of human beings does not lie in the possession of external things, but in the attainment of the higher mind and spirit, that is to say, in the development of what is the innermost part in us. It may mean pain and restraint, but it will lead us to joy and freedom.

Devotion is a sort of austerity (*tapas*) that is essential for a seeker after liberation. It is the contemplation of an unbroken current of a single thought, which is set to flow towards God, in whose light everything shines. This incessant flow of a single thought is the concentration in *bhakti-yoga*.

Human birth is the result of progress in evolution. The transmigrating soul as a result of its merits is blessed by God with a human form, to help him find the way for liberation. But among the countless privileged with this birth, there are few and far between, who develop intense love to release from bondage.

Though liberation is open to all, many do not feel any urge to seek it. Of those who aspire for liberation, many suffer from doubts and many others are scared away by difficulties. Only a few rare souls succeed in braving the perils and reaching the goal. This is due to their past *karma* both good and bad that has started giving results in this birth.

Devotion is both a means to the realisation of God and an end in itself. It is unalloyed faith in God. It is love that does not seek anything in return. It is natural that, when the mind is in that state, the way to liberation opens by itself. Moreover, "Devotion gives supreme peace to the mind."[41] That is why, it is said that,

---

40. *Śrīmad Bhāgavata*, VI.1.17.

41. *Śrīmad Bhāgavata*, I.2.22.

> The supreme duty of man consists in following such activities as will generate in him pure devotion to God, free from all extraneous motives, and unshakeable by antagonistic circumstances. By such devotion a person's mind attains to Supreme peace.[42]

The efforts of the person striving for liberation through God realisation never go waste. Lord Kṛṣṇa says,

> Ruin will not befall him either here (in this world) or there (in the next), O Arjuna! For not one who does what is good, dear friend, will (ever) come to a sad fate.[43]

A person who is very keen on striving for liberation will certainly attain it. Even one who is not keen on putting efforts to attain liberation, but who is attracted by it, will rise in the scale of evolution. Human life is an opportunity to develop the soul's divine nature.

When all other types of love are rendered less important, then one becomes conscious of Divine love.

Rabia[44] was once asked, "Do you love the Almighty?" "Yes." "Do you hate the devil?" "My love of God," she said, "leaves Me no leisure to hate the devil. I saw the prophet in a dream. He said, "O Rabia, do you love Me"? I said, "O Apostle of God, who does not love thee? But love of God hath so absorbed me that neither love nor hate of any other thing remains in my heart."[45]

Devotion and Liberation

"It (devotion) is superior even to liberation. It quickly burns up the soul's sheaths of ignorance as the fire consumes all objects."[46]

---

42. *Śrīmad Bhāgavata*, I.2.6.
43. *Bhagavad-Gītā*, VI.40.
44. A Muslim woman saint.
45. *A Literary History of the Arabs* by R.R. Nicholson.
46. *Śrīmad Bhāgavata*, III.25.33.

Ancient Hindu sages say that the individual soul has three alternative courses to be followed in the process of evolution: Heaven (the higher stages of life), liberation while still living (*jīvan mukta*), and final liberation. Amongst these, liberation while still alive means the attainment of Supreme devotion. Non-attainment of devotion is however transitory which is not due to lack of conviction on devotion but due to lack of desire to develop it. Culmination of devotion towards an object is easier. Devotion is an act of giving oneself totally to the object of devotion.

There is a natural yearning in him for something that is not for his sensual or intellectual pleasure, but it is for something beyond. All religions consider God in one form or the other as the object of devotion. So theists view that God is real and devotion to God brings liberation while still alive. "As long as one has not taken refuge in Thee, the Deliverer from all sins, so long will one have distress, desire, infatuation as also worldly pleasures."[47] To aspire for and to receive God's support is devotion, which releases one from all sorts of bondage which are the causes of desire, distress, etc.

> Hearing from Arjuna the news of Lord Kṛṣṇa's departure to Heavens, Yudhiṣṭhira (the eldest among the Pāṇḍavas) traversing the whole course of *yoga* step by step dissolved the lower principle into the next higher and finally effected the merger of his personal consciousness into universal.[48]

The meaning revealed is that, regardless of all the ornaments and garments, separated from all worldly attachments and having subdued even one's personal consciousness, the devotee should offer his speech as oblation into the fire of his mind, his mind into *prāṇa*, *prāṇa*[49] into *apāna*, *apāna* into death and death into the five

---

47. *Viṣṇu Purāṇa*, I.9.72.

48. *Śrīmad Bhāgavata*, I.15.40, 42.

49. *Prāṇa* and *apāna* are two facets of *prāṇa* ever active in the created world. It is like the inhalation and the exhalation of the Creator.

principles of earth, water, fire, air and ether. After having offered these five into the three *guṇas* (*sattva, rajas* and *tamas*), the devotee should submit the three into the one Great Principle; and having thus offered everything into the fire of the Self, he would effect the complete merger of the Self in the Eternal *Brahman*. Offering of oblations is the mystic merger of the lower principles in their immediate causes.

The doctrine of the development of the souls from the lower plane of life to higher ones is only a progressive psychic manifestation of life. "Dissolution takes place in the reverse order, so it is seen in the world also."[50]

The view is held that dissolution (at the end of a periodical mundane existence) takes place in the reverse order, with the pervaded principles (or effects) dissolving in their corresponding material causes. It is a well-known fact that the effects of things made out of clay like a jar or a toy of clay, etc. are restored back to clay, their material cause, on destruction. The silver or gold ornaments resolve back to gold or silver, their metal form, when melted. So too, the soul, a product of the Creator, would retrace its original source. This process leads to the attainment of the feeling of oneness with God. This state is known as the soul's liberation, that is, freedom from bondage. It is also the process of fusing the mind with God, which also means the total absorption of mind in God.

Souls do not have a self-manifesting power. They are always attached to God, though the sense of separation from God exists. If souls were self-manifesting, they could not have any relation with God. Because in *Bhagavad-Gītā*, Śrī Kṛṣṇa says, "And know Me also, O Bhārata, to be the embodied soul in all the bodies."[51]

What the Lord seeks to impress upon Arjuna is that the soul is a particle of His own Self. It is not different from Him. Human

50. *Śāṇḍilya Bhakti-Sūtra*, 92.

51. *Bhagavad-Gītā*, XIII.2.

being is a union of the Universal Infinite and the universal particular. Man, even though he appears as a part of the whole, is also the potential whole. To accomplish the universality is the ideal of man. Man's peculiarity is the possession of the inward principle, which impels him to the creative acquisition of a higher purpose in life. The lack of contentment in him is due to his idea of identification with the body. When this identification is removed, man becomes totally liberated.

To assert the point that souls are not self-manifesting, *Bhagavad-Gītā* points out, "As the one sun illumines all this world, O Bharata, the soul illumines all the bodies."[52] Though the soul itself is considered as different from God it is always attached to Him and dependent on Him.

The idea of diversity is produced in the soul by the internal organ (*antaḥkaraṇa*) which is a limiting adjunct to the individual soul. According to Vedānta philosophy, the mind, the intellect, the ego and *citta* are termed *antaḥkaraṇa*. With the limiting, adjunctive internal organ, the traverse of the whole course of evolution by means of different methods, in order to merge completely in the Supreme Being, is a long and difficult course. Devotion, on the other hand, raises the energy into its highest potentiality and draws the devotee to the spiritual path.

Through devotion (*bhakti*), man can easily retrace his reverse path to his ancestral source. Devotion acts as a catalyst in the progress of man's spiritual journey. Since the Vedic period, people are devoted to their object of worship.

Īśāvāsya Upaniṣad cites the situation of an aspirant who, having failed in all his efforts in getting illumination through other methods, adopted the path of devotion (*bhakti*). All his life he worshipped the material sun as personal God, but failed to see the spiritual entity behind the shining orb of the material sun. All his life he has been devoted to the contemplation of the Deity as

52. *Bhagavad-Gītā*, XIII.33.

manifested in the sun. Overfilled with devotion, he prayed: "Like a lid, Thy shining golden orb covers the entrance to the Truth in thee. Remove it, O sun, so that I who am devoted to the true may behold that."[53] Meditation upon the Supreme Being as residing in the sun is very often advised, because the manifestation of Divine Glory is associated with the sun. He reveals the true nature of all the objects by dispelling darkness. But to a true follower of the sun, his shining powerful rays obstruct his clear view of the true sun without rays. The aspirant, who likes to have the view of this true sun, prays directly to the sun himself, his heart filled with devotion. The knowledge the aspirant earned through other means only dispelled his ignorance. But his devotional prayers revealed to him the true nature of the personal God.

While devotion is the direct means to liberation, the knowledge earned through the path of action (*karma-mārga*) and the path of knowledge (*jñāna-mārga*) serve as subsidiary to it.

The aspirant of *Īśāvāsya Upaniṣad* intended to know the Truth as the Ultimate Reality in his personal God and prayed whole-heartedly throughout his life. After many hardships and failures through other means, he ultimately surrendered to his God and the material sun through the path of devotion (*bhakti*) and obtained illumination.

Devotion does not require a sequence of previous preparation of tranquillity, etc. The devotional way is easier to follow. The desire to get liberation alone is sufficient in this path. It is interesting to note that even the sub-human species are entitled to tread the path of devotion. To develop devotion, there is no need to practise severe austerities, to torture the senses or to suppress them forcefully. There is no harm to be done to the physical body. It is simply love of God. The supreme faith with reverence is the only qualification required in the path of devotion.

Prahlāda,[54] who learnt the path of devotion while still in his

53. *Īśāvāsya Upaniṣad*, 15.

54. A child devotee, son of Hiraṇyakaśipu, a demon king.

mother's womb, was endowed with supreme faith with reverence to Lord Nārāyaṇa.

The epic *Śrīmad Bhāgavata* says that the constant meditation and the constant love to God with faith is a sure way to get His blessings.

> Blessed are the *gopīs* of Braja,[55] who have their mind absorbed in the thought of Śrī Kṛṣṇa, and singing His glories with a heart full of love, eyes bedewed with tears and a voice choked with emotion even while milking their cows, pounding the corn for removing the husk, churning the curds, plastering the courtyard with cow-dung, swinging infants in the cradle, lulling their crying children to sleep, sprinkling water on the floors and doing everything else.[56]

It is said to mean that, like the celebrated damsels of Braja, a devotee should have his mind absorbed in God, who is the object of supreme love, the inner controller of all, the repository of all virtues and the devotee should be ever engaged in loving meditation on His virtues, glory and essence, even while attending to his daily round of activities.

Accepting with reverence the existence of God, His various descents, His utterances, power, virtues, glory, sports, greatness, etc. are some of the characteristics of supreme faith. He who cultivates absolute dependence on God, is said to be endowed with supreme faith. Leaving aside all the practices prescribed in the scriptures, the mere desire to have liberation is sufficient to approach God.

> To Him who at the beginning created Brahmā, and who gave Vedas to him, to Him the God, who reveals the knowledge of Himself, do I, desirous of liberation go for refuge.[57]

Devotion is to be understood as the "highest love to God and

55. Braja is a cowherd village in India.
56. *Śrīmad Bhāgavata*, X.44, 45.
57. *Śvetāśvatara Upaniṣad*, 6.8.

that nothing can topple it". Prahlāda, the son of the demon king Hiraṇyakaśipu, prays,

> O Lord, even though I may have to pass through thousands of wombs, let there be in me for ever, O Acyuta, unshakeable devotion to thee, in each of these births.

This unshakeable devotion to God is the source for liberation.

Nārada, Śāṇḍilya, Śaṅkara and Rāmānuja are all great devotees and are authorities on the doctrine of devotion. Śaṅkara, the great exponent of Advaita philosophy, says in his *Vivekacūḍāmaṇi* (Crest Jewel of Discrimination): "Among things conducive to liberation, devotion alone holds the supreme place. The seeking after one's real nature is designated as devotion."[58] Śāṇḍilya, the great sage, defines *bhakti* as "It is the highest love for God."[59] The great Nārada defines it as, "That verily is of the nature of Supreme love of God."[60] "God is the love Absolute. It is from this love that soul derives joy."[61]

God Himself is love. If one is desirous of joy or bliss, one should have to have it from God alone and from no one else. Devotion is nothing but the love to be cultivated towards the object of reverence. This means transforming of the whole mind towards God. Prahlāda, who possessed the highest devotion, said,

> The firm affection that the deluded feel towards the object of senses, such a firm affection may I have towards thee and may it never depart from my heart, remembering Thee.[62]

This love is of the highest order, because God is the Highest of all. The sense of love towards one, who is higher, varies from the

58. Śaṅkara's *Vivekacūḍāmaṇi*, 31.
59. *Śāṇḍilya Bhakti-Sūtra*, 2.
60. *Nārada Bhakti-Sūtra*, 2.
61. *Taittirīya Upaniṣad*, II.7.
62. *Viṣṇu Purāṇa*, 1.20.17.

sense of love towards one who is lower. The love towards an elderly person is different compared to the love towards a child. The love towards an elderly person is no doubt *bhakti*.[63] But in the case of God, it is the highest love of all. It is in the form of unceasing love and meditation.

"In the case of a devotee, even a little effort like remembrance of God destroys great sins, because all other means like expiation have been given up."[64] A devotee is always placed in a high order. He depends only on the strength of God's name. The frequent and continuous recollection of God's name is a simple practice, yet so powerful that it can destroy even great sins.

In the great epic *Rāmāyaṇa*, the effect of pronouncing Rāma's name is brought out during the slaying of Indrajit[65] by Lakṣmaṇa.[66] Indrajit, the demon prince, fought a fierce battle with Lakṣmaṇa. As the duel went on between the two powerful warriors, they were hurt by several arrows and many bows were broken. At last, Lakṣmaṇa took the deadly arrow named *aindra*, which he had obtained from Indra. It was like death at the time of the great deluge; and Lakṣmaṇa bent his bow and pulled the string to the utmost. While he did so, he uttered Rāma's name for its strength.

> If it is true that Rāma is unequalled in prowess, if it is true that he has ever been righteous, if it is true that he has ever been truthful, then, may this arrow kill Indrajit, the son of Rāvaṇa.

Lakṣmaṇa invoked the incantations with reverence to Rāma and sent the arrow towards Indrajit. It travelled like a streak of lightning and it mortally wounded Indrajit's head. Thus is the power of remembering Rāma's name with reverence.

---

63. In Hindu tradition, our relation to elders should have a trace of devotion.
64. *Śāṇḍilya Bhakti-Sūtra*, 76.
65. Rāvaṇa's son.
66. Rāma's brother.

Remembering of God's name destroys the great sins and brings purity to the intellect, clearing it of all doubts arising due to bondage. In *Bhagavad-Gītā*, the Lord Himself says, "Abandoning all religious duties take refuge in Me alone. I will deliver you from all sins. Do not grieve."[67] The sins, that are causes of bondage, are sure to be destroyed by taking refuge in God. This is possible only through devotion. When one is delivered of sins, one is liberated; that is the aim of one's life. "All are useful in liberation only through the production of the supreme devotion."[68]

So, all the methods adopted are useful and helpful when they lead one to the path of devotion, which is superior to all other methods.

> He who proclaims among My devotees this Supreme mystery shall come to Me, acquiring supreme devotion towards Me. There is no doubt about this.[69]

Abandoning all religious duties to take refuge in God does not mean not to do any duties. It means complete relinquishment of attachment to the fruits of actions done to fulfil the required duties. To renounce the fruits of actions is regarded as *sāttvika* which creates a *sāttvika* mind leading to true devotion. Yet, it is a fact that it is impossible to abandon actions entirely. But one can give up the fruits of work.

> Identification with Him is achieved through undivided devotion. Liberation is attained when the individual's internal organ (*antaḥkaraṇa*) is dissolved absolutely.[70]

The nature of the mind is described in *Bṛhadāraṇyaka Upaniṣad* as

---

67. *Bhagavad-Gītā*, XVIII.66.
68. *Śāṇḍilya Bhakti-Sūtra*, 84.
69. *Bhagavad-Gītā*, XVIII.68.
70. *Śāṇḍilya Bhakti-Sūtra*, 96.

> Desire, deliberation, doubt, faith, want of faith, steadiness, impatience, shame, intelligence and fear, all these are nothing but forms of mind.[71]

The *Śrīmad Bhāgavata* says,

> The mind of man under the sway of passions and greed will not attain to real and lasting peace through the restraint of the senses and other practices of *rāja-yoga*, as it will through the service of the Lord with loving devotion.[72]

Svapneśvara, the earliest commentator on *Śāṇḍilya Bhakti-Sūtra*, holds that the mind is capable of contraction and expansion. When it expands, it can perceive many things (several things) simultaneously: like the colour, the smell and the softness of a flower. When it is contracted, it can perceive only one. Like the sensation of pain, etc. the sense of egoism is also directly perceived in the intellect, because all the intellects associated with the individual souls have arisen from the ego-principle of God (*Īśvara*). Pleasure, pain, etc. are qualities which reside in the intellect. When reflected upon the soul, they are wrongly attributed to the latter.

Since the soul that sprung from God animates the intellect, it must be capable of grasping the external world made up of the elements: the subtle elements, the gross elements and the sense organs.[73] The power of grasping depends upon the three *guṇa*s (*sattva*, *rajas* and *tamas*), which act as limiting adjuncts in the sense organs. This limitation creates the sense of bondage in the internal organ (*antaḥkaraṇa*). This internal organ cannot be removed by knowledge. Just as it is impossible to destroy the soul which is the basis of all existence and manifestation. It is all-pervading by

---

71. *Bṛhadāraṇyaka Upaniṣad*, I.5.3.
72. *Śrīmad Bhāgavata*, I.6.36
73. Soul springs from God and enters the body to animate the bodily matter and to make it capable of functioning. When the soul enters the body it owns the body and identifies itself with the body. So it can be supposed that the intellect of the individual soul also has sprung from God, because of the connection between God, soul and body.

nature. It is bound to pervade the internal organ, which is by nature limited and finite wherever it is. Hence, the connection between them will always be present. It is just a case of mistaking one for the other, like seeing a snake in a rope. Devotion destroys this bondage and paves the way for liberation.

God is ever present in man and His bliss is always bestowed on the one who seeks it sincerely. But an individual soul can create a special relationship with God through this bliss-providing supreme devotion as a medium of approach. Bliss is the essential character of God and is established in liberation.

> Whoever has steady devotion to Thee, the root cause of all the worlds, what has he to do with the meritorious acts, wealth or desire? Liberation is already placed in his grip.[74]

As the modes of *rajas* and *tamas* are present in the mind, doubts arise in the mind. When these doubts are removed with the sword of knowledge, then one realises the Ultimate Truth.

In many ways, devotion is superior to the knowledge of the soul even though the latter clears the internal organ of its impurities. Liberation can be achieved only by the offering of the internal organ to God, that is, the absorption of all the functions of the mind into God. Devotion is the easiest method to absorb mind into God.[75]

Devotion leads one to the service of God, keeping his thoughts and spirits fixed on Him. When the unconditional love towards God develops in an individual soul, he transcends the limits of his consciousness and obtains liberation. Knowledge is weaker than devotion, so far as the attainment of liberation is considered. Supremacy of devotion is described in *Bhagavad-Gītā* as: "The worshippers of gods attain the gods, whereas My devotees,

---

74. *Viṣṇu Purāṇa*, I.2.20.

75. The merger or offering, that is, the sacrifices in the form of self-control or offering the sense objects into the fire of senses to burn them, etc. *Bhagavad-Gītā*, IV.26, 30.

however they worship Me, eventually come to Me and Me alone."[76] God takes those who worship Him dearly. "Whoever worships Me with devotion, they are in Me and I am in them."[77] Lord's grace of liberation to His devotee has been brought out in *Viṣṇu Purāṇa* by the Lord Himself. "As the mind endowed with devotion gets steady in Me, so through My grace attains liberation also."[78]

Devotion needs no previous preparation:

> He who with devotion offers Me a leaf, a flower, a fruit or water, I accept this offering made with devotion by him who is pure in heart.[79]

Devotion is the best purifier, because devotion is the fundamental characteristic of our internal organ (*antaḥkaraṇa*) and purity is its internal means. In *Mahābhārata* the Lord says,

> Whatever acts are consecrated by those whose intellects are concentrated in single-pointed devotion, all these, the Lord Himself accepts on His head.[80]

This means that God accepts and enjoys the previously mentioned type of offering as if He is obtaining the desired object far beyond the range of His hopes. Everything that man possesses should be dedicated (inner as well as outer belongings) to God, under the influence of devotion.

The relation between the soul and the internal organ (*antaḥkaraṇa*) will be there as long as the latter has an existence of its own. A crystal is colourless. The proximity of a coloured object gives it the colour. The object is the cause for bondage. Likewise, this soul, which is pristine, gets into bondage through the internal organ (*antaḥkaraṇa*) made up of the three *guṇa*s acting as a limiting

76. *Bhagavad-Gītā*, VII.23.
77. Ibid., IX.29.
78. *Viṣṇu Purāṇa*, I.20.20.
79. *Bhagavad-Gītā*, IX.26.
80. *Mahābhārata*, Śānti-Parva.

adjunct. It is not possible to remove the soul which is the very basis of all existence and manifestation. This relation cannot be removed because it is not possible to transcend the nature of either of them. The soul is all-pervading by nature. When in a body, it is bound to pervade the internal organ (*antaḥkaraṇa*), which by nature is limited and finite, wherever it is. As long as the relation between the embodied soul (*jīva*) and the internal organ (*antaḥkaraṇa*) is always present, the knowledge of the soul (*ātmā*) cannot bring liberation. The bondage can be destroyed only by the removal of the limiting adjuncts of the internal organ identifying itself to the soul.

In *Bhagavad-Gītā*, Lord Kr̥ṣṇa declares that devotion to Him frees the souls from all involvement in *guṇa*s. When the internal organ is freed from the effect of *guṇa*, it then becomes the cause of liberation, which is characterised by the Bliss of the Supreme Being. Lord Kr̥ṣṇa says,

> Of these, *sattva*, luminous and free from evil, from its stainlessness, binds, O sinless one, by attachment to happiness and knowledge.[81] Know that *rajas* is of the nature of passion giving rise to thirst and attachment. It binds fast, O son of Kuntī, the embodied one, by attachment to action.[82] And know that *tamas* is born of ignorance and that it deludes all embodied beings. O descendant of Bharata, it binds fast through carelessness, indolence and sleep.[83]

Thus describing the different functions of the modes and the effects of their domination in the mind due to different causes (starting from birth, food, surrounding, etc.), Śrī Kr̥ṣṇa points out that it is possible to transcend these three *guṇa*s through devotion and to attain the spiritual stature of God.

> And he who serves Me with an unswerving devotion transcends

81. *Bhagavad-Gītā*, XIV.6.
82. Ibid., XIV.7.
83. Ibid., XIV.8.

> the three *guṇas* (of *sattva, rajas* and *tamas*) and is fit to become *Brahman*.[84]

But this does not mean that knowledge of the soul is not necessary; as it is this knowledge which helps devotion by washing out impurities like lack of faith and lack of reverence. Faith and reverence are important factors in devotion. But the knowledge of *ātman* is not capable of destroying the superimposition of the characteristics of the limiting adjuncts of the mind on the soul because it is directly connected with it. These limiting adjuncts can be compared to a person suffering from jaundice and so cannot and does not prevent his sight from seeing a white object as yellow.

"When the seer beholds no agent of action other than the *guṇa*, and knows what transcends the *guṇa*, he attains to My state."[85] It is expressed here that the Self being pure in nature by itself gains agency through various actions by contact with the *guṇas* springing from the past *karmas*. When one perceives the Self and understands that the Self by itself is not the agent of actions, but is of the nature of infinite knowledge, then it attains to His likeness. This is easily attainable only through devotion, the highest love towards God. This highest love renders the mind totally absorbed in God. Because Lord Kṛṣṇa says,

> But by single-minded devotion, O Arjuna, it is possible to truly know, to see and to enter into Me, who am of this form (cosmic form), O harasser of foes.[86]

It is not possible to know God truly by mere study, teaching of sacred texts, etc., neither through meditation alone. Mere sacrifices, gifts and austerities do not cultivate devotion towards God. But by single-minded devotion, characterised by discipline and intensity, it is possible to know God directly and enter into His status.

---

84. *Bhagavad-Gītā*, XIV.26.

85. Ibid., XIV.19.

86. Ibid., XI.54.

Passages of *Kaṭha Upaniṣad* and *Muṇḍaka Upaniṣad* confirm that God or the Self cannot be obtained by instruction, nor by intellect nor by much hearing, whosoever He chooses, by Him alone is He obtained. To such a one He reveals His own form.[87]

As God is always dearer to a devotee, He reveals Himself to His devotee, whose single-minded devotion constantly flows towards Him.

> I am easy of access, O Arjuna, to that *yogin*, who is ever integrated with Me, whose mind is not in anything else but Me, and who ceaselessly recollects Me at all times.[88]

Here the *yogin* is one who has the steady abstraction of mind also called concentration or *yoga*.

One whose mind is not in anything else but in God at the time of meditation as well as during all other times is the real devotee; and God is accessible to such real devotees. Lord Kṛṣṇa says,

> To those ceaselessly united, who worship Me, I bestow that discernment by which they come to Me. Out of mercy for them, I abide in their heart; dispel the darkness born of ignorance by the brilliant lamp of knowledge.[89]

So when a person's mind is deeply attached to God and he is completely dependent on Him through intense devotion, he would reach God and would enjoy the Supreme Bliss and thereby obtains Liberation.

Liberation, Yoga and Sāṁkhya View

Mokṣa (the final liberation) is termed as spiritual freedom.[90] It is self-manifested and is not dependent on any action. It is the stage of Eternal Consciousness that changes when it is caught up in the

87. *Kaṭha Upaniṣad*, 1.2.23 and *Muṇḍaka Upaniṣad*, 3.2.3.
88. *Bhagavad-Gītā*, VIII.14.
89. Ibid., X.12.
90. *Citta vimukti*.

world of *karma,* but returns to its natural state in liberation, when it is free from the sense of contact. This is the feeling of freedom from the sense of bondage. Mental stability is a necessity to attain this state. Patañjali[91] defines *yoga* as the state of mental restraint. While restraint is involved in the initial stages and control in the more advanced stages, voluntary suppression is needed in the ultimate stage. Suppression here means to consciously dismiss unwanted ideas, impulses, etc. from one's mind.

Concentration is the first step for spiritual absorption. Through the practice of concentration, the mind becomes fully absorbed in the object of concentration and brings forward the full intellective function which is without defects.

Mind flows in two ways, either towards beatitude or towards sufferings. Steadiness in restraint is the peaceful flowing of the mind, freed from its fluctuating functions. This flow of beatitude is called *viveka.* The opposite is the flow of fluctuations leading to endless sufferings. Restraint of mental operation is dependent on the mental steadiness which can be achieved by practice and non-attachment.[92] This is the stepping-stone to achieve liberation.

> Practice is the effort necessary to maintain the mind in a state of concentration, so that the Light of Reality shines in its full splendour leading to liberation.[93]
>
> Practice becomes firmly established on being continued for a long time, without interruption and with earnestness.[94]

Mental control is essential to reach the state of liberation. So, Patañjali provides some suggestions to bring the mind under control. They are: (1) continuous practice for a long time (as prescribed in scriptures); (2) uninterrupted practice, even when the goal is not reached; and (3) earnestness and the spirit of

---

91. Author of *Pātañjala Yoga-Sūtra.*
92. *Pātañjala Yoga-Sūtra,* I.12.
93. Ibid., I.13.
94. Ibid., I.14.

reverence on this path. Liberation, the highest perfection in the process of man's evolution, depends upon the scale of mental advancement and intensity of practice of the person concerned. These will lead to spiritual maturity. This means that changes have to be brought about in one's mind, character and way of living through the long process of practices in the prescribed way. This change is fundamental and one must be completely prepared to continue his efforts until the goal of absorption or liberation is attained. One should be conscious of this spiritual freedom.

The term *kaivalya* is the word for *mokṣa* in Yoga and Sāṁkhya philosophies. *Kaivalya* is the adjective of the word *kevala*. *Kevala* means "to be alone" without being mixed with any other thing by itself and by its own will. The Self (the *jīva*) transcends the 24 basic principles (*tattva*),[95] gets free and stays by itself at the level of *puruṣa*.[96] This is *kaivalya*.

Patañjali defines *kaivalya* as the state of enlightenment (*mokṣa*) following the re-emergence of *guṇa*s, because they become devoid of the object of the *puruṣa*. In this state *puruṣa* is established in his real nature which is Pure Consciousness. *Kaivalya* is that state of self-realisation in which *puruṣa* finally gets established, when the purpose of his long evolutionary unfolding has been attained. In this state, *guṇa*s having fulfilled their purpose recede to a condition of equilibrium. Therefore, at this stage of *kaivalya*, the power of Pure Consciousness functions without any hindrance or limitation. He, the *Puruṣa*, is free of all bondage and his "Conscience power"[97] becomes Absolute.

---

95. According to Sāṁkhya philosophy, the 25 basic principles (*tattva*s) are *puruṣa, avyakta prakṛti, pradhāna, mahat, ahaṁkāra*, 5 *tanmātra*s (*śabda, sparśa, rūpa, rasa* and *gandha*), 5 *mahābhūta*s (*ākāśa, vāyu, tejas, ap* and *pṛthvī*), the 5 sense perceptions (*jñāna indriya*) and the 5 senses of action (*karma indriya*).

96. The supreme Soul; Absolute Awareness: The first of the 25 principles of Sāṁkhya philosophy.

97. *Cit śakti*.

Patañjali further states that in the last phase of this evolutionary process the power, the knowledge, bliss, etc. unfold from within the consciousness of the aspirant and become great in the end. At each stage of progress, new consciousness dawns on him. This new consciousness is infinitely more vital and glorious than the previous one. The person seems to be uncovering a great reality which is hidden within the deepest recesses of his own being. Transcending the transcendent state of consciousness, which can be attained within the realm of *prakṛti*,[98] he attains *mokṣa*.

This highest point is so perfect and overwhelming that it unites with the Divine consciousness. But the individuality is neither dissolved nor lost forever in that Great Reality.

Liberation is the state of consciousness in which *puruṣa* is completely isolated from *prakṛti*. Liberation does not mean that man lives alone, in solitary splendour on a peak of a mountain. This isolation from *prakṛti* is the complete unification with Reality. The more one transcends matter and isolates consciousness from it, the greater will be the union with the Supreme Being. The state of consciousness of *mokṣa*, leads to the highest point of bliss.

Liberation is the stage of Self-realisation.[99] And it is total, and incomparable Bliss.

98. Primordial matter.

99. *Ātma-sākṣātkāra*.

4

Brahman, the Absolute

fig. 1: Lord Brahmā
(Courtesy: Nancy Carpentier, Belgium)

Who verily knows and who can here declare it,
Whence was it born and when came this creation?
And did the "shining one" appear with its production?
But then, who knows whence it has arisen?
He from whom this creation came into being
Whether He upheld it or He did not,
He oversees it in the eternal region
He verily knows it or perhaps He does not know.

— *Ṛgveda*, X.II.129.6-7

TECHNICALLY speaking, *Brahman* is the first God of the Indian Trinity, composed of Brahmā, Viṣṇu and Śiva, because *Brahman* is the creator.

Ṛgveda speaks of Brahmaṇaspati, the Lord of prayer: "Present the sacrificer to the gods as you did Kakṣīvat, son of Uśij."[1] Prayers for protection are addressed to him.[2] He is identified with *Brahman*.[3] He is pure and beautiful in form with a ruddy appearance, has a clear voice, seven mouths, a beautiful tongue, sharp horns, 100 wings, and holds an iron axe in his hands.[4] He is said to be born of a great light and thunder in the highest heaven, and is himself the progenitor of the gods.

Sadasaspati, the Lord of the assembly at a sacrifice, is another personification of *Brahman*.[5] Without invoking Sadasaspati, a sacrifice cannot be offered.

Bṛhaspati is another embodiment of *Brahman*. He is the priest (*purohita*) of the gods with whom he intercedes for men. He is described as the blue-tipped golden flame of the sacrificial fire.[6] *Aitareya Brāhmaṇa* equates Bṛhaspati with *Brahman*.[7] So too *Śatapatha Brāhmaṇa* when it declares, Bṛhaspati is *Brahman*.[8]

The most important personification of *Brahman* is in Prajāpati. This epithet is not only applied to the first Vedic gods Soma, Agni and Indra, but also to the 10 primeval progenitors: Marīci, Atri, Aṅgīras, Pulastya, Pulaha, Kratu, Vasiṣṭha, Dakṣa, Bhṛgu and Nārada. Ṛgveda prays: "O Prajāpati, creatures are not outside

1. *Ṛgveda*, I.18.1. Kakṣīvat was the son of Uśij, a female servant of queen of Kaliṅga.
2. Ibid., II.23.5.
3. *Maitrāyaṇī Saṁhitā*, II.2.3.
4. *Ṛgveda*, VIII.29.3.
5. Ibid., I.18.6
6. *Maitrāyaṇī Saṁhitā*, I.8.6.
7. *Aitareya Brāhmaṇa*, I.4.3; IV.5.7.
8. *Śatapatha Brāhmaṇa*, X.2.2.3.

Thee, give us the things we desire, may we become lords of wealth."[9] *Taittirīya Brāhmaṇa* declares, "He should be worshipped before the other gods."[10] *Brahman* as Prajāpati is the most important Godhead as can be seen from such passages as: The *Brahman* is the first born of the All.[11] He is the whole, *Brahman*.[12] He is both the gods and men.[13] He produced creatures.[14] He is food.[15]

The fundamental concept of a creator as the Lord of the three worlds and yet above and beyond them is well brought out as can be seen in: The waters existed as the primeval elements; Prajāpati was on the waters, he desired to create, and through fervour created the universe. His first creation was the tortoise, the *Puruṣa*, who was actually prior to Prajāpati himself. From Prajāpati's flesh was created Aruṇaketu who took over the task of creation. Because of his desire, meditation and creative fervour Prajāpati is equated with *manas* (the mind).[16]

In the evolution of the concept of *Brahman* Prajāpati discharges the duties of the creator and preserver. Consequently, in the rituals Prajāpati combines both these functions, even if later on, Viṣṇu is given the attribute of the preserver. Prajāpati belongs to the first phase of the development of *Brahman* and is thus less abstract having more mythological potentialities than *Brahman*. Naturally, His early connotations are the creation of the different species, of the elements and of the prime progenitors. He meditates and performs sacrifices thus symbolising both *yoga* and *karma* as also

---

9. *Ṛgveda*, X.121.10.
10. *Taitirīya Brāhmaṇa*, II.8.1.4.
11. *Śatapatha Brāhmaṇa*, V.1.1.10.
12. Ibid., VII.3.1.42.
13. Ibid., VI.8.1.4.
14. Ibid., VII.1.2.1
15. Ibid., VII.1.2.4.
16. *Jaiminīya Brāhmaṇa*, I.269; *Bṛhadāraṇyaka Upaniṣad*, III.2.7.

the *karma-kāṇḍa* and the *jñāna-kāṇḍa*[17] of the Veda. While the philosophical *Brahman* evolved from the first, the mythological *Brahman* evolved from the second. Incidentally, the philosophical *Brahman* is neutral in gender while the mythological *Brahman* is masculine.

Hiraṇyagarbha is another personification of *Brahman*. Hiraṇyagarbha means the golden germ (or foetus). *Ṛgveda* calls *Brahman* as Hiraṇyagarbha declaring that in the beginning there was Hiraṇyagarbha, the sole lord of all beings.[18] Hiraṇyagarbha evokes the image of the primordial cosmic egg, which is golden, and out of which *Brahman*, the Creator, was born.

With the passage of time, Brahmaṇaspati, Sadasaspati, Bṛhaspati, Prajāpati, and Hiraṇyagarbha became synonyms for *Brahman*.

Brahman in the Vedas

The Veda recognises the Supreme Being overseeing all, but leaves unanswered the question of whence from what material this creation came into being. The Absolute of the Veda has ever remained shrouded in mystery. All speculations have failed to come to a definite solution.

The idea of the Absolute is as old as the Vedas:

Neither asat were there nor sat there was then
Neither was motion, nor the heavens that are beyond
What covered? Darkness? Whose governance ambhas
What existed then? The deep and profound Absolute.[19]

The word *ambhas* used here means "waters". Waters were not the first creation. The first cosmic principle is some very fine substance described here as *ambhas* that is, waters. Something cannot come

17. *Karma-kāṇḍa* is the ritual part of the Vedas. *Jñāna-kāṇḍa* is the philosophical part of the Veda.

18. *Ṛgveda*, X.121.

19. Ibid., I-1.

out of nothing. So before creation comes to being, the vast expanse of these electronic particles formed an ocean of substance perhaps the same as *ambhas* of the Vedas emanating from the self-aspect of the Creator, *adhyātma bhāva* of Almighty. This Almighty of Veda ever remained in mystery. Veda described it as "waters".

> *O Gracious Hero! May we learn anew to know thee as Thou art.*[20]

The great philosophers of the past and the present tried many theories and built philosophies, but have ultimately to confess their inability to solve the problem regarding *Brahman*.

Ṛgveda hints out in Nāsadīya-Sūkta (6-7):

> *Who does verily know, who here could say,*
> *Whence come forth, how this created,*
> *After are born gods of this creation,*
> *Who knows how it came into being,*
> *This creation how sprang forth,*
> *If it is supported or not*
> *Who its supervisor in heavens beyond,*
> *O! He verily knows or knows not.*

In the Puruṣa-Sūkta (Hymn on Puruṣa), the Veda gives a symbolic answer through an analogy of sacrifice. "A *yajña* was performed with the Primal Being. Spring was the butter, summer the fuel, and autumn the libation." Here, to a logical query to which a literal answer is required, no reply was given. This shows that the question is better left open.

Brahman in the Upaniṣads

Generally, *Brahman* is referred to for the Supreme Being. He is the Absolute of Philosophy, the Ultimate Reality, and the Ultimate Truth.

The difference between the words *Brahman* and Brahmā is that Brahmā is Prajāpati, the creator and protector of the universe.

---

20. *Ṛgveda*, VII-50.9.

He is the first projection of *Brahman*. *Brahman* is the God of religion, who protects as well as creates. All the religions though having various views accept *Brahman* as the God of religion.

Brahman is that which has *bṛhatva*, that is, the quality of greatness. *Bṛh* is the root of the word *Brahman* meaning "to grow", "to expound". *Brahman* is also referred as *Paramātmā* in the Vedas and the Upaniṣads. *Parama* means supreme, great. Just as it is not possible for anyone to see the soul of another person though one can feel that there is surely some life-giving principle existing in all, it is not possible to see this Supreme Being with our naked eyes.

Scriptures describe Him as "The more minute than the minute and greater than the great and is set in the hearts of all beings".[21] *Brahman* is beyond the vision of naked eye. His powers are beyond grasping because He is all-powerful. He is accessible only through His nature and quality. This is how the Vedas and the Upaniṣads praise *Brahman*.

> The reality of Supreme is not a question to be solved by a dialectic which the vast majority of human race will be unable to understand. Dialectic in itself and without reference to personal experience cannot give us conviction. Only spiritual experience can provide us with proofs of the existence of spirit.[22]

Upaniṣads hold that the Supreme *Brahman* is one without a second. Descriptions of *Brahman* given in different Upaniṣads and scriptures are likely to differ according to the plane of consciousness from which the sages describe the reality. All these descriptions are real. They describe one reality with different views, like the description of photograph of an object taken from different angles.

"The Truth is one. Wise speak it in many terms." In a conversation between Maitreyī and Yājñavalkya in *Bṛhadāraṇyaka Upaniṣad*, Yājñavalkya says,

21. *Mahā Nārāyaṇa Upaniṣad*, 12-1.
22. *Bhagavad-Gītā* by S. Radhakrishnan.

> As a lump of salt dropped into water dissolves with (its components) water, and no one is able to pick it up, but from wheresoever one takes it, it tastes salt, even so, my dear, this great, endless, infinite Reality is but Pure Intelligence. (The self) comes out (as a separate entity) from these elements, and (this separateness) is destroyed with them. After attaining (this oneness) it has no more consciousness.[23]

This particular consciousness is the character of the self as "pure intelligence". For it is knowledge itself. It has particular consciousness only when it joins itself to limiting adjuncts — the body and organs.

> For when there is duality, as it were, then one smells another, one sees another, one hears another, one speaks of another, one thinks of another, one knows another. When (however) all has become the very self of the knower of *Brahman*, then what should one smell and through what? What should one see and through what? What should one hear and through what? What should one think of and through what? What should one know and through what? Through what should one know "That" (the Immutable Intelligence) because of which all this is known? Through what, my dear, should one know the knower?[24]

Where everything has indeed become the self itself, whom and by what one should think? By what can one know the Universal Knower? The Eternal one is so subtle that the idea of oneness is derived from experiences.

To sage Yājñavalkya, Intellect itself is *Brahman*. *Taittirīya Upaniṣad* (II.4) supports this view though it proceeds further to the Bliss.

The same Upaniṣad indicates that the intellectual sheath that is more subtle pervades the mental sheath. The individual intellect is rooted in *mahat tattva*. *Mahat tattva* is the Total Intellect. The

---

23. *Bṛhadāraṇyaka Upaniṣad* II.4.12.
24. Ibid., II.4.14.

individual intellect is conditioned by the Total Intellect. Knowledge of *Brahman* is gained through intellect, reversing intellect to *mahat tattva*.

The word *Brahman* is referred to for the highest person. His greatness is devoid of all evils. He is possessed of innumerable auspicious qualities. He is surpassed in excellence. Hence, the Lord of all is *Brahman*. He is accessible through meditation on His attributes only. By realising Him, everything is realised. It is possible to know *Brahman* by means of creation, preservation and destruction of the world that constitute His characteristics. He is one whole without a second. This is how the Upaniṣads praise *Brahman*:

> *Oṁ. All those that are invisible are filled by Brahman*
> *All those that are visible are also fully permeated by Brahman*
>
> *The whole universe has come out of the whole Brahman*
> *Brahman is still full, although the whole universe has come out of it.*[25]

Aitareya Upaniṣad holds: "The whole world is founded on *prajñāna*. Therefore *prajñāna* is *Brahman*".[26] Just like *aham brahmāsmi* of *Yajurveda*, *tattvamasi* of *Sāmaveda* and *ayamātma brahma* of *Atharvaveda*, so too *prajñānam-brahma* is a *mahā-vākya*[27] of *Ṛgveda*. That is "wisdom is *Brahman*".

Pra means high, *jñā* means to know, that is, wisdom that again is *sāttvika prajñā* which is pure intellectual illumination. *Prajñāna* leads to *parā jñāna*. Intellectual illumination leads to the knowledge of Supreme. *Brahman* is also hailed, as *Brahman* is Bliss.[28]

Māṇḍūkya Upaniṣad (1-2): "All this is surely *Brahman*. The Self is *Brahman*." That is, one's innermost Self is *Brahman*. Sage

---

25. *oṁ pūrṇa madaḥ, purṇamidam, pūrṇāt pūrṇamudacyate*
    pūrṇasya pūrṇamādāya, purṇamevāva śiṣyate।
26. *Aitareya Upaniṣad*, III-3.
27. Great sayings.
28. *Taittirīya Upaniṣad*, III.6-1.

Śvetāśvatara says, "*Ātman* is *Brahman* who is partless, free from actions, tranquil, faultless and untainted. I go for refuge to that effulgent one, whose light turns the understanding towards *Ātman*."[29]

Īśāvāsya Upaniṣad observes *Brahman*: "It moves and It moves not. It is far and It is near. It is within all this and It is also outside this."[30]

The explanation given here is "for the ignorant, It is difficult to know, but for the wise It is near at hand, because they know It as their very self". *Īśāvāsya Upaniṣad*[31] also describes *Brahman* as "without qualities and attributes" and *Ṛgveda*[32] brings out the statement "neither existent nor non-existent".

Taittirīya Upaniṣad condenses the idea of *Brahman* as "supreme is that from which all beings are born, that by which they all live and that into which, when departing they enter".[33]

The Supreme Self is at once the transcendent, the cosmic and the undivided reality. In its transcendental aspect, It is the pure self unaffected by any action or experience, detached, unconcerned. In its dynamic cosmic aspect, It not only supports but also governs the entire cosmic action and the very self which is one in all and above all is present in the individual.[34]

Great philosopher Yadava Prakasha[35] holds that *Brahman* is of the nature of pure Universal Being endowed with three distinct powers of consciousness, matter and God. And through these powers, It passes through the various phenomenal changes which are held up in It. At the same time, they are one with It, just as one ocean appears in diverse forms as foam, billows and waves.

29. *Māṇḍūkya Upaniṣad*, VI.18-19.
30. *Īśāvāsya Upaniṣad*, 5.
31. Ibid., 8.
32. *Ṛgveda*, X.129.
33. *Taittirīya Upaniṣad*.
34. *Bhagavad-Gītā* by S. Radhakrishnan.
35. A master of Advaita Vedānta. The first teacher of Rāmānuja, who later became Rāmānuja's disciple.

Bṛhadāraṇyaka Upaniṣad describes *Brahman* as

> The absolute is never seen. But it is the seer (meaning It is the sight itself because Absolute is Intelligence). It is never heard but is the hearer. It is never thought but the thinker. It is never known but the knower. There is no other seer than It, there is no other hearer than It. There is no other thinker than It; there is no other knower than It. This is very "Absolute" that pervades the unmanifested ether (*ākāśa*).[36]

To support this *Taittirīya Upaniṣad* says:[37]

> He who knows It as existing in the cave of the heart in the transcendent *ākāśa* realises all his desires along with omniscient *Brahman.*

The Supreme *Brahman* as reflected in the body and organs characterised by ignorance, desire and work is the individual Self. The same *Brahman* as reflected in the Eternal and infinite power of knowledge is the *Īśvara* and in its unconditional, pure essence, It is Absolute. Thus, *Brahman* is called by different names from Hiraṇyagarbha down to the animals and plants on account of apparent limitations.

The supersensuous entity *Brahman* cannot be known through perception to an ordinary human being, just as it is not possible for one to see the self of the other. Still one accepts its existence because one feels it so.

Taittirīya Upaniṣad declares, *Brahman* is beyond words and thought[38] which means that the infinite cannot be explained fully by words and it cannot be known in its fullness by our limited mind. Words are inadequate and mind is incapable of comprehending its nature. Ordinary sight is in want of power.

Upaniṣads place *Brahman* as

> there is the *ātman*, not in man alone, but in all objects of the

---

36. *Bṛhadāraṇyaka Upaniṣad*, III.8-11.
37. *Taittirīya Upaniṣad*, III, Brahmānanda-Vallī, Section 7.
38. Ibid., Section 9.

> universe, the sun, the moon, the world and *Brahman* is this *ātman*. There is nothing outside the *ātman* and so there is no plurality at all. So, when this *ātman* as *Brahman* is known everything is known. The essence in man and the essence in the universe are one and the same and it is *Brahman*.

Though there is a contradiction between *Brahman* as unity and nature in its diversity, Upaniṣadic seers do not notice it when they experience and notice the diversity, they affirm it, and yet declare that it is all *Brahman*. From *Brahman* it has come forth and to it, it will return. He has himself created it out of himself and then entered into it as its inner controller (*antaryāmin*). When *Brahman* is known, everything is known. *Brahman* is in the expansion of consciousness.

It is said that there is that eternally existing tree whose roots grow upwards, whose branches grow downwards. The universe is supported in it and no one can transcend it. The strong flow of thought in the Upaniṣads is that *ātman* or *Brahman* is the only reality and nothing else. The pantheist view identifies the universal with *Brahman* while the theist looks upon *Brahman* as Lord controlling the world.

> That in which differences have vanished, which is pure existence, which is beyond the sphere of speech, which is self knowing, that is the intelligence called *Brahman*.[39]

Śrīmad Bhāgavata makes out:

> The one reality which is of the nature of undivided consciousness is called *Brahman*, the Supreme Self or God. He is the ultimate principle, the real self in us as well as the God of worship.

Brahman in Bhagavad-Gītā

In *Bhagavad-Gītā*, the word *Brahman* signifies a high state of self-realisation in which, through complete detachment from all

39. *Viṣṇu Purāṇa*, VI.7-53.

passions, man is self-contented within himself, and his mind is in a perfect state of equilibrium. Lord Kṛṣṇa, defining *Brahman* as a faultless state of equilibrium,[40] says that whoever is in a state of equanimity and equilibrium through detachment and passionlessness is said to be by virtue thereof in *Brahman*; for *Brahman* means a state of equanimity.

Furthermore, Lord Kṛṣṇa says that *Brahman* is the ultimate object of knowledge, which is without beginning, and it cannot be said to be either existent or non-existent.[41] This *Brahman* has his hands and feet, his eyes, head, mouth and ears everywhere in the world, and He envelops all. He is without senses, but He illuminates all sense-qualities; being unattached Himself and the upholder of all, beyond the *guṇa*s, He is also the enjoyer of the *guṇa*s. He is both, inside and outside of all living beings, of all that is moving and that is unmoved. He is both, near and far, however unknowable because of His subtle nature. Being one, yet appearing as many, the upholder of all living beings, the devourer and ruler of all, He is the light of all the light, beyond all darkness; He is both, knowledge and the object of knowledge, residing in the heart of all. Lord Kṛṣṇa declares to Arjuna,

> He who sees the Supreme Lord abiding equally in all beings, the imperishable amidst the perishable he sees (the Lord) indeed.[42]

Brahman is also identified with sacrifices. Since the Veda is sprung from the eternal *Brahman*, its eternal and omnipresent character is transmitted to the sacrifices. "Know that action originates from *Brahman* and *Brahman* originates from the Imperishable. Therefore the all-pervading *Brahman* is eternally established in the sacrifices."[43] Lord Kṛṣṇa clearly indicates that *Brahman* is the Veda

---

40. *Bhagavad-Gītā*, V.19.
41. Ibid., XIII.13.
42. Ibid., XIII.27.
43. *Bhagavad-Gītā*, III.15.

by using the words *brahmano mukhe*,[44] "Thus the various sacrifices are prescribed by the Veda."[45] When He says, "The ladle is *Brahman*, the oblation is *Brahman*, it is offered by *Brahman* in the fire, which is *Brahman*, *Brahman* alone he attains who sees *Brahman* in action",[46] He undoubtedly refers to God. Later in the fifth chapter Lord Kṛṣṇa uses the word *Brahman* in the sense of God: "The sage devoted to selfless action attains *Brahman* quickly"; "He who performs actions dedicated to the Lord and giving up attachment, is not touched by sin, as a lotus leaf by water"; "For *Brahman* is even and faultless".[47]

In the *Bhagavad-Gītā*, the personal God as *Īśvara* is the supreme principle, and *Brahman* is a principle, which, though great in itself and representing the ultimate essence of God, is nevertheless upheld by the personal God or *Īśvara*. Though Lord Kṛṣṇa says, "The highest imperishable principle is *Brahman*", He also declares, "For I am the embodiment of *Brahman*,[48] of immutable immortality, of the eternal religion and of absolute bliss",[49] thus establishing the principle of God above that of *Brahman*.

In many instances, Lord Kṛṣṇa speaks of attainment of *Brahman*-hood (*brahma-bhūta*), bliss of *Brahman* (*brahma-nirvāṇa*) and fire of *Brahman* (*brahmāgni*).[50]

Later in His teaching, Lord Kṛṣṇa as God declares,

> He who worships Me unflinchingly through devotion transcends all *guṇas* and becomes *Brahman*. I am the upholder of the immortal and imperishable *Brahman* of absolute bliss and of the eternal *dharma*.[51]

---

44. That is, for the attainment of the *Brahman*.
45. *Bhagavad-Gītā*, IV.32.
46. Ibid., IV.24.
47. Ibid., V.6, 10, 19.
48. Ibid., VIII.3.
49. Ibid., XIX.27.
50. Ibid., V.24; VI.27; XVIII.54; IV.26; II.72; V.24, 25, 26.
51. *Bhagavad-Gītā*, XIV.26-27.

Brahmā, the Unmanifest

It would not be out of place to introduce the concept of *avyakta* as it is used in the *Bhagavad-Gītā*. *Avyakta* primarily means "the Unmanifest".[52] In this sense Lord Kṛṣṇa defines *avyakta* as "This is said to be unmanifest, unthinkable, and unchangeable", and identifies with the supreme, which is himself. "That unmanifest which is called the Imperishable is said to be the supreme Goal, attaining which they return not; that is My supreme abode."[53] The most prominent characteristic of *avyakta* is that it is changeless and deathless, it is unmanifest and unthinkable. Lord Kṛṣṇa uses this word in the sense of unknowable. "Beings, O descendant of Bharata, have the Unmanifest as their beginning, are manifest in the middle, and have their dissolution in the Unmanifest itself."[54] But this *avyakta* is also referred to as a nature of God, which, under His superintendence, produces the moving and the unmoved — the entire universe.[55] God Himself is often referred to as *avyakta*, even though God is always superior to *avyakta*. "All the world is pervaded over by me in my form as *avyakta*."[56] Lord Kṛṣṇa calls this *avyakta* also as *akṣara*, the immortal, which is regarded as the last resort of all beings who attain their highest and most perfect realisation.

Thus, in *Bhagavad-Gītā*, Lord Kṛṣṇa uses the word *Brahman* in three senses: in the sense of *prakṛti*, from which the *guṇa*s are produced, in the sense of Veda, and in the sense of being an essential nature of God.

Even if *Brahman* is identified with *avyakta*, the latter being the highest essence of God, God naturally is the highest of all.

---

52. Etymologically, the word *avyakta* consists of two parts, the negative particle *a* meaning "negation" and *vyakta* meaning "manifested" or "revealed".

53. *Bhagavad-Gītā*, VIII.21.

54. Ibid., II.28.

55. Ibid., IX.10.

56. Ibid., IX.4.

5

The Universal Spiritual Entity, Sarveśvara

In all beings from immovable object to Brahmā the creator, in high and in low creatures, in the primordial elements, in *mahat tattva* and its evolutes, in the *guṇa* in a state of equilibrium and in guṇa in agitation in all these entities and conditions is present that one Supreme Spirit, the all-powerful Divine Person, the Lord of all, the Unchangeable Substance.

— *Śrīmad Bhāgavata,* VII.6.20-24

Those who resort to Me as the Supreme never meet with a fall (destruction) from that Abode of peace. The wheel of Time which I wield continuously, brings all beings except them under its sway. For, to them I am the beloved, the self, son, friend, teacher, well-wisher and Chosen Deity. — *Śrīmad Bhāgavata,* III.25.37-38

MAN has been a continuous enquirer. He works through his consciousness. He possesses a most wonderful apparatus of inquiry. He first became an inquirer, and used his apparatus for posing questions and solving them and he systematised the art of inquiry and developed a type of logic. From deductive logic, he developed inductive logic and then statistical logic. From gross observation, he moved to the highest precision. As he developed his enquiry, he realised the failures. These failures have not hindered man to continue enquiring.

Man's total range of enquiry may be classified under three

heads: (1) man's inquiry about his near and distant surroundings, (2) his inquiry concerning the nature of his own self, and (3) his enquiry about someone other than him and his surroundings. In the first case, he is the subject of enquiry, in the second, he is both the subject and the object of enquiry and in the third case, he is simply the subject.

It is this third type of enquiry that makes him enquire about the one who is more mysterious than he, and in this search realises that all his apparatuses are irrelevant, incompetent and insufficient to give any information in regard to that someone. It is here that man either accepts or rejects the third enquiry. When he accepts, he becomes humble because he recognises that all his means of enquiry are limited in scope because this someone or something is beyond the scope of his normal means of enquiry which are limited by many parameters. He understands that this unknown is changeless behind all that changes, is an indefinable behind all that can be defined and infinite behind all the finites that are in the scope of his enquiry. He is marvelled and enquiry being an inherent character, he wants to know the unknown. Or, he is afraid of this unknown and scared that his faculty of enquiry would be baseless, deny its existence and would not even accept to "hear" about it.

In Hindu philosophy, this unknown is called by different names: *Puruṣa, Īśvara, Paramātmā, Brahman* and so on. It is also considered as Supreme Reality.

Concept of the Universal Spiritual Entity

God is usually presented as the worthiest object of human endeavour. The soul (*jīva*) is embraced by God's sovereign supremacy. The moral creativity in life flows from the sustaining immanence of God in man. God is a life-giving and life-nourishing indweller. Without Him, the soul would practically cease to exist. God awakens the individual through His presence.

God is supernatural and immortal. Man is always in contact

with God. It can be said that to God, the worlds are his predicates. While soul is the individual spirit, God is the Universal Spirit.

God is perfection and He is pure essence. It is true, some scriptures do not admit the existence of God and others do accept and postulate the theory of God. A question may arise: If God exists, He should be perceptible. Why do we not see him? Of course, this is true. However, that does not mean that He does not exist. God is not an object of perception, because He is a super-sensuous entity. The Self, *ātman*, of another individual cannot be seen by oneself too, yet one accepts its existence. In the same way, the existence of God cannot be questioned, even though He is not perceived. The scriptures reveal the existence of God as true; and so they are the sole authority for knowing the existence of God. It is faith that prompts one to believe in something unperceivable.

Śvetāśvatara Upaniṣad says that the existence of God can neither be demonstrated nor logically proved. He is to be felt within one's Self. Rāmānuja also holds the same view. He says that God cannot be proved by inference, but is to be admitted on the authority of texts:

> Because the scriptures form the source of knowledge relating to Him.[1]

> The senses are great, but greater than senses is the mind, and greater than the mind is understanding. What is even greater than the understanding is He, the God.[2]

Bṛhadāraṇyaka Upaniṣad beautifully brings out God as:

> He who dwelling in the earth is within the earth, whom the earth does not know, whose body is earth, and who internally rules earth He is thy internal ruler and immortal Self. He, who is dwelling in the Self, is within the Self, whom the Self does not

1. *Vedānta-Sūtra*, I.3.
2. *Kaṭha Upaniṣad*, I.iii.10-11.

> know, whose body is the Self and who internally rules the Self, and He is thy internal ruler, the great God.[3]

God can be interpreted according to one's own ideals. For example, "in the beginning, my boy, this "Being" was alone, one only without a second. This one is God."[4] The word "being" is interpreted variously by different classes of people. An atomist called this "atom", a naturalist called "nature", a nihilist called it "nothing", the Advaita called it "Absolute existence" and so forth; to a theist, this "being" means God.

Śrī Rāmānuja places God as the character of *śuddha sattva*.[5] This is a spiritual substance characterised only by an unalloyed *sattva*; It is not like physical matter which has all the three *guṇa*s of *sattva, rajas* and *tamas*. This spiritual substance not only possesses the quality of *sattva* but at the same time is self-luminous in character. This spiritual substance, known as the body of God is not perceivable by man. But a *yogī* or a devotee, or a *paramahaṁsa*[6] can perceive this body of God.

In the introduction of *Vedānta Dīpikā*,[7] Rāmānuja briefly brings out that:

> God, who is the same as Supreme *Brahman*, is the cause of the universe. The universe, which is made up of matter and soul, is the effect produced by Him. Matter and soul form the body of God, and this body is capable of existing in a subtle as well as in a gross state. God with the subtle body constitutes the state of the universe before its creation and with his gross body, He forms the created universe itself. The individual soul enters into matter and thereby makes it live and similarly God enters into matter and soul and gives them their powers and their peculiar

3. *Bṛhadāraṇyaka Upaniṣad*, III.7-3.22.
4. *Chāndogya Upaniṣad*, VI.2-1.
5. Spiritual substance characterised by unalloyed *sattva*.
6. A *paramahaṁsa* is one who has controlled and subdued all his senses.
7. *Vedānta Dīpa* is the work of Rāmānuja, in which a brief commentary on *Vedānta-Sūtra* is brought out.

> characters. The universe without God is exactly analogous to matter without soul and in the world, as we know it, all things are what they are, because God has penetrated into them and rules and guides them all from within. Consequently, all things are representative of Him and all words denote Him.[8]

Religion means to realise. All religions realised that God is not just a person but the creator of the universe. He is regarded as the instrumental cause of the world, the Lord of all, the master of all and so forth. He is also designated by different names.

Is everyone anxious to know: Who is God? What does God look like? Can He come and talk to us? When we call him, would He respond to our loving smiles? and so forth. All these questions need satisfactory answers. But do we have the real thirst to know Him? Do we have the purity in our souls?

Swami Vivekananda points out:

> The chief thing is to want God. We usually want everything except God, because our ordinary interests are supplied by the external world. It is only when our necessities have gone beyond the external world, that we want a supply from internal, that is, from God. The want is that without which we cannot live. When the soul grows, then alone arises the feeling of the want of God and one feels to have him. The soul needs God to protect him.[9]

A vision of God, a glimpse of the beyond never comes, until the soul is pure, for God's universe is unalloyed purity.

Mere clay cannot project a beautiful building on its own nor can mere cotton transform itself into a cloth. Some dexterous person has to be present to transform the clay into bricks and construct the building. An adroit weaver alone can spin threads from cotton and weave the cloth. So too, a skilful agent has to be there to project this universe, full of souls and other matter. This

---

8. *Vedānta-Sūtra with Śrī Bhāṣya* of Rāmānuja. tr. M. Rangacharya and M.B. Varadaraja Iyengar.
9. *Religion of Love* by Swami Vivekananda.

skilful agent is named God. He is considered the Creator. But we cannot see Him, because God has no visible body; His body is said to be a spiritual substance.

Bricks, pots, buildings, etc. are other forms of clay. Rain, clouds, oceans, rivers are another form of water. They all belong to this world. Likewise, whatever we consider as universal body, His body is said to be a spiritual substance.

It is not possible to define God exactly. But He is within anyone's reach who approaches Him in the desired form with sincerity and a pure mind or attitudes. God is that One, who has special powers on His creatures.

The Sanskrit word for God is *deva* meaning "divine", "luminous", "to reveal", "to perceive". Yet, He is not perceivable through our normal sense perceptions. *Deva* also means "giver of precious things or ideas". The letter *da* means "to give". God is *deva*, because He is self-luminous and all other lights whether intellectual or physical are given by Him.

This mighty being is concealed in the souls of all beings. Many philosophers recognise God as "pure spiritual consciousness" that is whole, in the sense of perfect, extremely subtle and unalloyed.

"He that is *Brahman* (God), who is most subtle and though not voidness, is imaginable as voidness is regarded by holy persons (*bhakta*) as the Lord Vāsudeva."[10] Vāsudeva means:

(1) the God, who dwells in all beings, rules and protects them, and

(2) He, who provides a dwelling place (*vāsa*) for all in Himself. So He is Vāsu. Deva means effulgent, self-luminous. Vāsudeva is both *vāsu* and *deva*.

When we consider ourselves as physical beings, God is our

---

10. *Śrīmad Bhāgavata Purāṇa*, IX.9.49. Though *Brahman* is referred to as the highest Absolute, God in His super personality transcends even *Brahman*. This will be discussed later on.

master, father and we are his children. When we look upon ourselves as embodied souls, God is the universal soul and we are Its emanations.

Christianity declares, Blessed are the pure in the heart, for they shall see God.

Chāndogya Upaniṣad says, "When one reflects, then alone that one understands."

This reflection is only possible, when we cease to think that we are out of ourselves because, then alone we know Him as He is. God is the indwelling, indivisible spirit in man, that is, *pūrṇa* (the complete).

Suppose we look at the midday sun, we are dazzled and cannot look at it with our naked eye. We shut our eyes immediately. When we see the same sun through a smoked glass, we see it as a round, red globe. The smoke on the glass can be compared to the hankerings of our mind, which is full of desires. The more desires there are, the more layers of smoke are on the glass, through which we see absolutely nothing. We are unable to see God, because of these desires. When all the desires, clinging to one's heart, cease then man realises God.

From whom all beings are projected, in whom all live and unto whom all return can be called God. This is how the scriptures bring out God's virtue. To know this Divine Being, man should transcend the limits of physical, mental and moral conditions under which he works in his life. Man as man can never know God.

Ordinarily, in the existing state, we do not see anything real about higher things. When a man has seen something real beyond the senses, beyond the universe of senses, the Real is termed as God's vision. Seeing the Real means to realise some special entity in man's own Self as well as in the universe. That implies, understanding the supernatural existing entity. It is said that only then man has reached the world of God. The world of God is the elevated layer of consciousness very often called Heaven.

Sri T. Krishnamacharya[11] viewed that the material life or the physical enjoyment has become man's primary concern. Even a wise man becomes restless because he realises that he must be prepared to face constant struggle in this life. When by constant reflection on the causes of his restlessness he understands that his present mode of living would not provide him the inner harmony, he will search for an approach to overcome his restlessness. After many practical trials he will realise that love of the Divine would be the only solution. This is how man approaches God. Gradually, he realises that love to God, trust in God, and being in tune with God give him sufficient strength to face the bitter realities of life. When man submits himself to the power of God, the Divine protects him. God becomes his guide.

God is the one light that shines in the various forms, the one voice that speaks in various languages and the one life that thrills through every atom in the universe. Just as one thread passes through all the flowers in the garland, God breathes in all life and penetrates all beings. Just as electricity cannot be seen nor can be easily explained, God can neither be easily seen nor can He be easily explained.

Thiruvalluvar, a great Tamil poet of Tamil Nadu, beautifully pictured God in his *Kuraḷ* as, the letter *a* begins the alphabets, and (Sun) God is the origin of the universe. Just as the first letter of alphabet in almost all languages begins with *a* and its sound helps to pronounce all the consonants, God is not only the first in Being, but also the basis of all creation.

In *Les Miserables*, Victor Hugo, the great French writer defines God as: The infinite exists. It is true. This infinite has a *me*. This *me* of infinite is God. There is a *me* in the infinite above and there is a me below. The *me* above is God, and the *me* below is soul. Placing by the process of thought the infinite below in contact with the

11. Authors' father and Spiritual Master.

above is God. The invisible thread that connects the two *me's* is referred as God.

Rāmānuja places God as the character of *śuddha sattva*.[12] This is a spiritual substance (without being a matter) characterised only by an unalloyed *sattva*; it is not like physical matter, which has all the three *guṇa*s of *sattva*, *rajas* and *tamas*.[13]

Guṇa is an attributive quality of *prakṛti*, the cosmic matter and is viewed with three facets. They are *sattva* (illumination), *rajas* (activity), active emotions not easily controlled and *tamas* (inertia, dullness). *Sattva* is the quality of goodness and purity; it leads to happiness and harmony. *Rajas* produces restless activity and *tamas* results in indolence and inertia. The three qualities of *prakṛti* can be known only through their effects. They are not apparent in the un-evolved state of *prakṛti*, but become apparent in the evolved state of *prakṛti*. The soul in its pristine nature is not conjoined with the *guṇas*. It binds the soul when it resides in the body by virtue of the limiting condition of its living in the body. *Sattva* is superior to the other two *guṇa*s. Its characteristic nature is illumination because of its being pure. It leads to the illumination of the mind and senses. While generating knowledge, it also generates attachment to it, thereby binding the soul to the knowledge. *Prakṛti* and its *guṇa*s represent the limits of human freedom. When the quality of *sattva* is purified, the light of pure consciousness is reflected on it. When all the *guṇa*s are made inactive, inward illumination will flash giving life a fresh and new insight. Then divine birth takes place in man. *Prakṛti*, the cosmic matter, is characterised by the three *guṇa*s. It is the basic source of all things in the universe, both physical and mental. Besides *prakṛti*, Viśiṣṭādvaita admits the existence of transcendental matter named as spiritual substance, *śuddha sattva*, characterised by unalloyed *sattva* and described it as that which only possesses the quality *sattva*, being at the same time self-luminous in character. It is purely

12. Transcendental Spiritual matter, pure non-material entity.

13. See Chapter 1 on "Introduction".

spiritual in character. Its two important features are self-luminosity and manifesting itself always for others.[14] The body-form assumed by God in his eternal abode is constituted of this pure *sattva*, but subject to change like the material stuff.

This spiritual substance not only possesses the quality of *sattva* but also is self-luminous in character. *Sattva* (one of the qualities of *prakṛti*) is clarity and lightness. One of its functions is to provide knowledge. Knowledge is comparable to a light, which reveals the presence of an object. Right knowledge is an essential attribute of the soul (*jīva*). According to Rāmānuja, the relation of soul to knowledge is comparable to the flame of a lamp and its luminosity. Experience is knowledge. Clear knowledge leads to the experience of the soul. According to Viśiṣṭādvaita philosophy, the soul (*ātmā* also called *jīva*) is self-luminous,[15] because it is of the nature of knowledge. It is self-luminous, because it does not require another source for its manifestation. When the "I" is not identified with the body, which is the ego, erroneously taking the physical body as the soul, then the entity denoted by "I" is the true Self.[16] Self-luminosity of the soul is not to be understood in the sense that it reveals itself as "I" to all and at all times.

While an ordinary man cannot perceive the spiritual essence, known as the body of God, a *yogī*, devotee, *bhakta*, or a totally detached person (*paramahaṁsa*)[17] can perceive It.

In the introduction to *Vedānta Dīpikā*,[18] Rāmānuja briefly

14. These two qualities are also prevalent in knowledge.

15. *Svaprakāśa*.

16. Rāmānuja's commentary on *Vedānta-Sūtra* I.1, and Vedānta Deśika's argument in his *Śata Dūṣani*, 27.

17. *Paramahaṁsa* is one who is totally detached from the material world. *Parama* means "supreme, the highest", *haṁsa* means "desireless, a detached pure heart". He is the best among God-realised souls. Conquering the senses, treating pleasure and pain equally, subduing the ego, taking food just enough for survival, fixing God firmly in their heart, they live till the end.

18. *Vedānta Dīpa* is the work of Rāmānuja, in which a brief commentary on *Vedānta-Sūtra* is brought out.

brings out that God, who is the same as the Supreme *Brahman*, is the cause of the universe. The universe, which is made up of matter and soul, is the effect produced by Him. Matter and soul form the body of God, and this body is capable of existing in a subtle as well as in a gross state. God with the subtle body constitutes the universe in its causal state; and with His gross body, He forms the created universe. The individual soul enters into matter and thereby makes it live, while God enters into matter and soul and gives them their powers and their peculiar characters. The universe without God is exactly analogous to matter without soul; and in the world, as we know it, all things are what they are, because God has penetrated into them, ruling and guiding them all from within. Consequently, all things are representative of God and all words denote Him.[19]

Man's relationship with God is recognised since the time of Vedas. Puruṣa-Sūkta[20] says that one quarter of the *Puruṣa* (God) has spread out the cosmic universe and its living beings, while the other three quarters are in the immortal heavens. In a varied manner, this same idea is brought out in *Chāndogya Upaniṣad* (III.12.6) and *Maitrāyaṇī Upaniṣad* (VI.4) as "the three quarters of God (*Puruṣa*) sit root upward above." That means God is so great that He emanated only one part and His other three parts remain unchangeable. So in this world the true nature of God is not perceived, its beginning, its end and the nature of its subsistence remain unknown. Only by cutting this firmly rooted tree (*aśvattha*, the Indian fig tree) free with the strong axe of detachment, one would find that state from which there would be no return.

As expressed in Puruṣa-Sūkta, God is not only immanent, that is, forms the cosmic world, but also transcendent. The immanent part (the cosmic world) is not an illusion (*māyā*). It is an emanation, a projection and a development from God. The

19. *Vedānta-Sūtra with Śrī Bhāṣya* of Rāmānuja Acharya, tr. M. Rangacharya and M.B. Varadaraja Iyengar.

20. A Ṛgvedic hymn.

primordial matter and its manifestations have their basis, in essence in Him and are upheld by Him. The transcendent part is said to be the root from high; this root is itself in *Brahman* and is the basis of all in the lower world. But though *Brahman* is referred to as the highest abode and ultimate realisation, God in His super-personality transcends even *Brahman*. *Brahman* is only a constitutive essence in the complex personality of God. God upholds all the things in the world.

In *Bhagavad-Gītā*, Lord Kṛṣṇa says,

> there is nothing greater than I. All things are held by Me, like pearls in the thread of a pearl garland. I am the liquidity in water, the light of the sun and moon, manhood in man, good smell in the earth, the heat of the sun, intelligence in the intelligent, heroism in the heroes, strength in the strong and also I am the desires which do not transgress the path of virtue.[21]

From the theistic point of view, there is no contradiction in the different aspects of God as Preserver and Controller of the world, as the substance of the world, life and soul and as the transcendent substratum underlying them all. He who has true faith is attached to God.

God in His pure essence is ever free from all the impurities. He is of all the best qualities only, untouched by phenomenal disturbances with which His body is associated.

God, the Divine principle, is not beyond one's reach, but very near. He is not a detached spectator or a distant judge, but a father, a friend, a mother and a lover, who is with us all the time. These human relations find their fullest realisation in God; man is a co-sharer in the work of God.

Attributes of the Universal Spiritual Entity, God

It is difficult to give any definition or description of God on account of the inadequacy of our halting descriptions and

21. *Bhagavad-Gītā*, VII.7.11.

imperfect standards. He is also indefinable, because a complete knowledge of Him is difficult to acquire. The glory and nature of God are so vast that it eludes the grasp of our mind.

In the Upaniṣads, there is an account of the Supreme as the immutable and the unthinkable, as also the view that He is the lord of the universe. In the words of *Brahma-Sūtra* and *Taittirīya Upaniṣad*, the Supreme is that "from which these beings are born, that by which they live and that into which, when departing, they enter".[22] The Vedas speak of "the two birds perched on the same tree, one of whom eats its fruits, while the other eats not but only watches".[23]

God is full of auspicious qualities. He is the sum total of all ideal predicates, infinite and eternal, before and above all.

Some of His auspicious qualities are:

ONE WITHOUT A SECOND

The smooth working of the body with its constituents is possible, because there is only one soul pervading and controlling it. Similarly, the universe is pervaded and governed by one Supreme Being. If there had been more than one soul in the body or more than one Supreme Being in the universe, conflicts would have been inevitable. God is only one, without a second.[24] God has nothing similar to Him, nothing different from Him and no internal differentiation. Even if the soul (*ātmā*), which because of its being eternal and conscious, belongs to the same species and is very much like Him, even so it is not God. God is one and only one, though the wise call him by different names.[25] The one Supreme is called Brahmā, Viṣṇu and Īśvara according as He is creating, preserving and withdrawing the entire universe.

22. *Brahma-Sūtra*, 1.1.2, *Taittirīya Upaniṣad*, 3.1.
23. *Ṛgveda*, 1.164.2. *Muṇḍaka Upaniṣad*, 3.1.1., *Śvetāśvatara Upaniṣad* 4.6.
24. *Chāndogya Upaniṣad* 6.2.1.
25. *Ṛgveda*, 1.164.46.

Very often, a distinction is made between *Brahman* and Īśvara. While *Brahman* is the transcendental ground and abyss of everything, Īśvara is the personal God. The Absolute is a living reality with a creative urge. When this aspect is stressed, the Absolute becomes a personal God, Īśvara. In other words, *Brahman* is Īśvara when viewed as creative power. In the concept of Īśvara, the Absolute is brought into closer relation with the world.

In reality, *Brahman* and Īśvara are not two distinct entities, but only different names of the same reality. God is called Īśvara, because his nature, knowledge and wealth are infinite. He is the supreme Lord who sustains everything.[26] He is Īśvara who dwells in everybody's heart.[27]

FORMLESS

God is omnipresent, omnipotent and omniscient. Being all-pervading, he is in direct control of everything. He is the Supreme, while the individual souls are personal in an imperfect way.

A corporeal body is subject to heat and cold, hunger and thirst, disease, mortification, separation and other kinds of suffering. The individual soul is connected with the body in which it dwells and participates in the pleasures and pains to which the body gives rise. Since God does not share these afflictions, He has no form.

INCARNATION

God does not stand aside, leaving us free to make or mar ourselves. The Supreme manifests himself, but is not born in the ordinary sense. When the Lord is said to manifest himself at a particular time, on a particular occasion, it only means that it takes place with reference to a finite but extraordinary being. His incarnation (unlike the rebirth in case of individual souls) is the demonstration of the evolution of man's spiritual resources and

---

26. *Atharvaveda*, 2.4.

27. *Bhagavad-Gītā*, XVIII.61.

latent divinity. It is not the contraction of the Divine into the limits of the human frame. Having no birth nor death, His identity cannot be historically accounted for. He incarnates not only to put down evil but also to teach humanity the morals.

OMNISCIENT

God is omniscient because his knowledge is not dependent on the sense organs. He has the perfect knowledge which consists in knowing things as they are. Being eternal, His knowledge of himself is infinite and is characteristic of his being omniscient.

OMNIPOTENT

He is all-powerful, because there is no limit to his powers. His being Almighty only means that He can accomplish His work of creation, preservation and dissolution and can dispense equitable justice to the souls with inherent power without seeking external help. At the same time, it does not mean that He can do anything arbitrarily, or break his own laws and the laws of nature.

In creation, the world is developed in name and form, while it is in the undeveloped state in dissolution. Creation is a spatial and temporal expression. At the end of each of the world periods (*kalpa*) God takes back the whole world, that is, the material world becomes merged in non-distinct *prakṛti*. Dissolution does not mean annihilation. When a gold bangle is melted, gold remains. It only loses its name and form. Dissolution of the world is only the developed world (*vikṛti*) becoming undeveloped world (*prakṛti*)[28] again.

Creation and dissolution are only relative and signify different states of causal substances. Souls and matter have a twofold existence — a causal existence and an effect existence. In the causal existence, the souls are unmaterialised and Nature (*prakṛti*) is in equipoise whereas in the latter, the souls and the Nature obtain name, form and functions.

---

28. An evolute of *prakṛti* which does not serve as a cause of another evolute.

NON-INTRUSIVE

God is completely good and His love is boundless, He pours out his wealth of love in helping man to resist all that makes for error, ugliness and evil. Human beings can be influenced but not controlled. He is to be persuaded but not compelled. That is why, God acts with a particular delicacy. God is not a dictator.

God declares what is good and what is bad, supplies souls with appropriate bodies and gives them power to employ them. Man has the right to refuse the grace offered to him by God.

If the world has in it so much suffering and misery, it is not God that is responsible for it, but man who has the power to choose between good and evil. The practice of virtue will make man happy.

JUST AND BENEVOLENT

Every view of God represents some aspect or other of the relation of the human to the divine spirit. The different representations tell man what He is to mankind. In fact, the anthropomorphic conception of the divine is relative to man's needs. Each method of approach, each mode of address answers to some mood of human mind. In His love, He combines the apparently opposite virtues of justice and mercy. They differ only in name and serve the same purpose. The very justice of God is His mercy in disguise. God is merciful in that He provides for the souls all sorts of physical material with which to work while they live, and by means of which to enjoy the fruits of what they do.

MONOTHEISM AND POLYTHEISM

In Hindu theism, God is known by several names such as: Paramātmā, Bhagavān, Īśvara, Nārāyaṇa, Viṣṇu, Rāma, Kṛṣṇa, Puruṣottama and so forth. Yet God is God. There is no change in His status. He is given different names according to one's pleasures. Of course, all the names carry a special significance. Īśvara means "impartial Lord", who rules us. The term Lord brings out the quality of domination yet implies a sense of protection too. As He is the Lord, we are obedient to Him. If God is presented as father, mother, friend, etc. we feel our intimacy to Him.[29]

> The Lord abides in the heart of all beings. O Arjuna, causing them to turn round by His power as if they were mounted on a machine (wheel).[30]

Lord Vāsudeva, the ruler over all, lives in the hearts of all beings, that is, in the region from where all knowledge arises, which is at the root of all secular and spiritual activities. How does He exist? He exists by His special power (*māyā*). All the beings that mould on the mechanism of *prakṛti* in the form of body and senses are created by Him. They act in accordance with their *guṇa*.

Again, Śrī Kṛṣṇa says, "And I am seated in the hearts of all. From Me are memory, knowledge and their removal also. From Me proceeds everything."[31] We find the same view in the Upaniṣads too, like "He who is dwelling the Self — the God." Supreme Lord Īśvara is the innermost Self of our existence. All life is a movement of the rhythm of His life and our powers and acts are all derived from Him. If in our ignorance, we forget this deepest truth, yet the truth does not alter. If we live consciously in His truth, we will resign all our actions to God and will escape from our ego. If on the contrary we do not live consciously in His truth, even then this Truth will prevail. Eventually we will yield ourselves to the purpose of God, but in the meantime, there is no compulsion. Īśvara desires our free co-operation, when beauty and goodness are born without efforts. Then we become a transparent media for the light of God. He uses us for His work.[32]

---

29. Manifestation of devotional love appears in different predominant attitudes. The difference in attitudes can only be attributed to tastes and preferences. A father protects the children, a mother is compassionate towards them; the relationship with a friend is always closer. By presenting God as father, mother, friend, etc. the devotee seeks to be one with his own higher self, who is the Lord of his heart.
30. *Bhagavad-Gītā*, XVII.61.
31. Ibid., XV.15.
32. Ibid., by Dr. S. Radhakrishnan XVIII.61.

The word Īśvara also means "ruler". Īśvara's control over man does not rob him of his freedom of will. Man is the end for which the external objects of enjoyment exist. And Īśvara is the end for which man exists as the object of His control and support.

Also, Viśiṣṭādvaita scriptures declare that Īśvara creates the universe in accordance with the *karma* of the individual souls without any bias. The purpose of creation is twofold: (1) Compassion towards human suffering and (2) Divine sport. Creation of universe is a Divine sport from which Īśvara derives bliss (*ānanda*). It also serves the purpose of providing the individual souls, caught up in the ocean of bondage, an opportunity to escape from it and reach the final release. The individual souls cannot strive for the spiritual good without their being associated with the body, the sense organs and the intellect.

Is Īśvara all-compassionate and if the universe is His own creation, why should there be so much suffering in the universe? Why should there be disparity in the suffering and happiness of individuals? Hindu theistic systems explain this as being due to the *karma* of each individual which varies from one to another in accordance with one's past deeds. God dispenses good to those who have done good deeds and evil to those who have done wicked deeds. Hence, Īśvara is free from partiality. He is also free from the defect of being unkind.[33] The desires of Īśvara become fully achieved without any obstruction.[34] Īśvara is a particular *Puruṣa* who is untouched by the afflictions of life, actions and their results and the impressions produced by these actions.[35] He is the Supreme ruler of *Brahmāṇḍa*.[36] He is the reality generally referred to as God. "In Him is the highest limit of omniscience."[37] The point referred to here is that the omniscience

33. *Vedānta-Sūtra*, II.1.34.

34. Fundamentals of Viśiṣṭādvaita Vedānta based on Vedānta Deśika's *Tattva Mukta Kalāpa*.

35. *Pātañjala Yoga-Sūtra*, I.24.

36. A solar system.

37. *Pātañjala Yoga-Sūtra*, I.25.

of Īśvara is a relative thing and has a limit. According to Hindu philosophy the innumerable solar systems, scattered throughout the cosmos as so many centres in the consciousness of the one Reality are the manifestations of *Saguṇa Brahman*. No ordinary *puruṣa* (also called *jīva puruṣa*) can cross the infinite knowledge of the Īśvara of the system, just as a fountain cannot rise higher than the reservoir which supplies water to it.

According to *Yoga-Sūtra*s, even though He is referred to as God, He is one of the highest if not the highest rung of the ladder of unimaginable glory and splendour of Divine Consciousness. Not being conditioned by them, He is the Teacher even of the ancients.[38]

Īśvara is the one who inspires and gives knowledge to the teachers. Only Īśvara can do this, because He can also survive and continue through all the changes. This means He is the Supreme Teacher, the Real Teacher behind all the teachers, who are trying to spread the light of knowledge and Divine Wisdom in the world. It is the Divine Knowledge that is behind the evolutionary progress of humanity. The individuals merely become the instruments of the Supreme Teacher in whom all knowledge resides. He helps to enlarge the boundaries of human knowledge. His designation is *OṀ*.[39] Hindus consider this word as the most mystical, sacred and powerful *mantra*.

In short, Īśvara defined by *Yoga Darśana*[40] is not like ordinary souls in bondage,[41] but a special *puruṣa*. But still He is a *Puruṣa*,[42] residing in a body. As such, He resides in the body of all beings;

38. *Pātañjala Yoga-Sūtra*, I.26

39. Ibid., I.27. A *vācaka* is a name, which has a mystic relationship with the entity designated and has inherent in it the power of revealing the consciousness and releasing the power of the individual for whom it stands. Such a *vācaka* is *OṀ*.

40. Another name for *Pātañjala Yoga-Sūtra*.

41. Termed *jīva puruṣa*.

42. Derived from *purī* or "abode".

He resided there in the past and will reside there in the future. There has never been a time when He did not exist. But the qualities, which distinctly make Him special are:

(1) Without doubt, He resides as *puruṣa* in the body of each person in bondage possessing an individual egoism, but unlike him, Īśvara remains unaffected by the miseries of ignorance, egoism, attachment, aversion and clinging to life. Moreover, He is not affected by the good or evil actions resulting therefrom, by their fruits in the form of fortunes and misfortunes and the corresponding impressions left by them, which the ordinary *puruṣa* in bondage goes through.

(2) He is all-knowing. He knows the past, the present and the future, all simultaneously from microscopic to macroscopic details; and the degree of His knowledge transcends all limits of time, space and causality. Such Īśvara lies within the hearts of all persons as Master (Lord) and His name is *OṀ*. By the repetition of His name and meditation on Him as Teacher, through devotion, He dissipates ignorance from the hearts of His devotees, just as a *guru*[43] dissipates the mental or intellectual ignorance.

Nārāyaṇa

In Vaiṣṇava philosophy Nārāyaṇa, Viṣṇu, Vāsudeva, Kṛṣṇa, Sudarśana and many more names bear the same importance. The word Vaiṣṇava is used in the sense of "belonging to Viṣṇu". Viśiṣṭādvaita is a Vaiṣṇava philosophy. Nārāyaṇa is the personal God of this philosophy. He is the Ultimate Reality.

In Hinduism, the idea of several deities is based on pure monotheism. Different systems have sprung up adopting for their worship some particular aspects of the same God, naming him differently. Every Hindu is convinced that God is one, all-

43. *gu* = dark, *ru* = light.

pervading, beyond time and space, beyond name and form. But for practical purposes of prayer and meditation, He is represented as having different forms and denominated by different names. As man is the best of His creations, He is painted in the human form, but generally with four hands depicting thereby the idea of Divinity in this form. There are some prominent forms which are worshipped all over India.

fig. 2: Lord Nārāyaṇa
(Courtesy: Sumitra Sri Bhashyaṃ, U.K.)

Nārāyaṇa or Viṣṇu is that aspect of God which depicts Him as the Supreme Sovereign of the universe. He is worshipped as such and is regarded as personification of God in that form, who preserves the world with His divine power that is called Lakṣmī, the Goddess of prosperity, fortune and of wealth. His complexion is described as brilliantly bright, as radiating lustre of the sky with a bluish hue signifying splendour and infiniteness, as the blue colour of heaven is an indication of infinite expansion. In each of his four hands, he is holding something. In one hand he holds a sceptre, which is a symbol of supreme authority and of the unflinching laws of nature; in the second hand a lotus symbolises fortune; the third is holding a conch (the sound of the conch resembles the sound of *OṀ*), which serves as a trumpet to proclaim His kingdom, just and merciful. The conch is also used for pouring forth water, as a token of blessing which always emanates from the Lord. In His fourth hand, He is shown brandishing his *sudarśana cakra*, a disc of beautiful appearance, always prepared to serve as a weapon for killing the evil. He always bears a smiling face, puts on a yellow garment below his loins representing the earthly portion of the universe with a silver-lined waistband representing the boundary of glittering waters; He has a scarlet-coloured navel, which represents the fire *vaiśvānaragni*; His bosom of a dark bluish colour denotes the spiritual and ethereal portion of the universe. His head is covered with a crown studded with shining suns, moons and stars. He is seated on a royal bird, the royal eagle (Garuḍa) which is well known for its power of soaring high into heaven. Thus, the entire universe is shown as His person. He pervades the universe through every one of its atoms like a string permeates the beads of a rosary. Although God pervades the whole universe and shines everywhere in His glory, still His seat is in the heart of every man, every human being, and His worship consists in the deep emotion of love. He is the Lord of the universe: past, present and future. Nothing is hidden from Him. The Upaniṣads say:

> Knowing Him one is freed from chores. Verily such is the Lord of the size of the thumb resembling a smokeless glow of light, residing within the heart.

"The Kingdom of Heaven is in the heart of man", said Jesus. In the heart, He resides, in the heart, He is sought and in the heart, He shines, when meditated upon with love and devotion.

The word Nārāyaṇa is very significant in Viśiṣṭādvaita and the sound is considered as Supreme *mantra* called *dvaya* and *aṣṭākṣara*. *Dvaya mantra*[44] is thus called because it contains a set of two *mantras*: *śrīman nārāyaṇa caraṇau śaraṇam pradapye* and *śrīmate*

44. *Dvaya* from *dve* means two.

nārāyaṇāya namaḥ. Both the two *mantra*s are combined to form one *mantra*. On the other hand, *aṣṭākṣara*[45] is an eight-syllable *mantra*: *oṁ namo nārāyaṇāya*. At the commencement and at the end of any meditation (*dhyāna*), both the *dvaya* and the *aṣṭākṣarī* are repeated:

> *śrīman nārāyaṇa caraṇau śaraṇam pradapye* ।
> *śrīmate nārāyaṇāya namaḥ, oṁ namo nārāyaṇāya* ॥

Rāmānuja calls the *aṣṭākṣarī* as *mūla mantra*.[46] Chanting of the Nārāyaṇa *mantra* leads to liberation in which supreme happiness exists.

The word Nārāyaṇa and His supremacy as ultimate reality are expressed beautifully by Tirumaṅgai Āḷvār, a highly respected south Indian saint:

> *That which would yield status and wealth*
> *Wipe out all grief the devotees suffer,*
> *That which would with grace yields the heavens*
> *Vast lands and all good in this earth and,*
> *That which would beget many more than*
> *The mother herself would yield*
> *That word I have realised and*
> *That is the name of Nārāyaṇa.*

Nārāyaṇa is the one who comprises the entire universe of *cit* and *acit*.[47] He is the Supreme Self, *Paramātman*, that is, God in the soul, who is immanent in all. *Nāra* means "water", *āyaṇa* means "to move" or "place of movement, an abode". Before the creation of Brahmā, water was the abode of God. So He is called Nārāyaṇa. In the beginning, the cosmic soul had its abode in the water; and the cosmic soul moved in the water in the beginning.

Nārāyaṇa is same as *Brahman* of the Upaniṣads. Viśiṣṭādvaita

---

45. *Aṣṭa* means eight and *akṣara* is syllable. *Aṣṭākṣara* means eight-syllabled.

46. Rāmānuja, by naming *Aṣṭākṣarī* as *mūla mantra* considers it as the root of all the *mantras*. *Mūla* means root and *mūla mantra*, the root *mantra* of all the *mantras*.

47. *Cit* is that which animates the body, the life principle. *Acit* is that which does not have life.

gives more importance to Nārāyaṇa than to *Brahman* and regards Him as the instrumental cause of the projection of the universe. He protects His creation. So he is called Nārāyaṇa. His existence is always for the liberation of people. Because He protects all beings, He is also called Janārdana.

Subāla Upaniṣad describes Nārāyaṇa, the Supreme God, as *antarātmā* (the inner soul), and the inner controller of all beings in the universe.[48] To uphold the supremacy of Nārāyaṇa, *Mahopaniṣad* declares, "Nārāyaṇa alone existed in the beginning". "In the beginning,[49] dear boy, this was Being (*sat*) alone, only one, without a second."[50] Viśiṣṭādvaita interprets this Being (*sat*) as Nārāyaṇa. Pāṇinī, the Sanskrit grammarian, considers the term Nārāyaṇa as a specific proper name; and it is applicable to one specific being only, but not to any other entity like the general terms such as *sat, ātmā, Brahman,* etc. So it can be taken that the *Brahman* referred to in the Upaniṣads is the same as Nārāyaṇa. Several authorities are upholding the supremacy of Nārāyaṇa. He is also called *parā jyoti, parā brahman, parā tattva, parā brahmā*. The Puruṣa-Sūkta, the most authoritative part of Veda, because of its inclusion in all the four Vedas, supports the supremacy of Nārāyaṇa. Even the oldest epics, *Rāmāyaṇa* and *Mahābhārata*, Dharmaśāstras[51] expounded by great sages like Manu and Yājñavalkya, the Purāṇas as well as the Upaniṣads acknowledge the supremacy of Nārāyaṇa.

In his *Gītārtha Saṁgraha* the great Yāmunācārya, the preceptor of Rāmānuja, makes the point that the Supreme Lord is Nārāyaṇa. He is the seat of all power and auspicious attributes. He alone can give salvation as a matter of grace. This worthiness is attained through the practice of *bhakti*.

---

48. *Subala Upaniṣad*, III.
49. *Mahopaniṣad*, I.1.
50. *Chāndogya Upaniṣad*, VI.2.1.
51. Hindu Law Book on the Code of Conduct.

The mystic Āḻvārs[52] also defend the supremacy of Nārāyaṇa. In *Tirumoḻi* and other *prabandhas*,[53] the dominant feature of Reality is the identification of the Ultimate Principle (*parā tattva*)[54] with the God of religion; and this God is Nārāyaṇa. At the outset, Nammāḻvār[55] states: "That person who is endowed with infinite auspicious attributes *par excellence* is He, Nārāyaṇa." This implies, as *Taittirīya Upaniṣad* says, "that one reality is *parama puruṣa*, Supreme Person." To make it more specific, Nammāḻvār equates this Supreme Person with Nārāyaṇa. *Taittirīya Upaniṣad* as well as *Mahopaniṣad* use the term Nārāyaṇa because it connotes all the essential characteristics of the Ultimate Reality.

As Nammāḻvār explains, the word Nārāyaṇa means the Lord (*nāthan*) of the entire universe by virtue of His all-pervasiveness. He is the abode (*āśraya*) of countless souls possessing the characteristics of knowledge and bliss; and He is also endowed with an infinite number of auspicious attributes. In the *Peria Tirumoḻi*,[56] the mystic Saint Tirumangai Āḻvar hints at the special significance that the chanting of Nārāyaṇa will pave the way for liberation from bondage. He goes to the extent of saying "a mother who names her child as Nārāyaṇa would never go to hell". Nammāḻvār, in the later part of *Tirumoḻi*, states that "the Lord Nārāyaṇa is one, who controls the creation, sustenance and dissolution; and who as their inner controller directs Brahmā and Śiva; and who by manifesting Himself with them, protects the universe."

Everything in this world: life force, Brahmā, Rudra, earth, water, mind, sense organs, everything has its source in Nārāyaṇa.

---

52. The south Indian Śrī Vaiṣṇava saints.
53. *Thirumoḻi* and *Divya Prabandha* are Tamil devotional works written by saints. They are considered as Draviḍian authorities on devotion.
54. Ultimate Principle, the Supreme Being, namely Nārāyaṇa here.
55. One of the most important Tamil Vaiṣṇava saints.
56. A Tamil composition of devotional verses.

Sri T. Krishnamacharya's instructions for meditation on Nārāyaṇa: The one who meditates should picture the whole universe fitted inside Nārāyaṇa. This world of animate and inanimate objects is the body of Nārāyaṇa. Earth is the feet (*pāda*); space (*ākāśa*) is the navel (*nābhi*); Air (*vāyu*) is breath, Moon (*candra*) and Sun (*sūrya*) the eyes; Heaven (*antarikṣa*) his head; Fire (*agni*) his mouth, Sea (*samudra*) his living abode: *oṁ namo nārāyaṇāya*.

Why do people worship other gods, if Nārāyaṇa alone is the Supreme Deity? Nammāḻvār answers: The numerous deities referred to in the hymns of *Ṛgveda* are worshipped by other cults for securing desired results. Of course, the other gods confer desired boons to the worshipper. But all these deities are brought into existence by the Supreme Being Nārāyaṇa who as their Inner Controller (*antarātmā*) grants them power to confer the desired fruits. Thus, the worship offered to other deities ultimately goes to the Supreme Being Nārāyaṇa, who is actually the giver of boons sought for.

Another reason for supporting the exclusive worship of Nārāyaṇa is that the Supreme goal of life is the liberation of the soul from bondage (*mokṣa*). The sacred texts point out that Nārāyaṇa is the donator of *mokṣa*. Nammāḻvār preached that the Supreme Being Nārāyaṇa alone confers *mokṣa*. He considers Nārāyaṇa as the Ultimate Principle (*parātattva*) because He is the Lord of all beings (Sarveśvara). This means He is the Lord of all other deities including Brahmā and Rudra, the important Vedic deities, popularly acknowledged as higher gods. In other words, He is higher than the high.

Bhaṭṭa Bhāskara, another philosopher[57] explains Nārāyaṇa as follows: the term *nāra*, being derived from the root *nṛ* meaning "to lead", means he is the leader of all other creatures. Nārāyaṇa is the Supreme Soul (*Paramātman*). Vāsudeva in His immanent

57. Ninth century.

aspect dwells in all creatures as Indweller (*antaryāmin*).[58] He is the source of all souls (*jīva*). He remains in a potential form in the heart for the benefit of all souls. He is the creator, protector and dissolver of the universe. He is the only independent reality; all others are dependent on Him. He shines forever in His own glory.

Viṣṇu

Viṣṇu is another term signifying the concept of the Supreme Being. Viṣṇu means "that which pervades everything". It is therefore used as a synonym for Nārāyaṇa or *Brahman*.

"May we know Nārāyaṇa, for that may we meditate upon Vāsudeva? May Viṣṇu impel us towards it?"[59] This *mantra*, called *Viṣṇu Gāyatrī*, can also be translated as: "To Nārāyaṇa we bring worship, to Vāsudeva our meditations and in this may Viṣṇu assist us."

Padma Purāṇa says,

> Viṣṇu as Lord entered into *prakṛti*. The Sage Parāśara, who is regarded as one blessed with the knowledge of the Ultimate Principle (*Parātattva*) has affirmed the supremacy of Nārāyaṇa. The *Skanda Purāṇa*, which is classified as a *Śiva Purāṇa* and which gives primary importance to Śiva and Rudra, also declares the supremacy of Viṣṇu.

In the Hindu concept of the Trinity, Brahmā, Viṣṇu and Rudra, it is generally believed that Brahmā is the creator of the universe, Viṣṇu its protector and Rudra the destroyer of the universe. Nārāyaṇa assumes the form of Viṣṇu to protect all beings. Viṣṇu of the Trinity is the same as Nārāyaṇa, who is the primary cause of the universe.

Kṛṣṇa

Kṛṣṇa is another name generally used for Viṣṇu. In *Vedānta Ratna Mañjūṣā*,[60] it is said that Kṛṣṇa has got His name because he removes the sins of His devotees. The word Kṛṣṇa is derived

---

58. *Antaryāmin* = one who dwells inside.
59. *Nārāyaṇa Upaniṣad*.
60. *Vedānta Ratna Mañjūṣā*, Purushottama Prasada.

from *kṛṣ* "to scrape". Because He scrapes or draws away all sins and other sources of evil from his devotees, He is called Kṛṣṇa. The word also means "He who attracts all or arouses devotion in all." Kṛṣṇa, the teacher of *Bhagavad-Gītā*, not only arouses devotion in the mind of those who read *Bhagavad-Gītā*, but also attracts devotion in all. The same emotional sentiment is felt while reading *Śrīmad Bhāgavata Purāṇa*, in which the sage Vyāsa pictures Kṛṣṇa as an incarnation of Nārāyaṇa.

fig. 3: Lord Kṛṣṇa
(Courtesy: Claire Sribhashyam, France)

Sudarśana

Sudarśana means "leading to good". *Su* means "good", *darśana* is "one who shows or leads". Sudarśana is represented as a wheel (*cakra*) symbolising the wheel of the universe. The wheel depicts the rolling of creation. Sudarśana is prominent in *Ahirbudhnya Saṁhitā*.[61]

61. *Ahirbudhnya Saṁhitā* is one of the authoritative Pāñcarātra treatises, based partly on the Vedic and partly on the Tāntric system. *Ahirbudhnya Saṁhitā* is the collection of Vaiṣṇava doctrines contained in Vedas. This Saṁhitā has offered detailed interpretations of the names used for Viṣṇu in the Āgama treatise.

It says that after undergoing a long penance Ahirbudhnya[62] received from Saṅkarṣaṇa[63] the true knowledge and that this true knowledge was the Science of Sudarśana, which is the support of all things in the world.[64] There is nothing whatsoever outside the sphere of the power of Sudarśana. When *Brahman*, whose nature is knowledge and who is endowed with all qualities, resolves into the idea of splitting Himself into many, it is called Sudarśana. The knowledge of Sudarśana is spiritual and self-illuminating.

It enters into all things, reflects them and is eternal. When all the external movement of the objective world is ideally grasped in the word, it is said that the manifestation of the Sudarśana power is in it or the supreme thought-activity of God is in it. The realisation of God through the word or thought will only happen

fig. 4: Sudarśana Cakra
(Photography: T.K. Sribhashyam, France)

62. *Ahirbudhnya Saṁhitā* 5.34.5, 21.2; *Mahābhārata* 62.39.48.
63. Another name of Viṣṇu.
64. *Ahirbudhnya Saṁhitā*, III.2.5.

through the power of Sudarśana (which is part of Lakṣmī). Unity with God can mean union with Sudarśana.[65]

Śiva

Śiva means "auspicious". Śambhū is another name for Śiva meaning "giver of happiness". Nārāyaṇa, Śiva and Śambhū embody auspiciousness. All manifestations and all personifications belong to the same Supreme Being. Viṣṇu is Śiva; Śiva is Viṣṇu, who is Nārāyaṇa. The one light manifests in various forms.[66]

He who is known as Viṣṇu is verily Rudra; and he who is known as Rudra is *Brahman*. One entity functions as three gods Rudra, Viṣṇu and *Brahmā*. This one entity the Śaivaites[67] worship as Śiva, the Vedāntins as *Brahman*, the Christians as Christ and Mohammedans as Allāh. God rewards all, who strive to seek Him. Only the spiritually immature refuse to recognise other gods than their own.

> O Lord! All-pervading supreme Self, Lord of Yoga, who is there in the three worlds, who can penetrate thy mystery, know where, when, in what manner and in how many forms Thou engagest thyself in sport.[68]

The word *śiva* is derived from the root *vaśkantam* meaning Śiva always fulfils the desires of His devotees. *Mahābhārata* depicts this merciful aspect of Śiva, who is prepared to grant boons for which prayers are offered.[69] "May we know or realise the Supreme Person. For that, may we meditate upon Mahādeva and to that meditation may Rudra impel us."[70] Rudra here is referred to as "giver of knowledge" and not as the God of Destruction; because

---

65. *Ahirbudhnya Saṁhitā*, LI 69.78.
66. *Atharvaveda*, III.3.17.
67. Those who practise the cult of Śiva.
68. *Śrīmad Bhāgavata*.
69. Śiva's aspect of mercifulness is different from the aspect of Śiva as Rudra, the God of destruction.
70. *Rudra Gāyatrī Mantra*.

Rudra acts as the greatest help man can expect of God in the guidance of his thoughts in the right direction, that is, controlling and developing thoughts: the thoughts of the knowledge of God that lead to liberation.

In *Maitrāyaṇī Upaniṣad* of *Yajurveda*, many instructions on meditation[71] are prescribed for the meditation and worship of Rudra-Śiva.[72] The first is addressed to Rudra Mahādeva. The name Rudra is depicted as the power that rules knowledge and wisdom. Rudra is the giver of knowledge; and as such, He is the guide of the whole universe. Mahādeva is the name which usually describes His unrivalled Divine nature. The terms *Puruṣa*, Mahādeva and Rudra in *Rudra Gāyatrī* are typical of the characteristics of the same Divine Person implying His personality and spiritual quality — that of Śiva.

Śiva is another form of Īśvara, who is worshipped like Viṣṇu all over India by all branches of Hinduism. The idea of Śiva grounds on Advaita Vedānta. Soul appears as individual because of the reflection of the One universal spirit Śiva on mind. The universal spirit is Īśvara whereas His reflection is the soul (*jīva*), who when freed from lust, anger, fear, attachment, avarice, pride, passions, births and deaths, humility, grief, inertia, hunger, thirst, desire, timidity, misery, sorrows and pleasures becomes Śiva. The ultimate end of every branch of religion is the realisation of the individual soul as Śiva, which is realisation only in the Cerebral Lotus of the Thousand Petals[73] through *samādhi*.[74] Śiva is therefore pictured as seated on a tiger skin with his eyes closed in *samādhi* as *yogīśvara* as he is called too being even unconscious of the venomous serpents coiling round his arms and neck. His blue-coloured neck is a proof of His immunity to deadly poisons like evil, hatred, etc. To Him the deadliest of poisons is as welcome as

71. *Dhyāna Gāyatrī*.

72. *Maitrāyaṇī Upaniṣad* 2.9.1.

73. Called *sahasrāra cakra*.

74. Final stage of eightfold *yoga* discipline or any Hindu spiritual discipline.

nectar. He adores his snow-white body with snakes and scorpions. In the forehead, He possesses the third eye of spiritual knowledge. When this third eye is opened in *yoga* (through meditation), it burns the passions of lust and sexual desires with its gaze. He is all calm and peaceful and hence is named Śaṅkara one who bestows peace. When He wakes from meditation, He plays on His divine drum (*ḍamaru*) and dances His *tāṇḍava* dance in ecstasy of joy and bliss, which is His nature. He rides on a bull indicating that a person on attaining *samādhi* conquers the animal in him, suppresses his animal passions, dullness, stupidity and obstinacy. Śiva is therefore called Paśupati, Lord of animals. He wears a crescent moon on his head. This signifies his highly spiritual knowledge. The flow of knowledge from His head is compared to the holy waters of the river Ganges. He is believed to have his abode in the Himalayan high peaks: Kailāsa situated in the heart of the Tibetan solitude. Mānasa Sarovara[75] is located here, whose sight elevates a person spiritually through the impulse given by its natural scenery.

To a devotee the highest peak of Kailāsa is *Sahasrāra* (Thousand-petalled Lotus), and his calm mind is the beautiful lake Mānasa Sarovara. As all knowledge is the result of deep meditation, Śiva is called the originator of all branches of sciences, mathematics and philosophies. He begins to shine in the heart of a *yogī* and leads him gradually by instructing and enlightening him in the intricacies of the fathomless ocean of knowledge. He is the real *guru*, who always dwells in the heart of every person. Śiva can be approached through the practice of *yoga* with the help of His Śakti, Mother Goddess, manifesting Herself in the human body in the form of the psychic force. This power is commonly known as Kuṇḍalinī Śakti, which is translated as Serpent Power.

Śiva is also worshipped in the *tālī*[76] form of *liṅga*. The term *liṅga* in Sanskrit stands for an indicative mark, emblem or a

75. A lake on the Himalayan ranges.

76. A kind of mountain palm tree.

symbolical representation. Śiva-liṅga represents the Supreme Being denoted by the word Rudra Mahādeva — a symbol representing the worship of God with the whole universe emanating from Him. A *tālī* is a vegetative body manifesting without any differentiation in root, stem and leaves. Worshipping Śiva in the *tālī* form represents God in his spiritual[77] aspect with the entire creation within Himself.

Śiva is one of the Hindu ideas of Trinity[78] representing the principle of destruction and reproduction. The *tālī* form of *liṅga* indicates both: the disappearance and manifestation of all living beings, the involuntary emanation at His desire.

Śiva-Śakti is represented in the form of *liṅga* as a serpent coiled around Śiva-liṅga three and a half times having the tail in her mouth placed at the top. According to Śaiva authorities, the *liṅga*, usually called Śiva-liṅga, may be placed anywhere, but the blessings it radiates vary according to the cardinal points. In the east, it will confer royal dignity, in the south longevity, etc.

In the great epic *Rāmāyaṇa*, Rāvaṇa is depicted as a devotee of Śiva, taking with him a golden Śiva-liṅga, which he worshipped. Rāma's mother Kauśalyā and the priests of Rāma are also said to have worshipped Śiva.

> The forms we impose on formless are due to our limitations. Of course, we turn away from the contemplation of ultimate reality to concentration upon imaginative reconstructions. All gods, except the one unmanifest are forms imposed on Him. God is not one among many. He is the one behind the ever changing many, who stands beyond all forms, the immutable centre of endless mobility.[79]

But Rāmānuja says that on the ordinary human level worship of forms is essential because mind by nature is disturbed. It may go

77. *Adhyātma*.

78. *Trimūrti*. *Tri* = three, *mūrti* = image or face.

79. *Bhagavad-Gītā*, by S. Radhakrishnan.

astray to many things if there is no form for the worshipper to meditate upon.

Yoga-Vāsiṣṭha attempts to recognise the truth of all Hindu traditions, to adopt them and to weld them into something higher. Many names have been given to the Supreme Spirit by the learned such as Order (*ṛtam*), Self (*ātman*), the Truth (*Brahman*), etc. While the followers of Vedānta call it *Brahman*, those who proclaim the doctrine of void call it Void (*śūnya*) and the worshippers of Śiva naturally call it Śiva. The Holy One (*bhagavān*) conceived in different ways is one and the same.

Chāndogya Upaniṣad describes:

> Before creation, this universe was non-existent. Then it became existent. It grew, it turned into an egg, it lay for a period of one year and then it burst open. Of the two halves of that eggshell, one was of silver and the other of gold. That which was silver that is this earth. That which was gold is this heaven or celestial region.[80]

In the beginning, the universe was not accepted as existent as it did not differentiate itself into name and form; not that there was nothing in the beginning, because from non-existence (*asat*) the existential universe (*sat*) cannot emerge. When it is pitch-dark everywhere, nothing can be recognised. That non-being which existed before creation was without vibration and still prior to its expression as to an effort it began to be active and reached the status of Being. This being vibrated and became a seed ready to sprout into the name and form of the universe. Assuming greater concreteness it became the egg, which waited a year to burst into two halves upper and lower worlds.[81] The whole universe was hatched out of a golden egg, which lay a complete year before it brought forth offspring: the universe.

---

80. *Chāndogya Upaniṣad*, III.19 and 1,2.
81. The term year here is a time cycle before creation and not our calendar year.

The spherical dome of the heavens above, appearing to us as capping the earth on which we live, may be linked to an enormous semi-section of an egg containing the world. Perhaps, this golden egg landed itself as the visible symbol of the limitless, all-inclusive Divine Reality into which the manifold universe will be reabsorbed at the end. The *liṅga,* which is worshipped by the devotee of Śiva, is but a convenient replica of the universal semi-spherical emblem of the unlimited. Śiva-liṅga may be carved out of a stone, naturally found as stalagmite or shaped out of gold, or other metals. The *liṅga* is a symbol concealing a truth beyond it.

Śrī as Goddess

The word Śrī has carried the sense of divine glory and bliss through thousands of years. The tender regard of womanhood is one of the distinguishing characteristics of the Vedas. *Subhage,* meaning "O graceful one" is the courteous address for a Goddess as well as for a woman. The basic word *bhaga* has been used for *Bhagavan* (the Supreme Lord) as well as for *Bhagavatī* (the supreme Goddess). Śrī is also said to be the power of God, who serves Him uninterruptedly. Śrī is described as constantly serving Hari (God). It derives from the root *ṣam* meaning "giver of virtues, wealth" and "fulfiller of desires". And *ri* not only means "pure", but also "the power of speech". The Goddess Śrī who is commonly known by the name Lakṣmī is the most known among Hindus. She is the embodiment of auspicious qualities. It is commonly said that wherever prosperity, royal power and illustriousness are, there is Śrī. As an external quality, Śrī suggests beauty, lustre, glory, ruling power, etc. She is invoked to bring fame and prosperity.

The concept of Śrī can be traced back to the Vedas. Puruṣa-Sūkta and Śrī-Sūkta, the most significant parts of the Vedas elaborately describe Śrī. She is mentioned as Īśvarī (the feminine of Īśvara), the empress, while Īśvara is the emperor, the sovereign of the entire universe. "Lord in the highest form is always associated with power (*śakti*) called Lakṣmī or Śrī."[82] In the Vedas, she is associated with *padma* (lotus).[83]

fig. 5: Śrī Lakṣmī
(Courtesy: Sumitra Sri Bhashyam, U.K.)

The lotus suggests a growing and expanding world. The picture of lotus growing from the navel of Viṣṇu marks the beginning of a new cosmic creation. Lotus, in relation to Śrī Lakṣmī refers to the purity and spiritual power as well as to spiritual authority. In Hindu and Buddhist iconography, the lotus seat is a common motif. The gods, goddesses, buddhas and *bodhisattva*s sit or stand on a lotus flower. This symbol has a significance. Just as a water drop stays unconnected with the lotus on which it stands, these gods, goddesses, buddhas, etc. remain unconnected with the finite world and its limitations. Śrī floats freely as if it was in a sphere of purity and power. She is regarded as the consort of the great guardian of eternal law, Viṣṇu, who, as said in *Ṛgveda* (I.22.18), made three steps as the protector, upholding the eternal laws (*dharma*). His steps bring sweetness, peace and joy.

---

82. *Ahirbudhnya Saṁhitā*.

83. *padma priye padmiṇī padma haste padmālaye padma dalāya tākṣī. . . . Śrī Sūkta*.

The association of Śrī with Viṣṇu, Nārāyaṇa is so firm that it is always expressed as Śrī Viṣṇu, Śrīman Nārāyaṇa, Śrīnivāsa, etc. In Hindu mythology, Śrī's association with Viṣṇu is found in the context of the churning of the milk ocean by gods and demons, who seek the elixir of immortality.

In ancient tradition, it is said that creation proceeds from an infinite body of primordial water. The world and the multitude of universes arise from and rest upon this limitless expanse of waters. In its unrefined state, this watery world is formless and overwhelming. Creation can only take place when this mass of water is agitated and processed in such a way that form and evolution take place. Within the watery formlessness resides the potency or essence of life. When the primordial waters release the potency, creation can proceed. Gods and demons churn the ocean with the idea of obtaining the nectar of immortality. This action dramatically illustrates the process of distilling the essence of primordial waters.

In the myth of the churning of the ocean, Viṣṇu is the dominant God. Śrī emerged from the ocean. She is said to manifest herself (*prādurbhāva*) so she is not born in the ordinary sense during the time of churning the mythological milky ocean (*kṣīrābdhi*) for obtaining nectar. She is therefore designated as issued from milk.[84] Soon after her emergence, she chose the bosom of Viṣṇu[85] as her abode. She is given a respectable status and place as the dearest of Viṣṇu, because she enhances the glory of the Lord by her permanent association with Him.

She always accompanies Him in his incarnations. She is His associate and transforms her own person agreeably to whatever character Viṣṇu puts on.

In the Pāñcarātra Āgama School,[86] it is said that Śrī plays the

84. *Kṣīrodbhava, kṣīra* = milk, *udbhava* = emanated from.

85. This is narrated in many Purāṇas.

86. The religious treatises dealing with the modes of worship of God and matters relating to temples, particularly of Viṣṇu.

central role in the creation and evolution of the universe as the power of Viṣṇu. Śrī Tantra also called Lakṣmī Tantra[87] says that she undertakes the entire creation of the universe with only a one-billionth fraction of herself.[88] She is so transcendent that she is beyond the ability of the mind to circumscribe her. Only a minute fraction of her is manifest in the creation of the universe.

According to Śrī Vaiṣṇavism,[89] Śrī Viṣṇu is the Supreme Deity, who is mostly known as Śrīman Nārāyaṇa. He is always accompanied and attended by His consort Śrī. She does not play the cosmological role in Vaiṣṇavism, as she does in Pāñcarātra Āgama School, though she is inseparable from Viṣṇu. In Śrī Vaiṣṇavism, Viṣṇu or Nārāyaṇa is the central figure and is equated with the highest philosophical principle. Śrī Lakṣmī has acquired an intermediate place between Viṣṇu and His devotees.

The concept of Śrī as the Divine consort has great importance in the theology of Śrī Vaiṣṇavism, that is why this system is known as Śrī Vaiṣṇavism. Śrī is incorporated as a prefix of honour in all the major writings of Rāmānuja. His writings give the impression that Śrī is co-eternal with Viṣṇu, ever united with Him, one who never keeps away from Him.[90] During God's incarnation, She is always with Him.

Śrī Vaiṣṇavism equates the Godhead with the dual Self of Lakṣmī-Nārāyaṇa and Śrīyaḥpati. The divine mercy (*dayā*) flows from this dual relation of God and Goddess. According to Rāmānuja, Śrī is indispensable in approaching Viṣṇu. He describes Her as Gracious Mother, who intercedes with Nārāyaṇa on the devotees' behalf. In the *Śaraṇāgati Gadya*,[91] he says that Goddess Śrī, who is never separated from Viṣṇu, reflects all the

87. One of the important ritualistic practices of this school.
88. *Lakṣmī Tantra* of Pāñcarātra Āgama 14.3.
89. School of Viṣṇu cult.
90. She is called *anapāyinī*.
91. A devotional prose composition of Rāmānuja on "surrender to God".

characteristics of God: essential nature, form of divine personality, divine attributes, taking different forms for the worship of devotees, lordship, etc.; the characteristics appropriate to Viṣṇu's status and she is also liked by Him. In each of His incarnations, She takes the right form to suit the incarnation.

Sri T. Krishnamacharya instructed his children and students that while offering prayers in a temple they should first approach the Goddess to offer their prayers and obtain permission from Her to approach the God of the temple. Direct approach is not suitable to a man, who is tied to the bondage which is the human body. Goddess graces humans with compassion which is a stepping-stone to reach God like pure Love.

According to Viśiṣṭādvaita, Nārāyaṇa is not only the Lord of the universe, but also the Lord of love. As Śrīyaḥpati or Śrīnivāsa He is regarded as the father of all. Śrī resides in His heart and is thereby regarded as the Mother of all. The fatherhood and motherhood of God is designated to inspire the hope of universal salvation. A mother's tender love always works in a child's problems. God who is beyond *prakṛti* and *puruṣa* has a twofold spiritual form of his own: Lord and Śrī. They are philosophically inseparable, though functionally distinguishable. Śrī resides forever in the heart of Īśvara with her auspicious qualities and is indistinguishable from Him like the fragrance of a flower. Ontologically, Īśvara and Śrī are one, but functionally different owing to the redemptive needs of *jīva*. She changes His law of *karma* into the rule of love and tenderness (*kṛpā*). She makes God overpowering with compassion and affection (*dayā* and *vātsalya*).

The cosmic sovereign is ruled by love; and Śrī resides in the ever-blooming lotus of love and in the very heart of the divine nature. The Lord rules by law, Śrī rules by love; the majesty of the holy law of justice is eternally wedded to the all-conquering might of mercy. It is expressed here that, by the inner mediating link of compassion, goodness is changed into Godliness. Śrī melts the heart of the sinner by her infinite tenderness.

Śrī Vaiṣṇava theology points out that Śrī does not play any particular part in the creative function of Īśvara, unlike Śakti, the female counterpart of Śiva, who is the active power in creation. Śiva is only the inactive pure consciousness.

Certain branches of Pāñcarātra Āgama view that Śrī is the Creator, Sustainer and Destroyer of the universe. She has taken over the cosmic function of the three great gods, Brahmā, Viṣṇu and Rudra although it is stated that She acts according to Lord Viṣṇu's wishes. She is also the object of devotion. In this Āgama, Śrī is the most important object of meditation.

In Śrī Vaiṣṇavism, Viṣṇu is the great creator and Śrī is always established on His bosom along with the *Śrīvatsa* curl. Some groups of Śrī Vaiṣṇavas[92] look upon her as the first soul (*jīva*) and therefore as the first among the servitors (*śeṣa*). Regarding the position of Śrī in the three categories of *cit*, *acit* and *parameśvara*, the view of the older school[93] is that Śrī is identified with human souls and is therefore to be regarded as atomic in nature. Others, however, think that Śrī is as all-pervasive as Viṣṇu. She is the Mother of the universe. She is an important element in man's Realisation.

Taking into consideration the divine nature in the anthropomorphised conception, Nārāyaṇa, the father, stands for justice, while Śrī represents the motherly love that extends even to the one undeserving it most. A mother usually has greater concern for her weaker children. She always remains a mediator between Nārāyaṇa and all spiritual seekers. Prayers to Śrī, the Mother, for her grace must be the first spiritual action.

Vedānta Deśika[94] commenting on *Catuśślokī* of Yāmunācārya[95] considers Śrī as different from Nārāyaṇa but always associated

---

92. Hindus who believe in the unity and inseparability of God Viṣṇu and his consort Lakṣmī.
93. *Tattva Dīpa* by Ramya Jāmātru (1370-1443).
94. A disciple of Rāmānuja.
95. Preceptor of Rāmānuja.

with Him. She should not be identified with the power of illusion, *māyā*. She is conceived as existing in intimate association with Nārāyaṇa and like a mother exerting helpful influence to bring the devotees into the sphere of the grace of the Lord. Thus, Śrī Lakṣmī is conceived to have a separate personality of her own, though it is merged in the personality of Nārāyaṇa. All His efforts are in consonance with all Her efforts.

In his concept of Nārāyaṇa and Śrī, *Vedānta Deśika* also brought the paternal idea of the fatherhood and rulership of God in line with the maternal instinct of tenderness. Truth is eternal and uncompromising. But when it is transfigured by love, it mediates between extremes, links thoughts and actions and becomes a unifying power. Truth is based on non-contradiction and is expressed by "either . . . or" but love is based on harmony and is expressed by "both . . . and". In Rāmānuja's teaching compassion is more dominant because he was a true devotee.

The concept of Śrī is an essential part of God's easy accessibility. The Śrī Vaiṣṇava system of devotional practice has two objects: *bhakti* and *prapatti*. *Bhakti* is a continuous concentration on the Divine with knowledge (*upāsanā*), first becoming a spiritual being as God's servant and ending in complete self-surrender, the first stage of *prapatti*. For the humble folk, who have no training in philosophy, but are endowed with strong and undiluted faith, the grace of Śrī is the best help. This self-surrender is only attained through priceless divine concession. *Vedānta Deśika* further states that Śrī is neither the soul (*jīva*) nor God (Nārāyaṇa), but a separate person having Her being entirely dependent on God. Her relation to Nārāyaṇa can be understood on the analogy of the relation of the sun and its rays or the flower and its fragrance.

When religion is conceived in terms of will and justice, it demands adoration of the Creator as Father of all, but in the religion of redemption, justice is transformed into mercy. Śrī resides in the heart of religion as the embodiment of saving grace. She is the manifestation of pity (*kṛpā*) and compassion (*kāruṇya*) and She offers an eternal assurance to erring humanity that both the reign of righteousness and of redemptive mercy are at heart. Though He is the saviour, the Lord is the dispenser of justice according to merit; and justice is an insistence on the fulfilment of moral law through retribution and recompense. But retribution is transformed into forgiving love. Law is pervaded by love and overpowered by tenderness. Śrī lives in the blooming Lotus of the creative life, and is the heart of the Divinity. She depends absolutely on the Lord, belongs to Him only and the devotees depend on Her. As the bond of love, she mediates between the Infinite that is the Omnipotent and the finite that is impotent, and transforms the majesty of law into might of mercy. Sympathy and pity (*dayā*) has supernal beauty and sweetness. By her beauty, Śrī lures the Lord and turns Him into the Saviour; she draws the sinner by her sweetness, and the sinner is saved by entire submission to His will. Thus, in Viśiṣṭādvaita, the metaphysical truth of the Absolute as the Supreme Self is restated in terms of the non-dualism of Śrīyaḥpati as the Creator of the world and the Conserver of values. After salvation, the Lord and Śrī are one for the seeker, though they may appear as different and discrepant to the analytic intellect. The ethical idea of redemption and *dayā* are reconciled in ethical religion. It has its roots in justice and fruition in forgiveness. The Lord rules by law, and Śrī lives by love and the two are indissoluble and eternally wedded to each other. While in Judaism and other schools of monotheism controlled by ethical ideas, "law" dominates "love", in mystic religions "love" overflows "law". Ethical monism co-ordinates and controls the two sides by the non-dual entity of law and love. After liberation in one, who seeks God and is sought by Him, the faith in Śrīyaḥpati is changed into a soul-sight of the two as one, and just like the fragrance of the flower, the luminosity of light and the embodied soul, Nārāyaṇa and Śrī are indistinguishable.[96]

96. *The Philosophy of Viśiṣṭādvaita,* P.N. Srinivasachari.

In fact, for a true devotee, the ontological problem, whether Śrī is finite or infinite, is not so important since faith and love are his two walking sticks.

An interesting explanation of the essential unity of Viṣṇu and Śrī, notwithstanding their appearance as two persons at the same time, is given in *Lakṣmī Tantra*: "When Goddess arose from the ocean she was only visible to demons while gods saw only the male form."[97] "Even in dissolution (*pralaya*),[98] Lakṣmī and Nārāyaṇa became one as if it were a single principle. The whole cosmos is inside him both before and after creation."[99]

Concept of Hiraṇyagarbha (the Golden Egg)

Hindu deities like Indra, Agni, Vāyu, Varuṇa who are termed as cosmic gods — though they transcend the mortal stages — are yet below the grade of Hiraṇyagarbha, the first emanation of the Supreme Being. These minor gods may be linked to the sin because their tenure is limited in that particular stage. After their tenure is over, they descend to the lower world. A man however can reach up to the stage of Hiraṇyagarbha.[100]

Hiraṇyagarbha is the same total cosmic force emerged from the Supreme God. He is all-pervading, the father of Prajāpati, whose duty is to create. In *Bhagavad-Gītā*, Arjuna praises Lord Kṛṣṇa: "You alone are the great grand sire of all and also grandfather. Prajāpati is the father of Creators."

Jesus as God, Guru and Saints

For being saved from all their sins, it is to be noted that Islam and Christianity demand from their followers a lasting faith in the revered prophet and Lord Jesus Christ respectively. A Hindu regards God not as a prophet, but God as He is, in all His different

97. *Lakṣmī Tantra*, 8.49.
98. Dissolution.
99. *Ahirbudhnya Saṁhitā*, 4.78.
100. Hiraṇyagarbha is *Kārya Brahman*, that is, effected *Brahman*.

incarnations. Even though the Hindus consider *gurus* as God-sent messengers and highly revered persons, they look upon God as the Highest Reality; the *gurus* simply help the devotees by showing the path to reach this Truth. God alone can save them from their sins. Faith in God is all for them. Kṛṣṇa is an incarnation of Viṣṇu; and He is not a prophet. To a Hindu one should have faith in no one but God alone, whereas Muslims and Christians consider their respective prophet as a person separate from God, acting as an intermediary. This creates a vital difference in the understanding of Hinduism. According to a Christian or a Muslim, anybody who does not believe in his or her prophet is deprived of Divine clemency, whereas in Hinduism whoever believes in God would be liberated.

Conception of a Religion-free God

To one who believes in God, God is all. There is nothing outside and nothing can be differentiated from Him. He is an indivisible spirit present in all persons. He is the unifying principle behind all creations. All the moral and spiritual values are derived therefrom. All acts of sacrifice, charity and meditation are complete when conducted for His sake and offered to Him. God is distinct from the world, He is the highest Reality.

God appears in this world as the inseparable two — matter and spirit, object and subject, the Self and the non-Self (*ātman* and *anātman*) and so on. They imply each other. They are the separated parts of the original whole. Life cycle in the universe is nothing but the process of these two broken parts getting back to the original wholeness. The true progress lies in cultivating the supremacy of the soul over matter. So, the goal in life is to develop the morality of the soul — advancement of the soul.

Any specific system of belief in conduct, worship, faith, etc. is usually known as religion. It involves a code of ethics and a philosophy. Each specified religion has its own system of practices and ethical values, which have to be followed by its followers.

Religion provides some principles that guide a person in reaching his goal in spiritual evolution. It helps a person through leading him onto the right path or in the right direction to achieve this goal through higher knowledge (*jñāna*). It is the highest state of awareness. Religion does help in the process of mental elevation. It is like a supporting stick to many people. The principles adopted by the religions are usually methods to control the wavering tendencies of the mind.

Many people find it difficult to follow the principles, prescribed as religious duties, under the circumstances they live in. But this does not mean that they do not believe in God. They do have strong faith in God, but they are unable to follow the religious principles. This strong faith in God is itself the best support while treading their path of spiritual evolution. Faith does not prescribe any religious duty. Faith in the Absolute is a positive reaction of the mind. It makes the will strong. Faith as such is man's best friend.

To succeed in realisation, the elevation of the soul is very important. Without attaching himself to any religion, a man can keep his prayerful mind constantly, but his prayers should be conceived in terms of truth, goodness and beauty. As praised in Vedas, truth is the essence of Divinity. The knowledge of the Divine is an experience. Even the religious teachers proclaim that the devotee would be saved if he cultivates virtues like that of purity, self-control, detachment, truth and non-violence in their various forms. There is no need for religion to cultivate these virtues. He can worship his desired God (*iṣṭa devatā*) according to his own rights; and by every means of his power, he can acquire the grace of God.

According to the ancient Hindu sages, mind expands, when dependent on virtues, while it contracts, when dependent upon vice. A mental operation is like the light of a lamp; the lamp neither expands nor contracts. Only the light of the lamp will do so, depending upon the space, where it is kept. When this space is unlimited, the light of the lamp also becomes unlimited. When the consciousness is expanded as far as possible, through prayers and the following virtuous principles, the spirit in man also spreads out more light.

Soul is in the subtler layers of consciousness in man because it is a conscious entity. It is eternally real and dependent on God. Soul is atomic in size, dwelling in the heart like a point of light and is distinct from God, who is all-pervasive (*vibhū*). Man always craves for the power by which this all-pervasive God is to be known. To achieve this power he puts efforts to sharpen his mind. He not only craves to know God, but to become a perfect spirit to reach his goal. Man's life on earth is a journey towards divine perfection. In this journey, he has to cross over many obstacles. All the supports he takes from the codes of religion are only for this purpose. All forms of worship, ethical codes and laws are only for this ultimate purpose.

The ceremonies and rites are preliminaries for the development of moral qualities, they are only means for the purification of the soul. Rites and ceremonies prescribed in religion are initial steps to moral progress. They are intended to lead one to a virtuous life.

Development of virtues, self-culture, moral qualities and moral excellences are more important than ceremonial purity. Remaining independent of religion, one can develop moral excellences, live by developing the virtue of devotion to children, to family, to society, being kind to animals and so on. All these moral excellences should be practised with the idea of non-attachment. It is true that a tremendous effort of the human will and a variety of practices are required to bring the mind to non-attachment. "Purity, contentment, austerity, self-study and self-surrender to God are the *Niyama*."[101]

Whatever the conditions and circumstances are in which a man is placed, one can cultivate one of these practices to some

101. *Pātañjala Yoga-Sūtra*, II.32.

extent. In the beginning, they seem to be difficult. But gradually they become habits. Purity here not only means the purity of the physical body but also purity of thoughts, emotions and other mental faculties.

A virtuous life purifies and strengthens the soul. God is eternal perfection and to approach Him, the soul must be pure. The aim of man's life is to acquire the divine qualities and realise liberation. The first ascent of the soul's upward path consists in acquiring ethical purity. A bride is made to put on flowers and jewels before she meets the bridegroom. Likewise, virtues are soul's ornaments. The soul should be adorned with moral excellences before it meets the Supreme. Everything that hinders the transcendence of the soul should be carefully removed.

Practice of non-violence, truthfulness in all acts of life, not desiring for other's acquisitions, not deceiving anyone and good conduct do a lot of good in the elevation of soul.

God is attracted by devotional hearts. He chooses those who are pure in heart. One can deceive the world, deceive oneself, but can never deceive God. God knows the amount of sincerity in one's heart and sends grace accordingly.

It is natural that, when one is God-minded, one finds obstacles like vanity, extravagance, loss of faith, etc. The spiritual pride ruins the soul much quicker than the worldly vanity. Whether one is religious-minded or not one should be careful to cultivate a moderate dealing in all aspects of life.

Faith, love and prayer will bring positive reaction on the brain. All these work mysteriously. But they must be directed towards God with a strong belief. "Abandoning all duties, come to Me alone for shelter. Be not grieved, for I shall release thee from all evils."[102]

Discarding all duties to God with the firm belief that everything belongs to Him, one should surrender oneself to God.

---

102. *Bhagavad-Gītā*, XVIII.66.

When a person consecrates his life, actions, thoughts, feeling, love and prayers to God, He will guide him through the fight of life and one need not have fear. Giving oneself to God is the sure way of self-transcendence. Faith, love and prayers constitute unquestioning belief in God that does not require proof or evidence. To give oneself to God needs a strong will and trust in God. A weak man needs some help like religion as an external support. He has to take the support that gives him power to walk on the path of God. But a strong man can walk on this path on his own, because he is confident of his own powers. Whether one is religious or not, one has to put in efforts.

Any action done in a spirit of dedication is a worship of God. This is faith in God. All tasks of daily life, when done with an attitude of worshipping God, are sanctified. All utterances are prayers, when offered to God. They are all like self-giving to God. Nothing needs to be done. God accepts all tasks done with love and earnestness, however poor the offering may be. He grants our prayers, in whatever form we worship Him. He partakes whatever we offer. What is required is a pure and devoted heart. Śrī Kṛṣṇa says, "Whosoever offers me with love, a leaf, a flower, a fruit or even water I appear in person before that disinterested devotee of sinless mind, and delightfully partake of that article offered by him with love."[103] This means that God does not discriminate between one individual and another on different grounds. The only condition is that there should be love and purity.

Eternity is the only thing that can occupy and fill up love. Love partakes the soul itself. It is of the same nature as the soul. It is a divine spark. It is a point of fire within us, which is immortal. Nothing can limit love and nothing can extinguish love. God can add nothing to the boundless happiness of those who love each other. If He is the fullness of heaven, love is the fullness of man.

---

103. *Bhagavad-Gītā*, IX.26.

Love is like celestial respiration. It should be spread out to all. This is also the way God likes love to be utilised. The more love is drawn out from the heart, the more God will bring to the heart, where He resides. This treasure of love, when shared with all, will certainly please God.

Prayers need no religion. Certain thoughts are prayers. They are thoughts in the subtle layers of consciousness. Praying or saying prayers brings the tremendous power man needs. God by His own decree has placed His power in the hands of persons in such a way that unless they plead for it, His power is withheld. Wise people say: "Nothing is so powerful on earth as purity and prayers." Mahatma Gandhi said: "A prayer to God is poor man's medicine." Jesus said: "If you believe, you will receive whatever you ask for in prayer."[104] Prayers to God for the sake of others, the poor, the sick, etc. with love and faith floods the heart with life and the treasure of God.

Upaniṣads in general do not mention religion or duties. They particularly hint out desireless action and other methods of practice. The natural disability of the soul, that prevents it from walking on the path of God, is to be removed. Man has to transcend the limitations of physical, mental and moral conditions under which he has to work in his life. He can adopt any method to achieve transcendence.

Whatever may be the path man adopts, virtue, self-culture and purity of the heart are important. Veda does not lay stress in following a religion to approach God. The aim is to create unity in variety. God and His wisdom are for mankind in general. "Completely rid of passion, fear and anger, wholly absorbed in Me, depending on Me, and purified by the penance of wisdom, many have become one with Me even in the past."[105]

---

104. Mathew 21.22. "And all things, what so ever ye shall ask in prayer, believing you shall receive."

105. *Bhagavad-Gītā,* IV.10.

Exclusive love for God wipes out all the afflictions in man and frees his mind from all imperfections and vices; and his activities become as divine as that of God. One can adore and think of God according to his own conception. His mental freedom often works wonders.

6

Concept of Sin and Virtue

Shower your mercy on me my Lord,
You are the Viṣṇu who is the most merciful,
For this sinner is drowned in this endless sea of material life,
And merits your help Hey, Hari, Hey Puruṣottama.
— *Mukundamālā* 49 by Kulaśekhara Āḻvār

O Hari, pray make me Thine own out of sheer grace
who am the vessel of a thousand inequities,
who am fallen into the depths of the terrible ocean of worldly existence,
and who being resortless, have sought refuge at Thy feet.
— *Stotra Ratna, The Hymn-jewel of* Śrī Yāmunācārya 48

Concept of Karma

BEFORE going through the concept of sin in Hindu philosophy, it is necessary to review the idea of *karma*.

Karma is the law of action and reaction or cause and effect. Every action has a cause, and every reaction results from an action. The word *karma* comes from the root word *kṛ* meaning "to act", "action" or "deed". Any action, physical or mental is called *karma*. Every action has a reaction, that is, a result. The word *karma* includes both action and reaction or cause and effect. Moving, walking, talking, seeing, hearing, thinking, attraction, repulsion, willing, desiring and so forth that are actions of the body, the mind and the senses are known as *karma*.

The question of chance does not arise because of the Law of Karma. We may not be able to know the real causes behind the *karma* because of our limited knowledge, but what happened and what is happening is under the sway of this Law of Karma. The result of *karma* can be good, bad or mixed. That which is beneficial, to us as well as to others, is called good under certain conditions, while that which brings mental or physical injury is bad. Those that are partly beneficial and partly injurious are of mixed results. On the human plane, limited by time and space, it is impossible to find any action which is absolutely good or which produces absolutely bad results in every respect. Human plane is placed in between the highest and the lowest. So all *karma* is of mixed results.

Lord Kṛṣṇa says, "Works are always followed by their defects and demerits, just as the fire is enveloped with smokes."[1] While judging the results of an action, the predominance of good over evil is called virtuous, while the predominance of evil over virtue is called non-virtuous or sinful.

If the result of the action produces harmony, peace, tranquillity and happiness, this is due to a good action. Suffering, pain, misery, injury and unhappiness are the results of evil actions. All evil actions are considered sinful, whereas all good actions are considered virtuous.

Karma by itself is insentient. It is neither good nor bad. Every *karma* has a cause. The cause determines the nature of the effect. Beneficial effects are due to good actions (*puṇya karma*), and detrimental effects are caused by bad actions (*pāpa karma*). One who eats the food will get the effects of the food. One reaps what one sows.

Transferring *karma* of one individual to another is impossible. Only the one who does *karma* would reap its fruits. If someone else were to get the results, it would upset the law of *karma*. If God would transfer the *karma* of one person to another, He would be transgressing His own law of impartiality.[2]

---

1. *Bhagavad-Gītā*, XVIII.48.
2. Some Vedānta philosophers hold the view that the residual effects of *karma* of a realised or liberated soul would be shared by those who instigated *karma* in that person before his liberation.

Every *karma* starts from the soul (*jīva*). According to the law of *karma*, the reaction bounces back to the source, from where the action started. As Vedānta believes in the entity of the soul, the reaction of each action must return to the soul itself and influence the actor. All the causes of actions are motives or desires that lie within oneself.

It is the soul that does actions and experiences the effects. Even though the chain of *karma* is said to be without beginning, it has an end in liberation. While actual *karma* is the result of the actions of previous lives, the results of the actions of the present life add to the past *karma* with the results in the future life.

Karma is mainly of four kinds:

1. That which is stored (*sañcita karma*),
2. That which has been the cause of the present birth, body and character (*prārabdha karma*),
3. That which are sowing in the present life (*kriyamāna karma*), and
4. Future actions (*āgama karma*).

"Whatsoever a man soweth, that shall he reap", says St. Paul. Christ referred to the law of *karma* while his disciples question him: "Who did the sin, this man or his parents that he was born blind?" Jesus answered, "Neither hath this man sinned nor his parents." So, the man who was born blind could not sin in that life cycle. Only his actions in his previous life cycles are the cause of his blindness.

Karma creates nothing nor does it plan or design anything. Man creates his own actions. So, he is the cause of his own good and evil *karma*. He experiences the results accordingly. "Fear evil more than fire, as sin leads to sin."[3] Sin is the effect of wicked or immoral acts or deeds and is termed as *pāpa* or *aparādha*. It can be

---

3. *Kuraḷ* — Thiruvalluvar, 202.

expressed as the feeling of guilt accrued out of evil deeds that a person experiences in his own heart.

Concept of Sin

Sin as a word is difficult to understand, unless its attributes are taken into consideration. Evil, demerit, deceit, crime, etc. come under the word sin, though their meaning may differ. Sin can be understood better if its opposite "virtue" is also considered. Sin and virtue (*pāpa* and *puṇya*) together keep the human being sway in his life scale; and at the same time, they are essential for the human life.

Sin falls under the category of demerit (*adharma*). It is the doing of immoral acts. On the other hand, virtue (*dharma*) is the merit accrued out of the performance of good deeds or actions. Without virtue, demerit would not have existed. Both of them are the motives behind one's actions. It is very difficult to say whether an action is sinful or virtuous; the motive behind the action depends on the situation in which the action would be performed. It also depends upon the individual human nature.

A beautiful narration of how subtle the motive behind the action is can be found in the great epic *Mahābhārata* of the sage Veda Vyāsa. The story is about a game of dice as per the rules of stakes. The game was between Yudhiṣṭhira of Pāṇḍava, who was said to be the embodiment of virtues and Duryodhana of Kaurava. It is also said that a wise man becomes a fool, once he lays his hands on dice. It inhibits the good qualities in man and makes him commit wrong deeds. Yudhiṣṭhira knew well the consequences of playing dice. But it was a rule among kings not to refuse gambling, because it would bring a shadow on the bravery of the king. So the die was cast. Yudhiṣṭhira lost all his earthly belongings as his stakes. Then he gambled away all his brothers one by one and finally himself. After losing himself too, he waged his wife Draupadī and lost her too. So, when she was commanded by Duryodhana to be his slave, as per the conditions of the game, she wanted to know whether Yudhiṣṭhira lost her before he lost himself. She asked this question to the elders of the assembly, particularly Bhīṣma. She said: "Grandfather, you are the home of wisdom and learning. There is no one wiser than you are. Can you tell me if I am a slave?" Bhīṣma, who knew the subtleness of virtue and sin as also the code of conducts, said,

> I am indeed at a loss to give a proper answer to your question. The subtle shades of virtues and vice are hard to understand. A man cannot gamble anything once he has lost himself. But, a man has a right to his wife whether he is free or not. He can call her his property, even after he has lost himself. Accordingly, I cannot surely say that you are free. Though he was being defeated, Yudhiṣṭhira continued to play and he used you as the stake. I am unable to answer your question.

In many cases, the gross crimes committed are not considered as sin and the reasons are very difficult to explain. No one can explain the subtle meaning of sin thoroughly. Only the right answer to the virtue can bring out the right answer to sin. In some cases, best of good deeds are regarded as worst sins. Man has to live with sin as well as with virtue.

Sin can be attributed to different states of thoughts and actions. When thought moves down from the "supreme ideal nature" to the attitude of "self-centred ignoble nature", the inter-mediate thoughts on the way down can be considered as sins of different degrees. Thought is behind all actions. Sin is that thought which leads to the destruction of soul.

Sin is simply a demerit that pulls the soul down due to the impurity of mind. An impure mind makes one to do misdeeds that lead to pain, suffering, unhappiness, etc. Sin is due to vice, evil and immoral acts and thoughts. It is the thought that pushes man to act. When the mind is pure, man thinks in the right sense and does good actions that push him to the higher stages of life. When the mind is impure, man thinks in the wrong direction and does wrong actions, which make him sink low in the scale of life.

But on the human plane, man can only be moderate in all his dealings and in all the aspects of his life. In the world of relativity, within the limitations of time and space, it is impossible to find any action which is absolutely good or which produces absolute evil in any manner. Facing these facts, all are sinners in some way or the other. Food is a necessity for survival. All creatures get their food by violence. They have to kill and eat. Some kill animal life, some vegetable life. Animals are higher forms of life than vegetables. This is the reason why vegetarian food is preferred.

"This universe was enveloped by death alone, for hunger is death."[4] This means hunger makes man eat, which impels one to kill. The desire to eat forces one to kill. One sin leads to another, man's nature becomes fierce, and he sinks in low, increasing sins throughout his life.

Human nature is prone to many weaknesses. Sins can be committed by words in the form of lying, disparaging, bantering, etc. Aimless and hurtful actions and activities are consciously or unconsciously performed by hand. The feet are responsible for walking over places, where one ought not to go. The belly offends by taking wrong food. Man has to eat for his survival. He has to drink water to quench his thirst. For this, he has to injure some being. In whatever manner man may live, whether as an ascetic or a family man, it is impossible for him to practise non-injury to living beings to any extreme degree.

In water that one drinks, the fruits that one eats, as well as in breathing and talking many fine and invisible insects are killed. This way sins are committed.

Sins are innumerable like virtues. Different laws bring out different categories. Generally, they are classified in three ways: sins of action, of words and of thoughts. An evil thought or a harsh word is just as well of the nature of sin as a wicked deed.

4. *Bṛhadāraṇyaka Upaniṣad*, II.1.

"A single bad word will destroy all other good deeds. A wound caused by fire will heal within, but not the scar left by the tongue," says Thiruvalluvar in his *Kuraḷ*.[5] So, the great sages stress the need to cultivate a mind that would avoid sins, at least to some degree. The unrefined mental nature induces one to commit sins. A harsh word without any evil intention or a deed without any cruel intention is considered as a sin too.

All sins are rooted in the sins of desire or passion (*kāma*), hate or anger (*krodha*) and greed (*lobha*). *Bhagavad-Gītā* says that it is desire and anger born of *rajas*, insatiable in its demands, utterly evil in its working; know it like your foe, because these induce one to commit sins. "Triple is the gate of hell, destructive of soul — sensuality, hate and greed."[6]

Anything, a thought, a word or an action that is the cause for the destruction of the soul is sin. It is the duty of man to protect and elevate his soul progressively in the process of evolution.

Desires are evil only when their object is the illicit gratification of the self. As long as man is self-centred, his desires come into conflict with the law of universal love. This brings retardation to his spiritual progress. The whole course of evolution consists in the struggling of the soul (*jīva*) to know its own real nature. Not all desires but only unlawful ones are sins.

In *Bhagavad-Gītā*, Lord Kṛṣṇa says, "I am *kāma* in all beings, when it is not opposed to *dharma*. The real sins are the self-centred desires. All other sins are its numerous forms." Arjuna asks Kṛṣṇa: "What prompts a man to commit sins?" Kṛṣṇa replies: "It is desire; it is wrath, which springs from the passionate nature. It is a monster of appetite and sin. Desire leads to wrath, wrath leads to jealousy, jealousy to hatred. It is the desire that makes one to fan the spark of hatred, one of the worst sins. Desire is the enemy of the soul. It drags the soul towards sense objects. When the desired

5. *Kuraḷ*, 128, 129.

6. *Bhagavad-Gītā*, XVI.21.

object cannot be attained, this desire transforms itself into hatred owing to frustration. Frustration leads to violence. Violence in turn sinks the soul low in the life cycle scale."

"An inordinate desire destroys the home and leads to crime at once."[7] Crimes drown the man in the ocean of sins. So one must resist desires, which helps the soul to elevate in its spiritual path. Action by itself produces neither virtue nor sin, but the motive behind the actions does. The same is true for desires whose motives either exalt or degrade the soul.

The law of *dharma* declares that any thought or action done with bad motives results in sin. Doing injury to one's enemy may immediately give happiness, but it is bound to produce unhappiness in the future. Though doing injury to others goes against laws and is considered as sin, some injuries are permitted in scriptures and are not considered as sin. Injury to the life of animals in the performance of sacrifices does not produce any sin and must be regarded as being included in the merits. Certain injuries are recommended in Vedas as virtues. Yet, many saints consider that killing of life in the name of sacrifice is sin.

What is the good way? It is the path that reflects on
How it may avoid killing any living creature[8]
Not killing is the first and foremost good.
The virtue of not lying comes next.[9]
What is virtuous conduct? It is never destroying life,
For killing leads to every other sin.[10]

Even at the worst of one's own life, one should avoid killing. Lord Buddha offered himself to be killed, when a man tried to kill an animal for food. Later, this same man became a disciple of Lord Buddha.

---

7. *Kuraḷ* — Thiruvalluvar, 171.
8. Ibid., 324.
9. Ibid., 323.
10. Ibid., 321.

However great its gains, the wise despise,
The profit of slaughter.[11]

Not all injuries to living beings are sinful. Only such injury is sinful that is prohibited by the Vedic injunctions. But *Śrīmad Bhāgavata* considers all kinds of injury to living being as sinful.

Moreover, the great sages of the Vedic period earned super-sensuous powers of bringing back to life the sacrificed living beings after the completion of the prescribed ritual. So these were not considered as sins. They performed acts only for the sake of actions and not with personal desires. Certain rituals were duties that were to be performed for the uplift of society.

Upaniṣads say: "All merits arising from *dharma*, *artha* and *kāma*,[12] the good acts of life, if performed with selfish motives cause accumulation of sins." This means that actions performed with desires are sins. "He who performed duty (his duty) understanding the secret of work rises above good and evil."[13]

There is no sin in killing animals in sacrifices, which are performed for the attainment of heaven or such other purposes that bring good to the society. But in the sacrifices performed for injuring or molesting fellow beings, the killing of animals is sinful.

Attachment or bondage (*pāśa*) is sin, while attachment in the sense of protection to needy is a virtue. Any attachment expressed in the right sense will not taint the person concerned.

Sometimes wrong acts are done to uphold the righteousness.

---

11. *Kuraḷ* — Thiruvalluvar, 328.
12. *Dharma* signifies the merit earned by the performance of duties allotted to each person. *Dharma* is the quality, whose presence enables the soul to enjoy happiness. *Artha* is the acquisition of wealth. This should be acquired for the good of humanity and not for personal interests. The acquisition of *artha* should be in the rightful manner. *Kāma* is desire. All desires should be an act of service to God, to uplift society. The secret to keep away from sin is to perform all acts with a selfless motive.
13. *Bhagavad-Gītā*, II.50. The secret of work is to offer all actions to God.

These wrongs do not fall under the category of sin. Any action done for the sake of God or for the good of others will not fall on the scale of sin.

Insincerity, ungratefulness, attachment to those things, which impede attachment to God are considered as the worst sins from the religious point of view. All other sins may be redeemed, but never the ingratitude.

Egoism (*ahaṁkāra*) is the devilish propensity in man that impels him to indulge in corrupt ways and is the matrix of all moral evil. Moral evil intensifies into sin, when it is a deliberate transgression of the moral law. A wicked motive is worse than a wicked act. It deepens into vileness and taints the inner moral nature. On the other hand, virtue induces the moral agent to choose a course of conduct that avoids egoism. A good act is better than a good intention without action.

From the point of view of religion, sin is man's opposition to God, the opposition of flesh to the spirit. Man is both flesh and spirit. Spirit is his higher nature and flesh is his lower nature.

But Vedānta views that the tendency to sin is present somehow, but it is not the original sin. The soul (*ātmā*) is essentially pure. Sin is only an accident. Yet, the soul has the freedom to fall into sin or to be on guard to grow into Godliness.

It is significant to note from *Bṛhadāraṇyaka Upaniṣad* (I.3.1) the rivalry between gods and demons. Here we find that the descendants of Prajāpati, the Creator, were indeed of two kinds: gods and demons. They represent man's sense perceptions and the conscious and the subconscious activities. They became gods, meaning "shining ones", when they are illumined by thoughts and actions recommended by the scriptures. They turn into demons, meaning "self-indulgent ones", when they are impelled by their natural thoughts and actions, which are directed merely to secular goals. Naturally, gods are much fewer than the demons. Gods and demons rivalled for the ownership of these worlds.

The gods said to one another, "Well, let us beat the demons through Udgītha in the sacrifice." Udgītha is the way of chanting a Vedic *mantra* with perfection. In Veda, it is called Sāman hymn. Then the deities concerned with each organ, namely speech, nose, eye, ear, mind, skin and others, sang the Sāman hymn, one by one, to defeat the demons. But the demons, who knew very well that the gods would beat them with the help of these chanters, rushed at them and pierced all the organs, one by one, with evil. That is why it is found that one speaks what is wrong, smells what is wrong, sees what is wrong, hears what is wrong, thinks what is wrong, and so on. In this way, the demons tainted the deities with evil. So, there is always the conflict between good and evil in man.[14] The attachment to sense objects is the cause of evil that leads to sin. Unless this attachment is removed, there will be no end to the sins. But every soul is ultimately salvable and can attain liberation (*mokṣa*).

Between sin and virtue (*pāpa* and *puṇya*), one should aspire for the latter and shun the former. Every man reaps what he sows. Evil is expiated by suffering. But not every suffering is due to evil, just as in the case of the pain of childbirth. Good and evil are linked by causal necessity. Both are chains that keep the soul under control. The shackle for the good may be gold, and that of evil may be of iron, but the soul can free itself of these chains.

> When the struggle between right and wrong is on, he, who abstains from it out of false sentimentality, weakness or cowardice, would be committing a sin. But thou does not this lawful battle, then thou wilt fail thy duty and glory and will incur sin.[15]

Each one is assigned with particular duties to be performed in the course of one's life. Failure in adhering to these duties would be

---

14. The conflict is between the sensible and the submerged mind owing to the influence of *rajas* and *tamas*.

15. *Bhagavad-Gītā*, II.33.

a sin. According to Rāmānuja, sin is traced to past *karma* and nescience (*avidyā*), the cause of which is indefinable. The tendency towards sin is somehow there, but it is not an original sin. (It is killing or prompting to kill one to save thousands of people.)

Sin is without a beginning but has an end. Every soul can ultimately attain liberation by the saving grace of God if one prays for His mercy. God is holy and spotless. He is not tainted by any trace of sin.

> Physical evil is equated with suffering and may not be the effect of sin. Sin may result in suffering. But suffering may not be due to sin. Suffering may result from sin as a penalty. But moral evil arises from the violation of moral law. It deepens into sin, when duty, which is a divine command, is violated. Duty is the voice of God, in the will of man and it is a sin to omit what is commanded and·commit what is prohibited, as it is an offence against Īśvara. The sinfulness of sin is so deep that it cannot be exhausted by expiation.[16]

Rāmānuja and Vedānta Deśika hold that sin (*pāpa*) is of two kinds: one that is committed intentionally, and the other done unintentionally. The former can be overcome with suitable expiatory rituals.[17] Attempts to commit sinful acts will be as hazardous as walking on the sharp edge of a sword. Even if one succeeds in thriving on hidden wickedness, his fall is certain, either cutting the feet or falling into the pit. So one should save oneself from unrighteousness and sin. By offering our minds to God, doing all actions as an offering to God, all the sins are removed. This is the view of all religions. "Completely relinquishing all *dharma*, seek Me alone for refuge. I will release you from all sins, grieve not."[18]

---

16. *Philosophy of Viśiṣṭādvaita*, P.N. Srinivasachari.
17. *Kaṭha Upaniṣad* (2.24) refers to the need of overcoming such sins committed intentionally.
18. *Bhagavad-Gītā*, XVIII.66.

According to Āyurveda,[19] the senses are the causes of sins. Misuse of intelligence *prajñāparādha* leads to sinful acts. This means that the defective intelligence itself is a sin. According to Caraka,[20] the nature of transmigration is controlled by the good and bad deeds of man. Even the productivity of nature, its purity, pollution and all other things in which the nature is helpful and harmful to men are determined by the virtue and vice (*dharma* and *adharma*). They determine most of the human conditions that induce him to do good and evil deeds. Caraka admits that jealousy, vanity, anger, greed, ignorance, etc. produce improper sinful actions. But, he says that the main cause of all these is error of judgement. All the improper actions are due to improper understanding, confusion of thought and misdirected intelligence. That is to say, intelligence is used in a sinful way. The root cause of illness (considered as due to sins) is *aparādha*. Misuse of intelligence produces illness after a lapse of time. Caraka says that all climatic and other natural evils are due to the commission of sins. He says that in ancient times, people were virtuous and because of their virtuous ways of living, there was no pollution and so people were free from epidemics and diseases. As the time rolled on, the human conditions of life and the conditions of environment started sinking low and the attitude of people changed towards greed, leading to malice, lying, desire, anger, conceit, cruelty, etc. In their conduct, people continue to grow vicious and sinful in their thoughts and actions. A normal life ought to be a virtuous one, as vices and sins are the sources of all sorrows, suffering and diseases in this life and next.

The Universal Spiritual Entity is not the Judge of Our Sin

God is a pure entity. Already His name removes all sins. Sin is an anti-spiritual force. It is worldly bondage. As a clod of earth, dashing against a rock is shattered and crushed, the anti-spiritual forces, called sins, will be shattered and perished if they rush at

19. Indian medical science.

20. Author of *Caraka Saṁhitā*.

God. If God had ever sinned, man would have never freed himself to attain immortality by knowing Him. He is without worldly attributes. Remaining untouched by the world of virtue and sin (*puṇya* and *pāpa*), God has the power to make the soul evolve in the cycle of life as well as helping it to redeem itself from its sins.

> But superior to the unmanifested is the supreme *puruṣa*, who is all-pervasive and is, indeed, without worldly attributes. Knowing Him a man becomes freed and attains immortality.[21] Just as the sun, which is the eye of the whole world, is not tainted by the ocular and external defects, similarly, the Self is but one in all beings untainted by the sorrows of the world. It being transcendental.[22]

God resides within the Self. He is a pure spiritual entity untouched by external worldly activities. He is not the one to be linked with sin, definitely not.

But certain doubts do rise, if we consider certain statements: "He desired, let me be many, let me be born. He created all this that exists."[23] "That being willed. May I become many, may I grow forth. It created fire, etc."[24] Now the question may arise: Will God not incur sin through his desires? The answer is that God's desires are not touched by the Law of Karma (virtue or vice). He is the Ruler as well as the Protector. If He were subjected to *karma*, He would not have held the status of the Ruler. His purpose in creation is to redeem the sinful souls (*jīva*) to which he remains ever unconnected; yet, He keeps them within Him. Many do feel that when desire is considered as sin, the desire of God should also be considered as sin. In *Bhagavad-Gītā*, Lord Kr̥ṣṇa says, "I am *kāma* (desire) in all beings, when it is not opposed to *dharma*."

21. *Kaṭha Upaniṣad*, II.3.8.
22. Ibid., II.2.10.
23. *Taittirīya Upaniṣad*, II.6.
24. *Chāndogya Upaniṣad*, VI.2.3.

As said earlier, God's desire to project the world is for the redemption of each soul from its past *karma*. So even if He desires something, it is for the welfare of the beings. Because of that, it is said that the Supreme God is the Controller of all, the Lord of all, the Ruler of all. He is not magnified by good work, nor degraded in the least, by evil work. He is the Lord of all, the Ruler of beings, and the Protector of beings. "Works do not contaminate Me. In Me, there is no desire for the fruits of actions."[25]

Lord Kṛṣṇa says that actions of varying nature do not bind Him. It means that the activities of God are never tainted by the impulses of attraction and repulsion. He remains ever beyond these activities. It is His *prakṛti*, which does everything under His influence and supervision. Therefore, though in the worldly sense God is believed to be the agent in all activities, in reality, He remains forever totally untouched by actions, which are beyond the capacity of ordinary mortals.

God has transcended the limits of the material world and hence can never be linked to sin. Sage Parāśara[26] said that this universe rests on an infinitesimal fraction of God's energy. This reveals the measure of purity in God.

The power of Īśvara, the Supreme has different manifestations, according to their distinctive functions. He also takes different names such as *Brahman*, with attributes, Viṣṇu, Devī, etc. They are the gods (deities) known as the presiding officers of the created universe. God the supreme is the highest Reality. He is above all. There is the distinction between *Brahman* and God. The term God is used when He is spoken of as distinct from the world. The term *Brahman* is used when everything is included in Him.

The minor deities (also called gods) may be linked to bondage considered as sin, because of their limited tenures.

It is an assumption that the incarnation (*avatāra*) of gods is linked with sins. The manifestation of God in different forms for

25. *Bhagavad-Gītā*, IV.14.

26. Parāśara is the father of Vyāsa, the author of *Mahābhārata*.

the good of the world is called *avatāra* (incarnation). Incarnation is an aspect of God and is generally said to be a manifestation of Divinity through living beings. If God is linked to sin, even in an infinitesimal fraction, He is no more God, but a mere human being. God is the Highest entity whose grace is essential for the liberation of mortals. He has transcended all virtues. *Avatāra* is a part of God (*aṁśa*). But it is impossible to measure the infinite. Scriptures declare: "What is the whole, this is a whole. What has come out of the whole is also whole. When the whole is taken out of the whole, the whole remains whole."[27] The idea of whole and part does not apply to God. Even a fraction of God is whole by itself and is perfect to the full measure. *Avatāra* of God is complete by itself and is perfect to the full measure. It is absolutely perfect, whole and so does not enter in the context of sin.

Sin is inherent in the world. In a moderate sense, it is a necessary element. It is the opposition of the finite to the infinite. Sin is real in mankind. But it has no reality in the Divine being. As Ramakrishna once said,

> If God is taken as a serpent, sin is its poison. What we call poison is no poison to the serpent. It is a normal healthy secretion. The serpent does not die of its own poison. Similarly, God is not tainted by sin. If sin were ultimately real, it could never be destroyed. God who is powerless against sin is no God. If God is linked to the sin, how can mortals depend upon Him, for success in their moral good?

The moral quality in man fights against evil and sin. To help man, to achieve success in this fight, God always remains a guardian.

The forces of the impulsive nature of man dominated by the lower mind constitute sin. A divine incarnation symbolises the supremacy of merit over demerit (*dharma* over *adharma*). The conflict between conscious and subconscious forces is always active in every individual and in the whole universe. In the Vedas and

27. One of the peace chants of Veda.

the Upaniṣads, the term *deva* represents the higher mind and the *asura* represents the lower mind. In this conflict, God is the Rescuer.

> When Yama (the Hindu God of death) offers to the young Naciketas the boons, both earthly and celestial, which cannot be easily attained by mortals, Naciketas declines them all on the ground that they are not equal to *Brahman*, who is real, pure and sinless. As long as man has his end in death, he is bound by sin. Whatever is earthly and celestial is finite and has an end. It is linked to sin. So, he opted to know *Brahman* who alone is the inspiration for his sinless life.[28]

The great sage Nārada tells Sanatkumāra that he knows everything, every science, art and philosophy, but is still stricken with sinful sorrow. Then he learns from Sanatkumāra that knowing the wisdom of *Brahman*, the Pure, he will be released of all sorrows that are due to his sins.[29]

There is no infinite bliss that is tainted with sin. But the infinite alone can bring bliss, removing the sins.

Chāndogya Upaniṣad[30] explains how the great Indra tried to free himself from the bodily self that dragged him to commit sins. After realising *Brahman*, he became pure and attained the world of *Brahman*.

Upaniṣads also hint out that *Brahman*, the Absolute is ever free from sins. He shines in all serenity, ever Holy, showering His grace on the sinning masses.

> They say that lightning is *Brahman*. Lightning is so called because it dispels the darkness (due to clouds — sins, evils, etc. that obstruct the path of knowledge). He who knows thus that Lightning is *Brahman* dispels the evils that are set against him, for Lightning is verily *Brahman*.[31]

28. *Kaṭha Upaniṣad*, I.1.26 onwards.
29. *Chāndogya Upaniṣad*, VII 1.3.
30. Ibid., VIII 7.1.
31. *Bṛhadāraṇyaka Upaniṣad*, V.7.1.

Sage Parāśara[32] says regarding the creations of God:

> He (the God) is only the operative cause in the creation of beings. That from which the creative forces spring constitutes material cause. Leaving aside the material cause, the being that becomes embodied does not require the help of any other thing whatever. A thing is led into condition in which it is, O best of ascetics, only by its own potentiality.[33]

So, sin cannot be attributed to God. He has neither a beginning nor an end. As long as there is no end, the touch of sin will never be there. It is sin that brings an end to the beings. It is also said about God that "He is neither partial nor cruel."[34]

According to Madhva,[35] it is man himself and not God who is responsible for the evil and suffering in the world. If moral conduct is to play any part in the liberation of the soul from the cycle of rebirth, the soul must, in some way, participate in the corporeality and be affected by the human experience and action. Rāmānuja contends that the activity of the soul is not independent but depends on the five determining factors of the body, an agent, organisation, bodily functions and the direction of the Lord.[36] The soul pursues of its free will a course of action which is determined mostly by its own deep-rooted nature, inclinations and past *karma*. God has given man the power to do things in conformity with his own innate goodness or its opposite. The right to choose between right and wrong is his own, made on his own responsibility and at his own risk.

Like a carpenter, man acts with his own tools and hands but looks up to the architect for directions. The skill of the carpenter is his own. He does not owe it to his master. But the soul (*jīva*)

---

32. Father of Vyāsa, the author of *Mahābhārata*.
33. *Viṣṇu Purāṇa*, I.4 (51.52).
34. *Brahma-Sūtra*, II.1.34.
35. The founder of Dvaita Vedānta.
36. Rāmānuja's commentary on the *Bhagavad-Gītā*, XVIII.16

derived from the Creator, metaphysically, has the ability to do things. But for Him, he cannot move an inch. However, this does not involve God in the meshes of action and does not make Him responsible ultimately for the behaviour of the souls. God merely enables the soul to pursue a course of action, not arbitrarily, but in relation to his former life. He does not interfere with the bound soul's (*jīva*) decision in any way. The bound soul chooses out of its free will a particular line of action for good or for bad with sufficient knowledge of its moral worth. Consequently, it cannot blame anyone, least of all God, for the unpleasant consequences of his acts.

According to Madhva, the innate fitness of the soul (*jīva*) for good and evil, which makes it *sāttvika, rājasika* or *tāmasika,* is called *haṭha.*[37] *Haṭha* clings to the souls with the persistency of the green moss-like substance on the surface of water. This *haṭha* is the innate disposition. It finds divergent expression in internal and external behaviour through intensive effort.[38] All these three factors depend on God's will for their existence and functioning, like everything else in finite life. *Karma* which is its outcome can hardly operate and bear fruit without an intensive conscious effort on the part of the embodied soul. Human effort is thus made to play the key role in making man the architect of his own future.

Yet, God is not partial, because a partiality which interferes with right and wrong is a blemish. He allows the souls the full scope of expression of their individual nature, may it be good and evil. Madhva uses the principle of osmosis to explain how the evil of one helps the good of the others to increase. The resistance to evil releases the latent energies of good souls, helps them realise the good in their essential nature. For all categories of souls in *saṁsāra* (the life cycle of births and deaths) have an admixture of both, good and evil, in greater or lesser proportions in the

37. Not to be confused with haṭha of the word haṭha in haṭha-yoga.

38. Madhva in *Tātparya Nirṇaya* on *Mahābhārata,* XXII.84-88.

constitution of their physical and other sheaths composed of *sattva*, *rajas* and *tamas*. When evil souls are pitted against good ones, they react in keeping their evil nature by hating and traducing the good. By the law of spiritual osmosis, they shed the little good in themselves and absorb the evil that is in others. As the Divine law operates, the evil souls sink under the accumulated weight of their own evil into *tamas*, while the good souls, relieved of their evil, rise to higher planes of spiritual development.

Role of Sin and Vice

Devotion is pure uninterrupted love. It is one-pointed love towards the object of our approach. Devotion is love towards God. God is the light of love. To turn the mind towards devotion, one has to face many obstacles in his everyday life. Every person intentionally or unintentionally does certain wrongs in everyday life that lead to sin. This obstructs the moral perfection, which is the foundation for devotion. All the views should be considered from the point of view of human plane. Unfortunately, it is very difficult to live without committing sins in this plane that hankers for the progress on the path of devotion. But there is always the sunshine, after the dark night.

Instead of considering non-obstacles, one should consider the obstacles that one encounters in his path of devotion. If they are known, it is easy to avoid them, but there is no measure with which one can count the obstacles.

It is said in the scriptures that God moves man to actions according to the law of *karma* (action) and fulfils his desires. He gives knowledge to those who are ignorant, power to those who are weak, pardon to those who are guilty, mercy to the sufferers, paternal affection to children, sincerity to the crooked, goodness of heart to those who are wicked at heart. He cannot bear to remain separated from those who do not want to be separated from Him. He puts Himself at an easy reach of those who want to see Him. When He sees people affected, He has mercy on them and helps them. All His qualities are for the sake of others and not for Himself. Out of His motherly affection, He neglects our defects and tries to help us towards the idea of good.

He has the capacity to show a way, in which sins and vices are not obstacles in the path of devotion, because He cannot bear the separation of His devotee. He is the universal redeemer. He is within all beings to take care of them.

The aim of devotion is for the spiritual advancement of the soul. Spiritual advancement leads to liberation. Soul is the individual Self. It is an eternal entity and distinct from God, but one with God and totally dependent on Him.

Man is directed to commit sins, knowingly or unknowingly, that are incidental to the occupation he follows for his livelihood however honest and lawful it may be. *Bhagavad-Gītā* says that all undertakings are involved in sins. Warfare, agriculture, trade, industry, governance of people and all other means of livelihood involve in their pursuit, the practice of violence in some form or the other. Many pursuits cause loss of life to innumerable ants, insects, etc. everyday. Besides, many sins are committed by man in numerous other ways due to carelessness. *Karma* is mainly of two types: (1) actions, done for the acquirement of their results (*kāmya karma*), and (2) actions, done relinquishing the results, that is, doing an action for action's sake only (*niṣkāma karma*).

According to Vedānta Deśika, liberation (*mukti*) is possible when the individual soul becomes totally free from the shackles of *karma* in the form of both good and bad actions (*puṇya* and *pāpa*[39]).[40] The meditation on *Brahman* is enjoined as the means to achieve it. The main objective of such a meditation is to remove obstacles that stand in the way of realisation of *Brahman*. In so far as such a meditation is capable of removing all obstacles in the form of good and evil deeds, *brahma-vidyā*, meditation on *Brahman*

39. *Puṇya* is merit accrued as a result of performance of good deeds. *Pāpa* is sin accrued as a result of performance of evil deeds.

40. *Tattva Mukta Kalāpa*, II.41.

is also regarded as an expiatory rite even if the main objective is the realisation of *Brahman*.

Chāndogya Upaniṣad states that both good and bad actions are obstacles. Even *dharma* becomes *adharma* for an aspirant of liberation. *Dharma* is that which is a means to achieve a desired end. The Upaniṣad states further that all merits arising from *dharma, artha* and *kāma*[41] should be cast off.[42] Vedānta Deśika, based on Rāmānuja's interpretations, says that bad actions are of two types: one which is committed intentionally and the other done unintentionally. The former needs to be overcome whereas the latter does not affect the aspirant. So too the good actions done unintentionally will not affect the aspirant.

Yet, it is said that an aspirant should be like a lotus leaf unaffected by the water drops, be they pure or impure. In other words, to make meditation on *Brahman* efficacious not only for the removal of obstacles but also to obtain the realisation of *Brahman*, the devotee should not cling to the fruits of merits or demerits of actions done intentionally.

Patañjali has a slightly different view, even if he concludes that the aspirant should be detached from the results of good and bad actions. He classifies actions into two categories: mental and external. The external actions are achieved by the five motor senses (*karma indriya*). He divides the actions into black, white, white and black, and neither white nor black. The black actions are those committed by the wicked. They are also called *adharma*. Speaking ill of others, stealing other's property, etc. are external. Acting against faith, strength, meditation, intense concentration and wisdom[43] are internal. Faith, strength and other deeds can occur only in mental states. They are white deeds. In other words, resorting to study and meditation is white action. The white and

41. Three of the four *puruṣārthas*.
42. *Chāndogya Upaniṣad*, VIII.4.1.
43. *Pātañjala Yoga-Sūtra*, I.20.

black actions are actions achieved in the external world by the motor senses, however good they might be, because they are not altogether devoid of non-violence to other living beings. Finally, neither black nor white actions are those done by those who have renounced everything. Since it is practically impossible to live by renouncing all the results of actions (intentional and non-intentional), Patañjali concludes that one should minimise the results of good and bad actions through meditation (*dhyāna*) and intense meditation (*samādhi*). He advises the practice of *aṣṭāṅga yoga*[44] as also *dhyāna*. While *yama* and *niyama* purify the mind, *āsana, prāṇāyāma* and *pratyāhāra* reduce the influence of the senses on the external actions. *Dhāraṇā, dhyāna* and *samādhi* which Patañjali calls as *saṁyama* to bring forth their inseparability are meant to clear the aspirant from the consequences of the fruits of actions.

Jīva and Karma

As already said, the soul (*jīva*) is not a non-sentient entity (*jaḍa*). It is self-luminous, having the real knowledge, reflects the knowledge itself, innumerable in number and even in the state of liberation, it does not lose its individuality. The soul is also the knowing subject. So, it is the agent of action, motivated by God, who is Himself its ruler. The soul is not only the agent of action (*karttā*) but also the one who has the experience (*bhoktā*). The soul is the ultimate unit (*aṇu*), different from the body, from the sense organs, the mind, *prāṇa* and intellect (*buddhi*). In all actions that man performs, it acts as an agent, which can only be kept up, when it is associated with a body consisting of three *guṇa*s. As an agent, it acts and as one who has the experience, it experiences either the merit or the demerit (*puṇya* or *pāpa*) arising from the action.

Karma itself is neither good nor bad. They neither add virtue to the performer nor drown him into sin. But the motive behind

44. The Eight Limbs of Yoga : *yama, niyama, āsana, prāṇāyāma, pratyāhāra, dhāraṇā, dhyāna* and *samādhi.*

karma adds to virtue or vice. A good motive brings virtue to the performer. When actions are done with evil intentions, it gathers sins to the performer. The merit entitles one to certain transient enjoyments.

He, who accumulates objects of enjoyment only for his personal gratification, like the nourishment of his own body and senses and enjoys them for his own sake and deprives others of their share, accumulates only sins. This causes failure in the path of devotion. Because his actions are not inspired by the spirit of sacrifice nor did others get their proper legitimate share. He is called a sinner by the scriptures because both his earnings and enjoyments are sinful. That is to say, he who cooks food merely for his own sake eats only sin. This food of sin corrupts the mind. The corrupt mind causes failure to the devotion because of its impurity. So, *kāmya karma*s are those actions that are performed with certain motives, good or bad. A person who acts out of evil motives is considered as a man having an uncultured mind, which is itself an obstacle to devotion.

A person who performs actions with a disinterested spirit, keeping in view the happiness of others as the sole object, who shares his comforts with needy, who renders service to others (those in need) as a form of service to God, will be freed from the chains of past and present sins. This way sins will not stand as an obstacle to his path of devotion. The enjoyment attained by sharing with others what one has even to a small extent also makes the mind light with happiness removed of guilt and helps in real devotion. "By this renunciation (of the worldly objects) support yourself. Do not covet the wealth of anyone."[45]

If one is greedy to acquire the wealth of others, he will sail in the sea of sin which sure causes utter failure in his way to realisation. For Lord Kṛṣṇa in *Bhagavad-Gītā* says, "I am desire, when it is not opposed to *dharma*."

---

45. *Īśāvāsya Upaniṣad*, 1

Living in the world, one should gain the capacity to renounce the results of the actions performed and one should also try to share the fruits of actions with others.

When *karma* is performed without coveting for the fruits of actions for oneself and when it is done as an offering to God, the same *karma* will lead to the purification of mind. This type of action is called *niṣkāma karma*. Purification of mind is essential for devotion. Any action done for the sake of God will not have the consequences of virtues or sins.

A person who has not attained the state of mental purity must continue doing disinterested actions in a spirit of dedication to the Supreme so that sins and vices will not become obstacles to devotion.

As a chariot does not worry or concern itself with whether it travels in the right direction, so too if one leaves the results of action to the Supreme, whether it is of great importance or not, or whether it is virtuous or sinful, one will not be affixed to the sins. The human ego is the cause of sin. The only way to overcome the ego is to make it a habit thinking that God alone is the agent. Anger and greed are soul's highway robbers. Where these qualities prosper, sins will also prosper, obstructing devotional paths. ·

Man commits sins due to ignorance (nescience, *avidyā*). This ignorance differs in degrees in different individuals. It produces error in regarding a thing as what it is not. It is through this *avidyā* that one is attached to one's possessions as "mine" and the false experience of individual freedom. When a person realises that one's actions are to God, he ceases to have any attachment to anything and does not look forward for the fruits of his deeds. If one realises that he belongs to God, for God resides in him, his mind will be purified and thereby purifies the soul. When a person realises that God induces all his actions, he will not find obstacles to his devotion. But if he considers that he alone is the independent agent, he drowns in the sea of sin.

With the removal of *avidyā* (wrong knowledge), there will be no link to the sins, and true devotion will have no hindrances. Attachment to the fruits of actions is the main obstacle in the devotional path. The impure mind by itself is a great sin. A man with his mind full of sins, even if he performs good actions, is like a corpse adorned with ornaments. Just as the sky is mirrored in the ocean and it is not forbidden from being reflected in a pond, God's grace appears in all. Even the worst sinner can reform himself by thinking of God.

As said earlier, man lives on action. Desisting from action one cannot even maintain the body. Certain duties are prescribed for a man with due regard to status, stage of life, temperament and circumstances. They are his natural duties. Performance of such duties will not obstruct man's devotional path, because he will not be affected by the sins that are incidentally committed during the lawful discharge of these duties.

Day-to-day duties are known as legitimate duties. They are not defective even though they appear to be tainted with evils. Just as fire is mixed with smoke, which cannot be wholly separated from it, day-to-day actions are tainted with demerit also. They involve in one way or the other, the destruction of some life in some form or the other. No action is completely free from blemish. So man must perform actions renouncing the evils of mineness, attachment and desire for the fruits of action. This way sins will not hinder the progress of devotion. Duties are to be performed for duties' sake only.

"One should not abandon one's innate duty even though it may be tainted with blemish, for even as fire is enveloped in smoke all undertakings are clouded with demerit."[47] The *Bhagavad-Gītā* also points out that man's disinclination to act out of fear in involving himself in sins is itself an obstacle in his path of devotion. Man should enter into action whether it is good or bad. "Man

47. *Bhagavad-Gītā*, XVIII.48.

does not attain freedom from action without entering upon action, nor does he reach perfection merely by ceasing to act."[48]

None can remain inactive, not even for a moment, in order to keep away from virtues and vices. Action is necessary for the maintenance of life. To live man should take up to action. Man alone is qualified to perform either good or evil actions. Other beings do not possess this qualification. Action performed in human life has a tendency to cause bondage that is a sin. Attitude of renunciation must be practised, to avoid failure in the devotional path.

There should also be human efforts to remove sins in the path of devotion. Though each individual is controlled by God's power, man is free to act independently. He is free to overcome virtues and sins, by making a sincere effort in the right direction using his physical and mental power. He should exercise these powers spontaneously. "Doing work without attachment man attains the Supreme."[49]

God's abode is that universal state, where there would be a total absence of torments in the form of likes and dislikes, good and evil actions, feeling of joy and sorrow and all other evils. While human birth is an open door to reach this abode, devotion is the ladder to climb up to this abode which incidentally is open to all, whether one believes in God or not. Devotion shows and directs towards the right path. The embodied soul (*jīvātman*) is held in bondage by the latencies of good and evil deeds performed in countless lives of the past known as the shackles of *karma* and on reaching the human state; it again starts its career of fresh deeds under the impulses of egoism, desire and attachment. So it gets more and more entangled. To be freed from such shackles, the mind should be trained to become stable and the intellect should become determinate and one-pointed. This will clear off all the obstacles in achieving the goal of Realisation.

---

48. *Bhagavad-Gītā*, III.4.

49. Ibid., III.19.

7

Peaceful Emotion, Śānta Rasa

May the sustainers of eternal truths
Be conducive to harmony.
May our thoughts and actions
Contribute to our happiness,
May the virtuous men of experience and wisdom
Confer peace and progress on us,
May the ancient sages be kind to us
And respond to our invocations in our social ceremonies.

— *Ṛgveda*, 7.35.12

THIS chapter reflects faithfully Sri T. Krishnamacharya's commentary on *Rāmāyaṇa*, *Śrīmad Bhāgavata*, the Upaniṣads as also on the meditative hymns of Vedānta Deśika on *sudarśana cakra*.

Birth of Human Emotions

Man is born with serenity and peace; then he gradually develops and nourishes love, wonder, and other eight emotions. As a child, he maintains a harmonious relation between them, independent of his will-power. Becoming a slave to desire leading him to greed, he develops and nurtures certain emotions like repulsion, anger and fear more than serenity and love, clouding thereby his inborn peaceful emotion. The stimulating determinants and the transitory states of these determinant states attract him to such an extent that he ignores the presence of peace (*śānta*) in him. In his daily life, he gives more attention to the *rasa*s like wonder, heroism, mirth, fear, anger and repulsion than to love and serenity. To protect serenity (*śānta*) and to maintain it free from impurities, the emotion of love should be developed by reducing the importance given to other emotions. The mind, which houses all the emotions (including that of peace, *śānta*) and the consequences of the stimulating factors and the transitory states, clouds the inborn peace (*śānta*) forcing man to tread away from his fundamental basic emotions. He gives more weight to pride, haughtiness, the sense of invincibility, contempt, disdain, arrogance, anxiety, anguish, fear, despotism, repugnance, malice and other subsidiary variations of his fear, anger and repulsion. Man gives little or no importance to detachment, desire for meditation, humility, tenderness and sympathy, which are the supporting factors of his peace (*śānta*) and love (*śṛṅgāra*), and he plunges deep into those emotions that lead him away from peace.

Through his own fault, through misuse of liberty and intellect, through disobedience to God, man loses the paradise of pure unalloyed happiness. Spiritual life, therefore, consists in the restoration of the lost values. The resignation of the self to the Supreme will mean a progressive attempt at transcendence from the individual to the universal peace and can be best achieved by a strict ethical discipline as well as by the cultivation of what constitutes the whole of human life. Prayer, contemplation and virtuous deeds are some of the means to achieve this end.

God blessed humanity with three invaluable riches:

1. A human body with its intellectual and discriminative capacities,
2. A life force to enjoy the unique advantages of the human body (to obtain liberation), and its benefits, and
3. An inborn peace to use it as a measuring rod to pave the way for liberation.

The Almighty also blessed humanity with a unique, enviable and incomparable world of experience to live, enjoy and yet be detached from it. To enable man to achieve, the Almighty gave him the wealth of nine emotions: eight to live by and to enjoy and one to be detached from the world of experience.

This world is nothing but a bunch of these emotions consisting of many variations, interpolations, determinants and transitory factors all concealed in the form of objects of experience. Man should use this unique opportunity to blossom his existence into peace and serenity by creating and maintaining a logical proportion of the eight emotions so that he is liberated. One of the best tools he possesses is devotion and its accessories. Unless he reorganises his emotional set-up, unless he develops selfless love, unless he recognises the importance of peace and unless he transforms each of his eight emotions into devotional emotions, he will be sailing against the winds.

The relation between *śānta* and the other eight emotions can be understood by tracing the origin of creation in Hindu mythology:

Before the creation, Lord Nārāyaṇa or Viṣṇu,[1] the Supreme Lord, was reclining on a bed of the coiled Serpent Ananta,[2] which was afloat on a perfectly calm milky ocean.[3] The milky ocean was calm; the Serpent Ananta was immobile and Lord Viṣṇu was Serene. Completely engrossed in Serenity[4] and out of Pure Love,[5] Lord Viṣṇu, out of His navel, brought forth Brahmā[6] and instructed him to create a universe. Since Viṣṇu brought forth Brahmā from Himself, He provided Brahmā with half of His Serenity and Love. Brahmā obedient to Viṣṇu, created a universe of an immeasurable number of species, humans, animals, plants, rivers, mountains, etc. He was marvelled[7] by the wonder of the universe he had created, for which he used one-fourth (that is, $^1/_8$ of Love he

1. Viṣṇu means that which pervades. Nārāyaṇa means He, who is the dwelling place for the soul.
2. Ananta is the name of the Primordial Serpent. It also means timeless and eternal.
3. *Kṣīrasāgara. Kṣīra* = milk, *sāgara* = ocean.
4. *Śānta* (Serenity).
5. *Śṛṅgāra* (Aesthetic Love).
6. That is why, Lord Viṣṇu is also called Padmanābha.
7. *Adbhuta* (Marvel)

obtained from Viṣṇu) of his force (love). Brahmā was proud[8] of his creation. His heroism absorbed another fourth ($^{1}/_{8}$) of his Love. He realised that the universe was inert. Out of compassion,[9] he infused life into each created being, for which he used another quarter ($^{1}/_{8}$) of the Love that he had obtained from Viṣṇu. Viṣṇu, satisfied with the created world, infused all beings with serenity in form of a soul. This is the reason why Hinduism says that serenity is a birthright and that God is in every being, human or animal.

God bestowed all created beings with serenity and peace; He graced man with the same emotion of serenity and peace. By definition serenity is constant, unique in its value, unchangeable and unalloyed, whereas love is variable, because it is born out of two emotional set-ups (of the parents), and gives birth to other emotional values. At the time of conception, man obtains love from his parents. Thus, man's basic emotional set-up shares equally in serenity and love. Consequently, serenity and love are his birthrights. For generations to come, until the dissolution of the universe, all beings inhere this proportion of serenity and love. Being created by Brahmā, they all possess wonder, compassion and heroism too.

Man develops these three (wonder, compassion and heroism) at the cost of his love. His attraction to the world of experience in wonder forces him to sacrifice a fourth of his love. He uses another fourth of his love to develop compassion and heroism.

All created beings benefit from their God-given gift. Owing to the power of reasoning and discrimination that man received from God, he considers himself superior, becomes contemptuous and arrogant giving himself self-importance. He uses the other beings for his delight and entertainment.[10] For this, man sacrifices one-sixteenth of his God-given gift of love.

---

8. *Vīra* (Heroism).
9. *Karuṇā* (Compassion).
10. *Hāsya* (Mirth).

Arrogance and disdain born out of delight and entertainment develop doubt, cowardice and anxiety breeding fear[11] in man, at the cost of another sixteenth of his God-given love.

Fear leads him to anger[12] through selfishness, hatred, violence, etc. He sacrifices yet another sixteenth of his God-given love and serenity. This is the reason why, the more man tends towards anger, fear and contempt, the less he loves, as he sacrifices the pure emotion of love to feed and breed anger, fear and contempt.

Anger boils faster in man than in animals and leads to repulsion.[13] Like foam and smoke coming out of a volcano, the boiling anger gives rise to malice, hostility, repugnance and revulsion in man. Again, he sacrifices one-sixteenth of his God-given love and serenity.

These emotions are part of man's daily food, and like the food he eats, they should be used in a harmonious way:

- *Śānta*, serenity is half of his complete emotional set-up, the other half being love.
- This other half is harmoniously shared by the other emotions.
- *Śṛṅgāra* (love) 1/4th of the value of his love.
- *Adbhuta* (marvel) 1/4th of the value of his love.
- *Vīra* (heroism) 1/8th of the value of love.
- *Karuṇā* (compassion) 1/8th of the value of his love.
- *Hāsya* (mirth) 1/16th of the value of his love.
- *Bhayānaka* (fear) 1/16th of the value of his love.
- *Raudra* (anger) 1/16th of the value of his love.
- *Bībhatsa* (disgust) 1/16th of the value of his love.

---

11. *Bhaya* (Fear).
12. *Raudra* (Anger).
13. *Bībhatsa* (Repulsion).

Table 1: Distribution of Rasa Shares in a Harmonious Structure of a Human Mind

Rasa	*Emotional* base = 32	*Variation and extrapolations*
Śānta (Serenity)	16/32	Peace, bliss, death, holiness, liberation, calm, detachment, profound meditation, etc.
Śṛṅgāra (Aesthetic love)	4/32	Sympathy, tenderness, joy, friendship, unity, love, harmony, etc.
Adbhuta (Wonder)	4/32	Stupefaction, surprise, delight, enchantment, enthusiasm, exaltation, etc.
Vīra (Heroism)	2/32	Pride, haughtiness, nobility, fairness, loyalty, victory, invincibility, etc.
Karuṇā (Compassion)	2/32	Pity, haughtiness, nobility, fairness, loyalty, victory, invincibility, etc.
Hāsya (Mirth)	1/32	Laughter, contempt, disdain, humour, sarcasm, arrogance, self-importance, etc.
Bhayānaka (Fear)	1/32	Anxiety, anguish, doubt, fear, cowardice, indecisiveness, etc.
Raudra (Anger)	1/32	Aggressiveness, violence, cruely, hatred, selfishness, despotism, self-centredness, etc.
Bībhatsa (Repulsion)	1/32	Repulsion, disgust, rejection, repugnance, malice, brutality, cruelty, etc.

fig. 6: Legend for the emotional set-up
(Courtesy: Cristina Blanchelande, Monaco)

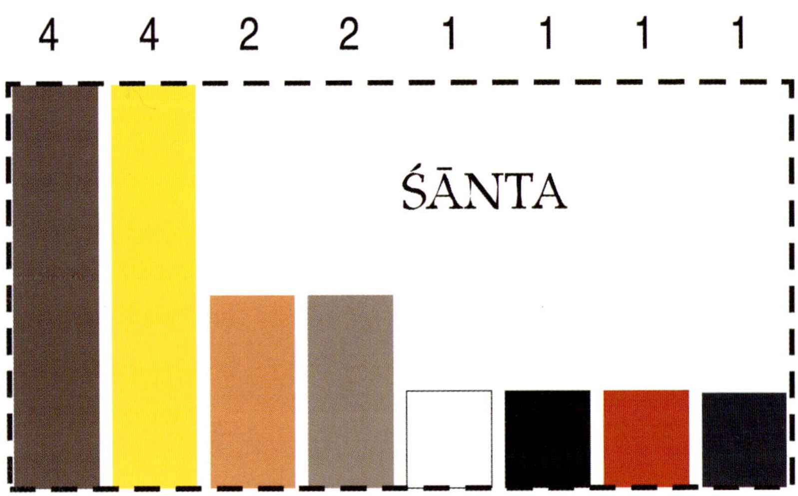

fig. 7: Distribution of *rasa* shares in a harmonious structure of a human mind
(Courtesy: Cristina Blanchelande, Monaco)

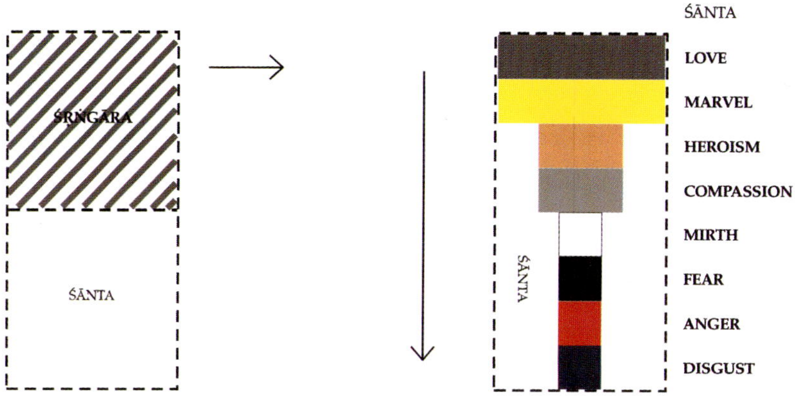

fig. 8: Sequential onset of emotions from birth to infancy (Courtesy: Cristina Blanchelande, Monaco)

Each time man increases the value of his lower emotions, he sacrifices compassion (*karuṇā*) and love (*śṛṅgāra*), but not serenity (*śānta*), even if it is not expressed or used. For example, disgust (*bībhatsa*) and heroism (*raudra*) will first supersede compassion (*karuṇā*) before annihilating wonder and love. So also, fear (*bhayānaka*) and mirth (*hāsya*) will annihilate heroism (*vīra*) first before annihilating wonder and love.

Man is thus born with eight petals of emotions issued from the flower of serenity: love, wonder, compassion, heroism, mirth, fear, anger and repulsion.

Although man conceals his serenity and sacrifices his love to develop heroism and other lower emotions, he is not past all hope, since serenity is always constant and love cannot be entirely annihilated, both being his birthright. When man maintains the above proportions constantly, he is said to maintain a harmonious emotional set-up, because human life, unlike animal life, is based on all these nine emotions. Moreover, it is possible for man to convert all lower emotions into devotion and bring to forefront his two main emotions: serenity and love.

Bṛhadāraṇyaka Upaniṣad, Chāndogya Upaniṣad, as also *Śrīmad Bhāgavata* and *Rāmāyaṇa,* refer to sixteen parts, sixteen tongues of fire, one-sixteenth of *Puruṣa,* one-sixteenth of the sun and so on. The most important weapon that Viṣṇu holds is a *cakra,* also called *sudarśana cakra*. The word *cakra* means disk. *Sudarśana cakra*[14] is the disk that leads to the good; by destroying the bad, it brings the good to the forefront. This *sudarśana cakra* has sixteen spokes or rays and is the measuring rod to maintain the human emotions. As far as emotions are concerned, man's mind is built up on sixteen layers.

In the case of harmony, half of man's mind is covered by serenity, one eighth each by love and wonder, whereas only one-sixteenth each by heroism and compassion, and the remaining eighth is covered by mirth, fear, anger and repulsion equally. Some of these emotions have a reciprocal relationship:

- When man increases his repulsion, he loses his wonder.
- When he increases fear, he loses heroism.
- When he increases anger, he loses compassion.
- When he increases disdain, he loses love.
- When he loses love, he loses peace.

In other words, man conquers disdain by love, violence by compassion, fear by courage and repulsion by wonder. All the four lead him to peace, serenity and calmness.

Each of the eight emotions has its specific stimulating factors, determinant causes and transitory emotions.[15] None of these should exceed one-sixteenth of the value of the main emotion. Any increase in these values will naturally increase the concerned *rasa* which will hinder the opposite *rasa* leading to a decrease in love and a

14. See Chapter 5 "Universal Spiritual Entity, Sauveshvara".

15. *Uddīpana bhāva, ālambana bhāva* and *vyabhicārī bhāva*.

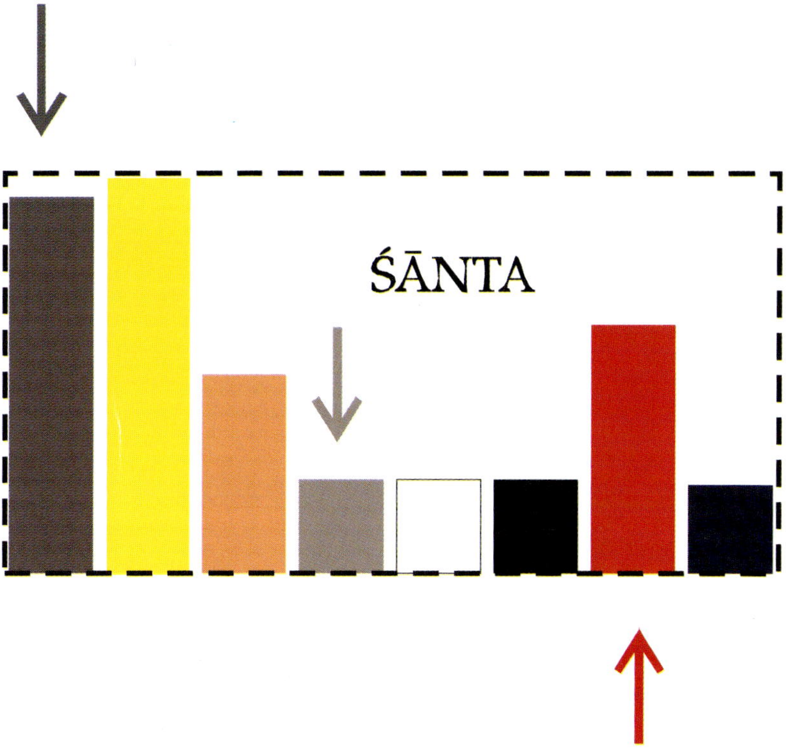

fig. 9: Reciprocal relationship of some of the emotions
(Courtesy: Cristina Blanchelande, Monaco)

consequent shrouding of serenity and peace. Man should remember that many stimulating factors as well as determinant causes overlap more than one *rasa* and increase their intensity. This leads to the loss of the fundamental measure of *śānta* and *śṛṅgāra*. The interactive relation between the stimulating factors is such that one stimulating factor can excite another even if the second factor is not present in the field of direct experience.

The variations of emotions, their extrapolations, the determinant causes, the stimulating factors as well as the transitory emotions constantly feed the main emotions (*rasa*). Very often not even a permanent vigilance is sufficient to maintain the inborn emotional harmony. For this reason, all Vedānta commentators, irrespective of their school of thought, strongly recommend the conversion of the lower emotions into devotion so that the field of love increases; this automatically paves the way to serenity and peace, because love and selfless love are the only human emotions capable of removing the clouds from the field of *śānta*.

Hinduism, including Buddhism and Jainism, advise devotees to contemplate on images depicting peace, serenity, bliss and contentment. Contemplation on Śrī Rāma with his consort Śrī Sītā, on Śrī Kr̥ṣṇa playing the flute with the cow listening to Him, on Viṣṇu with his consort Śrī Lakṣmī, on Padmanābha reclining on the Great Serpent, are some of the examples, as also meditation on the meditating Buddha, or on Jaina *tīrthaṁkara*.

Repeated and continuous contemplation on these images that reflect peace, serenity, bliss and contentment, will kindle, as a stimulating factor, the same *rasa* in man. Man will thus free himself from his slavery to the lower emotions.

fig. 10: Lord Kr̥ṣṇa
(Courtesy: Sumitra Sri Bhashyam, U.K)

fig. 11: Lord Gaṇeśa
(Courtesy: Gabriel Liechti, Switzerland)

fig. 12: Lord Buddha
(Courtesy: Nancy Carpentier, Belgium)

Peaceful Emotion: Śānta Rasa

Śānta means peace. When the mind is quiet without any agitation, man experiences peace. *Rasa* is essence. The essence of peace is *śānta rasa*. So, *śānta rasa* is the peaceful state of mind. It is spiritual harmony.

Śama means calmness of mind and is the permanent emotional disposition of *śānta rasa*. Emotions and sentiments are internal mental states and are associated with knowledge. Man perceives objects through his mind. As he perceives them, he experiences certain feelings. Feelings are different from perception. Feelings give rise to emotions. Each individual has his own type of emotions and sentiments.

According to Vedānta epistemology, the subjective experiences of will, emotions, etc. are different mental constituents, forms or states that are experienced by being directly and illusorily imposed upon the self-revealing consciousness. *Śānta* is one such state of experience in spiritual joy. The state of *śānta rasa* is blissful and is the essence of bliss itself.

Śānta is the undisturbed, unperturbed, unagitated state of mind, though mind is in emotional state. The absence of mental conflicts uncovers the state of mental tranquillity. *Śānta* springs from an absence of ego. In fact, the absence of ego and desire leads to peace of mind.

Peace is the perfect calm that comes from the cessation of all agitations of the mind. The cultivation of the habit of restraining the sense organs from their natural tendency to enjoy objects helps obtain peace of mind. It is the calmness of the mind characterised by the complete cessation of its determinations and agitations. The thoughts are well balanced with purity of heart and conduct. The mind is calm, peaceful, serene and placid. The mind seems to feel as if it is motionless, but, it is in fact experiencing bliss.

The immediate experience of the highest bliss, which

constitutes the essence of Self due to perfect control of the internal and external sense organs, is the result of the *śānta* state of mind.

Śānta rasa is the annihilation of egoism. Egoism is the feeling of identification with one's body, senses and mind. It is due to this that man comes to regard himself as the doer, in relation to what is being done by the mind, intellect and body. Therefore, completely eliminating this feeling of self-identification with the body is what is meant by annihilation of ego. When the state of annihilation of ego is achieved, the mind becomes calm. When the mind becomes calm, man's physical as well as psychological sheaths (gross as well as subtle frames) become strong enough to face any events in life without any mental agitations. So *śānta rasa* is considered essential in man's life.

Even though the soul is free from the emotions, the embodied soul (*jīva*) is under the influence of nine emotions (*nava rasas*). Amongst them, *śānta* is the queen. It is the quintessence of all *rasas* and is the real nature of *jīva*.

Saint Tyāgarāja[16] in one of his compositions sings:

Without calmness there is no happiness of anybody,
Be he one who has controlled his senses or a Vedāntin (philosopher)
Be he possessed of family or children and of material wealth or rich in spiritual sādhanā (practice)
Like japa (repetition of cryptic sounds) or tapas (austerity measures)
Be he well versed in all Vedas and Śāstras (Hindu scriptures) knowing well their inner significance,
Be he one who has performed yāga and karmas (sacrifices and actions of duties),
Be he a great devotee of God.[17]

16. One of the great music composers of southern India (1767-1847) and a devotee *par excellence* of Lord Rāma.

17. "Spiritual Heritage of Tyāgarāja" by C. Ramanujahari.

There is no use in acquiring the whole world when the mind has not reached the state of *śānta*. The blissful essence in *śānta* transcends all material gains. In a peaceful state, the Self realises its freedom by subduing the self of egoism (*ahaṁkāra*) or ego sense, and attunes its will to that of Īśvara, viewing every action performed as a service to God.

In Hindu philosophy, great importance is given to mental stillness and poise. The highest knowledge is where all cognitions dissolve into the *śānta* state, mostly considered as the silence that surpasses all understanding. It is the condition where the perceiving transitions of the mental activities drop off and submit themselves into a detachment *par excellence*.

The highest sensory enjoyment is in the culmination of *śānta rasa*. To the enjoyer of *rasa*, the world seems to be full of *rasa* and the enjoyer feels that the world is born of *rasa*. Having obtained the taste of the joy of *rasa*, man becomes blessed. That *rasa* is the essence of bliss, *śānta rasa*, in peace. This taste springs from *Brahman* himself. The experience of *śānta rasa* brings the highest joy to man. This experience is the experience of *Brahman* the supreme.

Mental restraint plays an important role in *śānta rasa*. Patience, forgiveness, etc. bring tranquillity to the mind. To experience *śānta rasa*, one has to consciously transcend the body, the mind and the intellect through concentration.

Considering the knowledge of Ultimate Reality as the true essence and adopting the required methods to reach this goal are the determinant causes (*ālambana vibhāva*) of *śānta rasa*.

The sentiment of quietness is based on the permanent emotional disposition of an absence of desire that is the cause of liberation. Calmness of mind is the permanent disposition, *sthāyī bhāva*. Considering the knowledge of ultimate reality as the true essence and adopting the required methods to reach this goal are the principal determinants. Pilgrimage centres, holy rivers, forest areas on top of mountains that bring calmness to the mind and the company of holy persons are its stimulating factors.

Śānta is the natural condition of the Self in which it renounces attachment to worldly objects and exists in its inherent bliss. It is devoid of the sense of difference, unperverted by emotions, and manifested as the supreme bliss and consciousness of oneself.

Śānta rasa is the matrix of other *rasas*. They emerge from it and merge in it. When their causes appear, they emerge out of it and disappear with the disappearance of the causes. It is free from pleasure and pain, joy and grief, aversion and envy and permeated by impartiality to all.

According to *Bhagavad-Gītā*, *śānta rasa* is the equanimity of mental state. It denotes constant equipoise of mind free from partiality and prejudice in the midst of objects, actions and incidents, etc. that are likely to throw one off one's balance, such as joy and sorrow, gain and loss, victory and defeat, praise and blame, honour and ignominy, friend and foe, etc.[18] "Evenness of mind is called *yoga*", says Lord Kṛṣṇa to Arjuna. The *yoga* is in *śānta rasa*, because *śānta rasa* is the state of mental equilibrium, which is attainable in calmness alone. When *sattva* phase takes over the mind, *śānta rasa* emerges, bringing mental poise.

Bhagavad-Gītā mentions the state of *sthitaprajña*[19] meaning firm wisdom, as the *śānta rasa* stage. This wisdom is in winning the blissful *Brahman* that is full of beatitude. This state is called *śānta*. The sentimental experience of spiritual harmony is *śānta rasa*.

Śānta rasa is connected with the Hindu God Nārāyaṇa who is the embodiment of peace. It is white (milky white) in colour. Before the creation, there was only a waveless milky ocean (*kṣīra-sāgara*), Lord Nārāyaṇa lying on the bed of Serpent Ananta created Brahmā from His navel and Brahmā created the world.

Śānta Rasa and Bhakti

Bhakti is the love of humanity in relation to God. Devotees

---

18. *Bhagavad-Gītā*, II.48.
19. Ibid., II.54.

experience this divine love in many ways. This experience of divine love is a joy kindled by the love essence called *bhakti rasa*. Love is always for love's sake; to give love to God without asking anything in return from Him is *bhakti*, and the joy of *bhakti* is *bhakti rasa*.[20]

The lowest form in which this love is apprehended is what the devotees call the peaceful. When one worships God with his love in gentle, peaceful, calm attitudes, he experiences a kind of individual joy that is *bhakti rasa*. Worshipping God with *śānta* is a stage of *bhakti*. *Bhakti rasa* flows smoothly with the current of man's nature in *śānta rasa*.

Śānta is the undisturbed state of mind. The strong feeling of emotion calms down in this stage to enjoy the bliss essence of God. The devotional emotion is an indivisible flow of illumination that relates man with God. This emotion is kindled in the mind when all types of emotional disturbances calm down, which is a prerequisite to meditating upon God. *Bhakti rasa* affects the body and mind with intense delight. Affection (*anurāga*) is its dominant phase (*sthāyī bhāva*). It (*bhakti rasa*) predominates *śānta rasa*. *Bhakti rasa*, that relates man to God, is also spiritual. It is peaceful love. It is the quieter form of devotion in which man feels himself to be of God's people.

While passing from lower grade to higher grades, all the *rasa*s change their aspects to spiritual essence. The perfection of *rasa*s is in their spiritual aspects. In their culmination, they all become *śānta*. *Bhakti rasa* is hidden in all the *rasa*s, but emerges only in their culmination point after reaching the state of spiritual essence and in the peaceful form. Just as the dispersion of the sun's rays in falling rain form an arc containing the colours of spectrum in consecutive bands, *bhakti rasa* disperses all the *rasa*s peacefully. This means all the *rasa*s originate from *bhakti rasa* and in their spiritual highest level, become *śānta rasa*, to retrace their path and mingle with devotional emotion.

---

20. Emotional Devotion.

Emotions and sentiments are not only interactive in *bhakti rasa* but they have equanimity of value. *Bhakti rasa* expresses its *bhāva* in the *śānta* state. The higher stages of *śānta rasa* make one the beneficiary of peaceful bliss who slowly becomes a devotee of God through his unmotivated love-essence which is the emotion of love[21] in its spiritual aspect. No doubt, love is *śṛṅgāra rasa*. But the culmination of *śṛṅgāra rasa* is in *śānta rasa*, balancing its emotional and sentimental aspects. *Śānta rasa* is the foundation of *bhakti rasa*, because *bhakti* begins in the harmonious state of emotion and sentiment.

The activities of the mind can be compared to the waves of an ocean. Every wave is attended by a fall and the next moment a rise. This process goes on continuously. But at the depth of the sea, these waves are calm. In the ocean of the mind, thought waves rise and fall, which results in the emotional upsets that make a person lose his mental balance. The mind is an ever-changing whirlpool. It waxes and wanes. It is happy one moment and unhappy the next. Sometimes it is strong and sometimes it is weak. These changing mental operations can be subjugated with effort. The act of subjugation is *śama*, which is also the dominant phase (*sthāyī bhāva*) of *śānta rasa*. *Śama* means self-control that is, control of one's senses.

The source of bliss is in the soul (*ātman*), which is to be heard first, then thought about it and then meditated upon peacefully. This act of meditation on *ātman* is the first stage of *bhakti*. *Ātman* is the spiritual bliss centre that presides over the body frame of every living being and is full of essence (*rasa*). Man has not realised this bliss centre, because of his emotional mental upsets due to different reasons. Like the sun that illuminates the whole world, this bliss centre illuminates man's body in its various functions. Everyone feels this illumination inside him, though unable to express it because of mental upsets due to agitated emotions. This

21. *Prema Rasa.*

blissful centre is attained only through *bhakti* and the joy gained therein is *bhakti rasa*.

Once a man attains this spiritual centre that is within him, he can experience the Supreme Soul, *Paramātmā*, who rules this spiritual centre in man, the *ātman*. According to *Bhagavad-Gītā*, desire, anger, greed, etc. are gateways to perdition. "As a fire is enveloped by smoke, as a mirror is covered by dust and as an embryo is encased in the membrane, so are the embodied beings covered with desires."[22] These are to be subjugated. As attachments and repulsions recede slowly by subjugation, the mind starts gaining peace. Peace helps to meditate on the soul, *ātman*. These peaceful meditations kindle *śānta rasa*, waking *bhakti rasa*. So, *śānta rasa* is the lower stage of *bhakti rasa*. The nature of *ātman* is in the form of supreme bliss and it must be experienced in its essential nature and enjoyed in *śānta rasa* that kindles the *bhakti rasa* that relates man to God, Creator or the Infinite.

That which is Infinite, Great, beyond all, is true happiness. There is no joy in that which is finite. Happiness lies in infinity. Efforts should be made in particular to know the Infinite alone. The Infinite alone transcends all relations and includes within its range all the desires, hopes and aspirations of man. Hence, this *Brahman* is unequalled, unlimited and unsurpassed bliss. This unsurpassed bliss is experienced through *bhakti rasa*. This supreme happiness is filled with *bhakti rasa* which transcends *śānta rasa*.

The joy of the world is momentary, perishable, the roof of suffering and alloyed with suffering. The joy, that is the essence of God, is not of that nature. It is superior even to the *sāttvika* form of joy (*śānta rasa*) and altogether different from it. It is eternal and ever unchangeable because it is the same as God and there is no reality other than that. Only *bhakti rasa* can provide this bliss.

Joy is of different forms. They are dull, active and

22. *Bhagavad-Gītā*, III.38.

illuminating.[23] *Śānta rasa* is derived from illuminating joy. So meditation on God in his *sāttvika* form ignites *śānta rasa* in us and takes the mind to the super-sensuous joy of eternal blessing with the experience of *bhakti rasa*.

Rasa is that which is enjoyable. It is not a non-existing factor. *Rasa* is that which gives pleasure and joy. In realising the Self within even if we negate all objects of the body, mind and intellect, is not an inert void, an empty non-entity, but is a positive experience. This idea is indicated by the Upaniṣadic saying, "*ātman* is full of *rasa*".[24]

Self in self is the Supreme and this is the origin of *rasa*. The joy in this *rasa* is so perfect in itself that all the sensuous objects put together can never give even a trace of this eternal joy in perfection. This is *bhakti rasa*. Having experienced the spiritual centre as one's essential nature, one becomes blessed.

The nature of emotional attachment that is associated with *śānta rasa* is such that the devotee, by his tender love for God, induces the same in him so that the emotion of love may be regarded as a consciousness of bliss. *Śānta rasa* is also a special kind of consciousness dissociated from ignorance and reveals itself in the form of emotion. This form of peaceful emotion is solely intended to please God and is regarded as natural love, known as *bhakti rasa*.

When the Supreme Reality is *Brahman*, it is then *Brahmānanda rasa*, that is, Emotion of Supreme Bliss of *Brahman*. The universe has its source and sustenance only in this bliss, its spiritual centre.

Once *bhakti rasa* dawns on the heart of a person, it does not disappear, though it may increase or decrease at times. It is not produced, but manifested by favourable conditions. It subordinates similar and dissimilar emotions to itself and predominates over

23. According to the influence of three *guṇa*s.

24. *Taittirīya Upaniṣad* by Swami Chinmayananda.

them. It is manifested in quiet love,[25] loving servitude, friendly love, etc.

There is an eternal urge in the soul for union with God. Finite love cannot make it perfectly happy, it is an imperfect manifestation of deep lying innate love for God. God is the embodiment of all kinds of *bhakti rasa*. He excites different *bhakti rasa*s in different devotees according to their permanent emotional dispositions. Natural love for God being transcendental, *bhakti rasa* is also transcendental.

25. *Śānta Rasa*.

8

Benefits of Devotion

By singing His praise, even heinous sinners like murderers of holy men and parents and teachers, as also men of low and impure birth, are redeemed. — *Śrīmad Bhāgavata*, VI.13.8

Introduction

"If God is realised in this very life, well and good. If however He is not realised in the course of this life, one will be a great loser."[1] It is possible for man to attain knowledge of the Supreme in this life, because he can think, argue and he can also choose a goal and struggle to reach it. This is not possible for an animal. So, if a human being does not try to visualise God, it will be a great loss to him.

Śrī Kṛṣṇa says in *Bhagavad-Gītā* that having attained a human body, one should constantly devote oneself to the practice of adoration and should not forget Him even for a moment. "Having attained this transient, joyless world, worship Me."[2] Joy is not permanent in this world of afflictions. This world is stricken with the threefold afflictions called *ādhyātmika*, *ādhibhautika* and *ādhidaivika*.[3] The only remedy left for the human being to cross

1. *Kena Upaniṣad*, II.5.
2. *Bhagavad-Gītā*, IX.33.
3. *Ādhyātmika duḥkha* is related to the body and the mind, such as sickness due to birth, desire or anger, and so on. *Ādhibhautika duḥkha* is caused by the natural influences such as other men, beasts and birds, or inanimate objects. *Ādhidaivika duḥkha* is caused by supernatural influences such as spirits, miseries due to heat and cold, wind and rain, etc. *Ādhidaivika* means caused by the gods (the corresponding deities). All three forms of miseries exist in the Self, so long as it is identified with the body and the mind."

over this ocean of sorrows of life is to dedicate his mind, intellect, senses and body to God and God alone. It is possible to attain Him through the practice of the means proposed in *bhakti*. God-realisation alone draws man out of all types of sorrows and pains. The fulfilment of the object of human existence lies in the realisation of God alone. "Having known Him, he transgresses death (that is, bondage) and there is no other means to attain Him (other than devotion)."[4] "He who knows *Brahman* attains the highest."[5] As we know, *bhakti* is the unceasing meditation done with love on the Supreme Being, purely as a divine service for the pleasure of God and not in expectation of any rewards thereof. "Fix your mind on Me, be My devotee, thus fixing the mind on Me and having Me for the supreme goal, you will attain Me."[6]

Devotion as an emotion (*bhakti rasa*) is like a continuous stream of oil. It is supreme divine love. Devotion manifests itself in one when one has made oneself fit for such a state by constant practice. Practice here consists in directing the mind towards God. The attempt to fix the mind steadily in God is called practice. It is like a beautiful channel for the flow of thought-currents in the direction of God.

Progress in practice leads to different stages of *bhakti,* when the aspirant comes to the definite conclusion that God alone is the Supreme object of love. His mind naturally recoils from all objects of this world and the world after; and he devotes himself with exclusive love and supreme reverence to the constant remembrance of God and God alone. Divine love makes man enjoy the bond existing permanently between him and God. The supreme happiness enjoyed by a God-realised soul is incomparable. Only the unconditional deep-rooted love for God serves as a means to know Him in His true form, to have His vision and to attain Him eventually by stages. This implies that all this is only possible

4. *Śvetāśvatara Upaniṣad*, III.8.

5. *Taittirīya Upaniṣad*, Ānanda Vallī, II.1.

6. *Bhagavad-Gītā*, IX.34.

through God's grace, and in order to earn it, one has to be deeply devoted to God. Only to such a person, who loves God and who craves to have His vision, God showers His grace and reveals himself. "This Self cannot be attained by the study of Veda, nor by meditation nor through much hearing. He is to be attained only by whom the Self chooses. To such a person the Self reveals its nature."[7] "When Self is revealed, the vision of God is at its reach."[8] "The one who is devoted to God is most dear to Me."[9]

There are many stages of devotion. Devotion requires the foundation of knowledge (*jñāna*). As knowledge develops, the stages of devotion also ascend, till man sees God everywhere and in every object.

Devotion Reduces the Consequences of the Activities of Other Emotions

Whatever joys are recognised in this world and however intense they could be, they will not fall under the category of true happiness. For there is none among them, which is superior to all other forms of happiness and remains ever unchanged. That which exists today and ceases tomorrow can never be true happiness. *Chāndogya Upaniṣad* declares, "That, which is infinite or great beyond all, is true happiness. There is no joy in that which is finite. Happiness lies in infinity. Efforts should be made in particular to know the infinite alone."[10] The right approach to feel the experience of joy in the infinite is devotion to Him. Devotion itself is an emotion, which is a mental state. When emotions arise, they are to be felt. Devotion as an emotion is different from other types of emotions. It is untouched by the influence of the three *guṇas*. "There is not a creature, either on earth or again among the gods in heaven, that is free from these three *guṇas* born of

7. *Muṇḍaka Upaniṣad*, III.2.3.
8. *Kaṭha Upaniṣad*, I.2.23; *Bhagavad-Gītā*, XI.55.
9. *Bhagavad-Gītā*, VII.17.
10. *Chāndogya Upaniṣad*, VII.23.1.

prakṛti."[11] When the devotee concentrates his mind on the Supreme, with the mind being rooted in *sattva guṇa* (principle of harmony), which lies beyond the modes of *tamas* and *rajas* (principles of darkness and activity), he derives the pure *sāttvika* form of joy or unmixed joy, because this *sattva* is free from the two other *guṇa*s. This joy paves the way for the emotion of devotion, *bhakti rasa*.

The embodied soul becomes impure due to the dominance of *rajas* and *tamas*. Unless these two *guṇa*s are transformed to the state of *sattva*, the soul remains impure, that is, veiled by mental dirt. Lack of purification of soul is the cause for disturbing emotional activities. Like the health of the body, the health of the soul should also be taken care of. The health of the soul must be evoked from within. Consumption of right food purifies the physical body. The soul becomes pure by providing right thoughts to the mind. This is to be done by leading a virtuous life. The healthy soul is strong enough to remain inattentive to insignificant emotional activities though they arise in the mind very often.

Emotions are of varying types, starting from the insignificant one to the highest spiritual one. All the nine basic emotions (*rasa*s)[12] evoke various emotions and sentiments. Except peaceful emotion, *śānta rasa*, all other emotions are the results of the temporary predominance of *rajas* and *tamas*. All the *rasa*s can be turned into love. Devotion is an aid to purify the emotions. The causes of the gross type of emotions are many. Just like one's sins and past *karma* cause the evocation of various emotions, in the same way ignorance, *avidyā*, which is the natural disability of the soul, is a cause too.

Inadequate mental training obstructs the proper grasping of information from the sense perceptions leading to erroneous understanding, invalid knowledge, confusion of thought and so

11. *Bhagavad-Gītā*, XVIII.40.

12. *Śṛṅgāra, vīra, karuṇa, hāsya, bhayānaka, bībhatsa, adbhuta, raudra, śānta.* See Chapter on "Concept of Emotions or Nava Rasa". See Chapter on "Peaceful Emotion, Śānta Rasa".

on. This in turn leads to wrong emotions and their consequences, which can be illustrated by an example. Ten persons crossed a river. One among them, desiring to know whether all of them had reached the other shore safely, counted all from one to nine except himself. All of them were in great fix, as the tenth person could not be traced. A pilgrim came to their rescue, counted all of them from one to nine, and declared the tenth person, as "you are the tenth".

A child, while observing that the words give rise to ideas in its mind, finds out that the application of a particular word to a particular thing is based upon the expressive power of the word. In the same way, if man understands the application of emotions in the right sense, he can reduce the consequences of the activities of other emotions. He should learn to convert all types of emotions into that of love.

Groups of desires and tendencies that cling to one's intellect also evoke different types of emotions. Consciousness itself, owing to the difference of the limiting adjunct, takes the form of happiness, sorrow, desire, hate, etc. which evokes emotional activities. Consciousness is like an ocean ever giving rise to multiple ripples hindering the perception of the ocean bed. Consciousness is restricted due to emotional agitations. *Bhakti* is love to God which purifies all types of emotions through rightful moral activities. "God speeds you (in your journey) in crossing to the farther shore beyond darkness."[13] A man who has attained moral perfection develops a new power of understanding, which enables him to know and see things justly. Proper understanding annihilates wavering emotions. Devotion to God is the best method for the purification of emotions, while a good will-power is for self-purification.

The application of moral codes in our daily life develops our capacity of right understanding. Right understanding paves the

---

13. *Muṇḍaka Upaniṣad*, II.2.6.

way for right knowledge, which cleanses the mind and the intellect of all their distractions and defaults providing them stability. The disciplines prescribed in devotional practices help one to learn conquer one's lower mental attitudes. This naturally reduces the consequences of the gross types of emotions. Development and cultivation of virtuous dispositions illuminate the soul, increasing the spiritual motivation. Since every virtuous act is a way of expressing one's love, it reinforces the hidden strength of the soul. Devotion is a pure, subtle and ever expanding experience. One, who has once experienced it, will ever think of that alone. So there would be no room for other types of emotions. The vision of God or the Supreme requires control of the mind, concentration of all the mental faculties.[14]

When the mind is freed from the restlessness coming from dejection, fear, anxiety, grief, agony, etc. it becomes calm. When it becomes calm, its capacity to be attentive becomes steady and controlled. One can obtain this state of calmness through the practices of virtues like forbearance, politeness, love, etc. All these virtues also purify the mind. When the mind is purified, the insignificant emotions subside on their own. Lord Kṛṣṇa says, "Through single-minded devotion, however it is possible to truly know, to see, to enter into Me."[15] Single-minded devotion is pure, serene and full of harmony, with no other activities in the mind except love for God. *Bhakti* itself cleanses all types of gross emotions. Through the cultivation of devotion, the soul would be freed from the clutches of the sense objects.

The fire of right knowledge reduces all other types of emotions except that of devotion leaving no trace of agitated emotions. There is no purifier equal to right knowledge. Devotion, which is of the nature of love, is an emotion in itself, but is a serene benevolent one. Moreover, the emotion of devotion dissolves

14. The Indian psychology includes feeling, thought and the will-power in the mind.

15. *Bhagavad-Gītā*, XI.54.

other emotions and helps one's self to merge into God just as the river merges into an ocean, losing its identity.

Devotion is a mental disposition in the sense of loving devotion to God. Though there is an emotional element in *bhakti*, it is intellectual, because it presupposes some knowledge of the Divine Being. Devotion is a discipline involving the development of certain ethical virtues and the observance of moral duties, etc. for the acquisition of spiritual knowledge. Each of these practices brings a change in the mental attitude, making the mind strong to face any situation with calmness.

Realisation Reduces the Consequences of Kleśa and Karma

Kleśa means afflictions, a misery. *Kleśa* is an evil in the sense that the afflictions result from the latent tendencies of past lives; *karma* means action. To survive, man has to do actions. It is not wrong, if it is said that the *kleśa* of hunger makes man perform different actions. So *kleśa* and *karma* go hand in hand.

The human body, which is considered as the abode of enjoyment, is also the seat of miseries. Individuals have been going through all kinds of miseries from life to life. The misery of old age, the pain of disease, the misery of living torn away from beloved people, the miseries of unfulfilled desires, and so on always hunt man. Yet, he does not want to get rid of these miseries. Yudhiṣṭhira, the eldest of the Pāṇḍavas, says, "Day after day, there enter into the temple of death, countless lives. Looking on this spectacle, the rest of them, those who remain, believe themselves to be permanent and immortal. There can be nothing more wonderful than this."[16] *Kleśa* and *karma* are for embodied souls only. God is untouched by these. Patañjali says, "Īśvara is a special *puruṣa* unaffected by the vehicles of afflictions, actions and fruition."[17] Īśvara is not bound by *kleśa*s, *karma*s, etc. like the embodied souls, who are still involved in the cycles of evolution.

16. *Mahābharata*, Vana Parva, Yakṣa Praśna.

17. *Pātañjala Yoga-Sūtra*, I.24.

The embodied souls are nourished by Īśvara and evolve from stage to stage, until they become free from *kleśa* and *karma*. In Īśvara, the highest knowledge and power culminate. His desires become fulfilled without any obstruction. Even during the great deluge, the Supreme Lord alone survives. He is the Creator of the Universe, the individual souls and the matter. Though He has no interest of His own, yet He is under the necessity of conferring benefits upon His creatures who are caught up in the ocean of bondage. Free from bias He creates them in accordance with their *karma*. "The reservoir of *karma*, which is rooted in *kleśa*, brings all kinds of experiences in the present and future lives."[18] As long as this root exists, it will continue to ripen and produce its inevitable misery and suffering in life. One cannot strive for the spiritual goal without being associated with the body, the senses and the intellect. So, God creates opportunities for the souls to work out their destinies and make them fit to know Him. Man has to struggle hard, passing through many stages to reduce *kleśa* and *karma* to the vanishing point, to make himself capable of knowing God.

Man's will is ever free, though he is dependent on God. It is this conviction of dependence on the Supreme that obliges man to lead a moral life. Not everything in this life is predetermined. Within the limits set by birth, environment and tendencies, man has still an ample scope to carve out a future. "This body is called a field, *kṣetra*."[19] Every soul,[20] entirely different from the body, is a cultivator to whom a plot of ground is given. The extent of ground, the nature of soil, the changes of weather to which it is exposed are all predetermined. But the cultivator is free to till the ground, to manure it, to raise suitable crops, or to neglect it and allow it run to waste. Similarly, there are elements of freedom as well as elements that have been predetermined in the lives of all beings.

18. *Pātañjala Yoga-Sūtra*, II.12.

19. *Bhagavad-Gītā*, XIII.1.

20. Lord Kṛṣṇa uses the word *kṣetrajña* — *Bhagavad-Gītā* XIII.1.

The body, *kṣetra*, is material, mutable and perishable, whereas the soul, *kṣetrajña*, is conscious, immutable, eternal and imperishable. Though they are entirely different from each other, due to ignorance, they are identified as one. This ignorance leads man to bondage. "Matter (body) is perishable, but God is imperishable and immortal."[21] *Śvetāśvatara Upaniṣad* uses the word *hara* to designate the individual soul, because it seizes the matter (body) as an object of its own experience.

The individual souls have certain limitations (*upādhi*). They are physical, mental and moral conditions, under which they have to work. These limitations, which are imposed on them by *avidyā*,[22] delude human beings into the belief that they are independent, and thus they become victims of miseries. These miseries are termed as *kleśa*s.

According to Sāṁkhya philosophy, the misery is taken to heart and constitutes a real torment. The scriptural means of terminating the misery are uncertain. They are not final. The only method of putting an end to the misery is seeking the knowledge of "the evolved", "the un-evolved" and "the knower". When all the three are understood, the cessation of suffering results. Patañjali in his *Yoga-Sūtra* enumerates five types of *kleśa*s: *avidyā, asmitā, rāga, dveṣa* and *abhiniveśa. Avidyā* is ignorance, *asmitā* is the sense of egoism, *rāga* is attraction, *dveṣa* is repulsion and *abhiniveśa* is strong desire to live. The inquiry into the causes of *kleśa*s brings a change in the inner faculties of the human being (that is to say, an inner change in the human consciousness) and awakens the spiritual faculties.

The five modes of ignorance (*viparyāya*) water the ground (the body according to *Bhagavad-Gītā*) and make the sprouting possible. Deprived of the moisture provided by these forms of ignorance, the ground becomes barren. The deprivation of dampness is from

---

21. *Śvetāśvatara Upaniṣad*, I.10.

22. *Avidyā* is the natural disability of the embodied soul which prevents it from apprehending reality as such.

wisdom. All types of *kleśa*s are due to the error of the intellect or wrong knowledge.

The five modes of ignorance are ignorance (*tamas*), delusion (*moha*), great delusion (*mahāmoha*), blindness (*tāmiśra*) and extreme blindness (*andhatāmiśra*).

AVIDYĀ

Avidyā[23] means "absence of knowledge". *Avidyā* is the breeding ground for the other four *kleśa*s. In *avidyā*, the non-eternal, the impure, the evil and the non-soul is considered as the eternal, the pure, the good and the soul respectively. It is also the absence of awareness. "Spiritual ignorance is the imposition of the idea of the Self on that which is non-self."[24] When the soul gets involved in *avidyā*, it begins to identify itself with the body, with which it becomes associated.[25]

This identification increases as the soul gets more and more attracted or attached to physical experiences, until the turning point is reached and the upward climbing in the opposite direction begins. This turning point may depend on a sudden alertness, or an excessive suffering, or an unexpected encounter with a wise person. In its transcendental approach, the soul extricates itself from matter, which results in the realisation of its real nature. For the soul, the cyclic process of manifested life begins with the association of its consciousness with the body through the direct agency of *avidyā*.

ASMITĀ

The word *asmitā* is derived from *asmi* which means "I-am". "I am" represents the awareness of self-existence. *Asmitā* is the expression of the I-consciousness. When it gets involved in the body, it loses its real nature and the feeling of "I am" modifies

23. Here *vidyā* is used in the sense of right knowledge.

24. *Viṣṇu Purāṇa*, VI.7.10.

25. This idea of identification is also said to be owing to *māyā* (illusion).

into "I am this". The two processes, the loss of awareness of its real nature and the identification with the body-mind-complex, are simultaneous. The moment consciousness identifies itself with the body-mind, it not only loses its pure state but also binds itself by the limitations of *avidyā*.

When the pure perceptibility of the soul is active, intellect becomes its perceiving instrument. The transformation of these two into an apparent identity is the affliction called *asmitā*. *Asmitā* manifests through the physical body in the grossest form of the *kleśa* and through the intellect in the subtle form.

RĀGA

Rāga is the attraction that one feels towards any person or object of experience immediately after any kind of pleasure or happiness is derived therefrom. One may be devoted to a particular pursuit, because it gives oneself intellectual satisfaction.

DVEṢA

Dveṣa is the repulsion felt towards any person or object, which is a source of pain or unhappiness. The essential nature of the soul is blissful and therefore anything that brings pain or unhappiness in the outer world makes the mind recoil from that thing or person. *Dveṣa* (repulsion), and *rāga* (attraction), form a pair of opposites. Love and hate have but an alternative connotation. The pleasure due to *rāga* and the pain due to *dveṣa* are bondage of the individual soul.

ABHINIVEŚA

Abhiniveśa is the desire to live or the fear of death. This strong attachment to life, which is universal, is well established even in the learned. The fear of death in the form of an idea of annihilation of the Self, which cannot be expressed by perception, inference and scriptural teaching, carrying its own potency, indicates the pain of death experienced in previous births. This experience seems to exist in the extremely ignorant and even in the wise, who have fully understood the impermanence of life, because the habitual potency caused by the experience of the pain of death is same for both.

Even though it is said that only to the ignorant the world consists of a multitude of sorrows, to the wise, the world is full of bliss, and that the world is dark to the blind and bright to the one with eyes — the five afflictions bind the wise too.

Avidyā may take the meaning of "loss of Self-knowledge". It is bondage; and this bondage can neither be destroyed by weapons, nor by wind, nor by fire, nor by the millions of acts enjoined by the scriptures by nothing except the wonderful sword of knowledge and by the grace of God. *Avidyā* manifests in desires. When the mind has relinquished his desires for enjoyments, man is awakened. The mind becomes tranquil, producing calmness in the heart.

"A desireless man sees the glory of the Self through the serenity of the sense organs, through the purity of mind and thereby becomes free from sorrows."[26] The Self is difficult to be known by ordinary people, who are possessed of *avidyā*, as *avidyā* is the cause of impurities of the mind. The impure mind sheltering afflictions is unable to discriminate between the real and the unreal.

All *kleśa*s can exist in two states: active and potential. In the active state, they can be recognised easily by their outer expressions. In a person, who is in a fit of anger for instance, it is easy to see that aversion is in full swing. If this same person subjects himself to a rigid self-discipline, he will develop the capacity to keep himself free from anger. This type of action reduces the *dveṣa* to its potential state. The function of *dveṣa* ceases in the potential condition, but its germs are still there, which may be made active again on favourable conditions. The affliction of *dveṣa* becomes suppressed but not completely destroyed.

While Patañjali advises the practice of *kriyā-yoga*[27] to attenuate

26. *Kaṭha Upaniṣad*, I.ii.20.

27. Austerity, self-study and resignation to Īśvara constitute *kriyā-yoga* — *Pātañjala Yoga-Sūtra*, II.1.

the *kleśa*s progressively until they become quite dormant, incapable of being aroused by ordinary stimuli from the external world, Rāmānuja prescribes *sādhanā-saptaka*[28] to destroy *kleśa*s. As they can be made active again under extraordinary conditions, *kleśa*s should not only be reduced to an inactive state but should be completely annihilated. Patañjali advises meditation, *dhyāna* as a means to annihilate them, even if they are in the subtle form of latent impressions. All the disciplines prescribed in the spiritual path serve to attenuate and annihilate the *kleśa*s. Meditation (*dhyāna*) serves to reflect on the deeper problems of life, to change one's habits of thought and attitudes; it helps to solve the problems effectively for the realisation of one's objective, namely Self-realisation, which finally leads to the realisation of God. Whatever spiritual discipline man applies, even though they all involve certain spiritual exercises outwardly, they polarise and harness all his energy to achieve this purpose.

*Kleśa*s can assume innumerable forms of expression; and if one of its expressions is suppressed, it will assume another form. So all *kleśa*s should be annihilated as a whole. *Kleśa*s involve man in the never-ending cycles of births and deaths and the miseries of life. According to Hindu philosophy, *kleśa*s are the underlying cause of *karma* man generates by his thoughts, desires and actions. *Kleśa*s and *karma* are related to each other as cause and effect. Each human soul goes through a continuous series of rebirths reaping the fruits of thoughts, desires and actions done in the

28. Purification of the body by consumption of *sāttvika* food, which leads to the purity of mind (*viveka*); Getting rid of sensual attachment or anger for securing mental tranquillity (*vimoka*); Repeated reflection of God, who is immanent in the human souls (*abhyāsa*); Performance of the religious duty, which will provide inner mental strength (*kriyā*); Development of ethical virtues such as honesty, integrity, compassion, benevolence, non-violence, etc. which will give inner purity (*kalyāṇa*); Freedom from despair due to disappointments and unexpected calamities (*anavasāda*), and lastly, not to be overpowered by excessive joy, so that tranquillity of mind is not disturbed (*anuddharṣa*). See Chapter on "Sevenfold Discipline of Rāmānuja or Sādhanā Saptaka".

past and generating new causes which will bear their fruits in this or a future life. So in every human life two processes are at work simultaneously: the working out of *karma*, which will bear fruit in the future and the memorising of latent impressions linked with either attachment or repulsion. The result of each thought, desire, emotion and action is memorised in *karmāśaya* (the reservoir of *karma*). *Karmāśaya* is the subtle body, which is the medium or vehicle in man's inner constitution and is referred to as the causal body (*kāraṇa śarīra*) in Vedānta. The reservoir of *karma* serves as a container of all impressions emerging from human thoughts, desires, feelings and actions, just as all experiences, which passed through the sense organs, are recorded in the brain and can be recovered in the form of memory.

The causal body is the effective cause of the present and future lives; and the experiences, which constitute those lives, flow to a great extent from it. Yet, the real cause of these experiences is the *kleśa*, because they are the driving force for the generation of *karma*. The causal body merely serves as a mechanism for adjusting the effects of these *karma*s. For example, the motivation to get pleasure is the real cause of an action. The type of action depends on the type of pleasure one expects. So, one decides to act in compliance with certain parameters of the way, the time and the place, which are the adjusting factors between the motivation and the pleasure. If the motivation is annihilated, there would naturally be no search for pleasure nor would there be any action to take pleasure, which is no more searched for.

Every soul has to go through the experiences of the fruits of *karma* set for the present life. Every action bears fruits, but it requires a suitable time and environment for its fulfilment. Until then they remain a latent force.

Karma is a natural law and works with a mathematical precision. The law of *karma* states the conditions under which one has to work. It does not command man to work or not to work, but sets the conditions for action or non-action. The serving of a succulent dish sets the conditions for eating or non-eating. The cause of pleasant or unpleasant consequences of eating the dish is not the dish, but the motivation to get the taste of this succulent dish even though one attributes the cause to the dish. The law of *karma* is certainly very strong even for the man, who is on his way to realisation. The fruits of actions determine one's birth, experiences and many intellectual gifts, but they do not determine man's will or affect its strength of application in a particular direction.

Once the wheel of *karma* is set in motion, it will gather momentum at every instant without providing any escape from the inevitable results of action, until the motion of the wheel is brought to a standstill. Right knowledge is one of the means to put a stop to this motion. *Karma*, which one has to pass through in the existing life, cannot be destroyed. But future *karma* can be destroyed by the fire of knowledge. The root of afflictions exists as long as one fails to realise the unaffected nature of the soul. As soon as the true nature of the soul is discovered, *kleśa*s disappear. "When a person realises Him in both high and low, the knots of his heart are loosened, his doubts dispelled and his *karma* exhausted."[29] A devotee, who always lives absorbed in the thought of God, will not be affected by any of the *kleśa*s and *karma*. He will be beyond afflictions due to his nearness to God. A child forgets hunger and bodily pains when playing with his toys. Similarly does the devotee take pleasure in God without minding the afflictions. God is his wealth, power and everything.

Wisdom dawns through uninterrupted contemplation on God. Like the fragrance of sandalwood, the perfume of the soul, the abode of God is covered with microscopic particles of endless peaceful impressions embedded in the mind. When the constant frictions of the knowledge of God purify it, it is clearly perceived.

The moment the knowledge of God is perceived all the seeds

---

29. *Muṇḍaka Upaniṣad*, II.2.8.

of *kleśa* and *karma* become incapable of sprouting, for the ground is rendered barren, deprived of the moisture of *avidyā*. When *avidyā* is dried up, all sorts of *kleśa* are dried up too. Yet, even for the one, who has realised the nature of God, the body would continue to live, because of the force of his past impressions, just as the potter's wheel continues to rotate for a time even after the potter has ceased to make it go round. The past impressions are of prior *karma* which has begun to take effect. Wisdom[30] as an intellectual function has the capacity to destroy all *karma*, except that, which has begun to take effect; it would automatically become sterile. "For him, only so long is the delay as he is not liberated from the body and then immediately he is merged in Being."[31] The results of actions are of two types: (1) That which has already become operative, and (2) that which has not yet become operative, that is, the results of actions that have been accumulated in previous births and those that have been earned in the present life till the attainment of right knowledge. The first is called *prārabdha karma*. In a realised soul it gets exhausted before the fall of his body. Since he is realised, he will not have the consequences of the second type of *karma* (those that are yet to become active). There is no time gap between the fall of his body and his attainment of release.

> Verily, the embodied self (the self which thinks he is the body and the body is his) is held by pleasure and pain. There is no cessation of pleasure and pain to the one who is embodied. But the pleasure and pain do not indeed touch one who is bodiless.[32]

As the evolution of human consciousness progresses, man gives up his identification with the body. Then he can remain as if untouched by *kleśa*s, because he understands that *ātman* is nearest

30. According to Sāṁkhya philosophy, virtue (*dharma*), wisdom (*jñāna*), non-attachment (*vairāgya*) and lordship (*aiśvarya*) are the four functions of the intellect (*buddhi*) that help one disable all its defects (the five *kleśa*s).

31. *Chāndogya Upaniṣad*, VI.14.2.

32. Ibid., VIII.12.1.

to him and that the soul is really not affected by *kleśa*s. *Kleśa*s are not independent of each other, but form a series beginning with *avidyā* and ending in *abhiniveśa*. How *kleśa*s are experienced depends upon the particular cause. The effect is always related to the cause, and the quality of experience is determined by the cause. As long as the root of afflictions exists, it will ripen and bring results in experience. The birth, the lifespan and the life experience when produced by virtuous actions of the past are possessed of pleasurable fruits. When the same are produced by vice, the fruits are painful. "To people who have developed discrimination everything is misery on account of pains, resulting from change (*pariṇāma*), anxiety (*tapa*), mental impressions (*saṁskāra*), and the interaction of *guṇa*s (*guṇa-vṛtti*)."[33] In fact, all the experiences are either activities or potentially full of misery to the wise, whose spiritual perception is awakened.

The spouse, children, wealth, etc. give happiness to an ordinary man and develop attachment in him, which in turn gives rise to a causal body consisting of attachment. On the other hand, if some harm is done to this happiness, the pain thus caused develops repulsion, which would give rise to a causal body consisting of repulsion. Since *karmāśaya* is rooted in *kleśa*s, it ultimately gives rise to pain only. "The pleasure which arises from the contact of the senses with their objects, which is like elixir at first, but like poison in the end, is said to be *rājasika*."[34]

As man fondly enjoys worldly pleasures with his senses and mind, considering them as eternal joy, impressions of those enjoyments are left in his mind, due to which he seeks once more to obtain those very enjoyments. Aiming at this he impulsively perpetrates various sins through attachment. In order to reap the evil consequences of such sinful acts, he has to undergo terrible sufferings. This situation may be compared to that of a moth,

33. *Pātañjala Yoga-Sūtra*, II.15.

34. *Bhagavad-Gītā*, XVIII.38.

which on account of its attachment to colour — the object of sight — finds pleasure in deliberately making a dash at the flame of a lamp mistaking it for an embodiment of joy, and so in the end it suffers by getting burnt and dies.

The momentary pleasure that appears to be pleasurable binds man through attachment. Therefore, a seeker of beatitude should not allow himself to be enticed into these types of delightful traps. Just as the adding of fuel to the fire increases the flames, the more one desires the more one accumulates pains. There is no pain equal to desire.

Even if a poison-mixed sweet dessert gives an enjoyable taste while eating, it would undoubtedly produce many types of miseries in the end. Anxiety is a sort of fear that starts with the first appearance of a painful experience even if this experience is pleasurable. During enjoyment of pleasure, the hidden attitude of repulsion peeps out to give its experience. If there is wealth, there is always the fear of losing it or the threat to one's security. There always is the fear of losing the beloved ones. These fears emerge into consciousness only when a crisis occurs in one's life, even though they are always present in the subconscious.

The expression of joy due to pleasures or misery due to displeasure leaves a corresponding impression on the subconscious which is often evoked by memory. In order to reactivate these impressions and to revive the experiences one engages in new actions. These new actions ripen by providing another set of experiences (pleasure or displeasure) which in their turn leave corresponding impressions on the subconscious mind. Thus, the cycle of impressions, new actions to revive the experiences and new impressions, continues endlessly. Even if ordinary people do not seem to be affected by these cycles, they do affect a man of discrimination, because his mind is capable of distinguishing between right and wrong and the corresponding consequences. *Viveka* (discrimination) is an illuminated state of mind. When discrimination dawns on the mind, man begins to reflect on the value of life and detach himself from the current of ordinary thoughts and desires. He cares more for finding the Reality which is hidden behind the course of phenomena.

"*Prakṛti* is said to be the cause of the agency to the body and sense organs. The Self is said to be the cause of experiencing pleasure and pain."[35] *Prakṛti* works through the three modes of *guṇa*s. The Self in its pristine nature experiences "itself" by "itself" as nothing but joy. But, when dwelling in the body, it is in conjunction with *prakṛti* and experiences the qualities born of *prakṛti*. The contact of the soul with the three *guṇa*s (*sattva, rajas* and *tamas*) existing from beginningless time and the soul's attachment for worldly objects, which are evolutes of the *guṇa*s, are the causes for the *kleśa*s. These are due to the conflict between the natural tendencies caused by the domination of one of the *guṇa*s and the states of mind. The function of the *guṇa*s is ever changing and so is the mind. *Guṇa*s become the chain of mutual support in each and every action of the mind. Because of their influence, the actions of mind are classified under three categories: a tranquil mind, a disturbed mind and a mind of inertia. In the same way, the experiences are classified as of happiness, of misery and of delusion. During conflict, one of the *guṇa*s dominates to suppress the other two. Because of the conflict of *guṇa*s and their constant existence in the human body, all types of experiences become miserable to a man of wisdom.

To a man of the world immersed in his illusory pursuits of pleasure, life may appear as a mixture of pleasure and pain, joy and sorrow. But to a wise, whose spiritual faculties are awakened, life would appear as full of miseries. The so-called happiness seems to be a sugarcoated pill, containing only pain and suffering inside the pleasurable coatings. This awakening forces the wise to seek for a permanent solution to eradicate the *kleśa*s.

If the cause of the *kleśa*s is known, then the remedy can also be

35. *Bhagavad-Gītā*, XIII.20.

found. The soul in its pristine state is untouched by *kleśas*. But dwelling in the body, which is impermanent, in relation with the world of experience, it experiences the qualities born of this objective world. It accepts the body as its own, just as a rope takes any colour dyed to it indifferent to the qualities of the thread. Linked with the material body (*prakṛti*) and the subtle body (which is the result of *kleśa, karma* and *saṁskāra*), the soul thinks itself to be *prakṛti* and its evolutes, of which the body-mind-complex is constituted. So, if one wants to realise the real nature of the soul, one must first understand what it is not — it is neither the body-mind-complex nor the matter. The understanding or application of this knowledge is the removal of *avidyā*, which in turn removes the other *kleśas* (*asmitā, rāga, dveṣa, abhiniveśa*) and provides the perfect knowledge of the soul.

> One should ascend higher and higher restraining successively the sense activities and mental activities from the gross to the fine till at last one is lost in *samādhi*.[36]

> The dissociation of soul and body brought about by the dispersion of *avidyā* is the real remedy and that is the liberation of the *jīva*.[37]

How to obtain enlightenment by avoiding future sufferings? When the knowledge of discrimination dawns on the mind through the practice of uninterrupted devotion to God man's attitude towards *kleśa* changes. In this illuminated state of mind, the devotee is capable of discriminating the Real from the unreal. Continuous practice of devotion following the principles of *sādhanā saptaka* and *kriyā-yoga* removes the impurities of the mind to a great extent. The practice in *bhakti-yoga* provides the devotee an inner source of illumination. The increase in wisdom goes hand in hand with an increase in illumination leading finally to the vision of the Supreme. That is why, it is said that the permanent establishment

36. *Kaṭha Upaniṣad*, I.3.3.

37. *Pātañjala Yoga-Sūtra*, II.25.

of the mind in God is the effective cure for the root cause of bondage and suffering, since it would disable the natural tendency of the mind from seizing one thought or the other.

The moral codes set in devotional practices do help in bringing the mind under control. When the mind is controlled, the intensity of concentration increases together with spiritual freedom. With the firmness of spiritual freedom all *kleśa*s would be washed off. By proper perception and meditation on God, the mental impressions melt away. Just as gold is purified by thorough heating on fire and comes out discarding the impurities, revealing its own lustre, so too, the mind discards its impurities and reveals spiritual illumination through meditation. At this stage the devotee is established in God. He gradually but totally gives up desires for external thoughts. When external thoughts are eliminated, the unobstructed realisation of Reality occupies the mental plane. Restraint of mind and contemplation on God are the surest remedies for all types of *kleśa*s in the worldly existence. "Seated on the same tree one of them the personal Self sunken in ignorance and deluded grieves for forgetting his own divine nature. But when he sees the other the Lord as also His glory, he becomes free from dejection."[38]

Just as the sun is not tarnished by the dust and dirt of the material on which it reflects, so too, when the individual comes to realise the transcendental reality of his Self, the suffering and enjoyment disappear and he attains the unbroken eternal bliss of his Self.

Bhagavad-Gītā speaks of *niṣkāma karma*, that is, action for action's sake, in which all *karma*s of the performer are said to be consumed in the fire of wisdom. This technique ceases to add new impressions (*vasana*) to the accumulated stock. When practised perfectly *niṣkāma karma* can only stop generating new *karma* for the future; it cannot destroy the root of impressions — the causes

---

38. *Muṇḍaka Upaniṣad*, III.1.1.

of *kleśa* — which is inherent in the manifested life. The *karma* already accumulated will not disappear by any method. Man must wait patiently till the *karma* is completely exhausted. The paradox of an ordinary man's life is that he confines himself within his own framework and yet is limited in his capacity to alter its important trends. On the other hand, one who practises meditation regularly can make changes in the layout of his framework. Through the uninterrupted practice of meditation, one acquires a state of discrimination, which would pave the way for the awareness of the Real. It is the state when the soul awakens from its long spiritual sleep and becomes mature to find its real state crossing over the ocean of conditional existence. This stage leads to complete liberation, destroying bondage. After attaining this stage, the devotee never again falls into *avidyā* or another *kleśa*. After attaining liberation, one would continue to act, but with the distinction that actions would be done with an identification with the Supreme and not with that of the individual ego.

One who is given to good culture acquires the same characteristics of refinement of mind and emotions. He will acquire refined ways of thinking. From the development of good culture, the mind becomes transparent. A transparent mind acquires both, one-pointedness and steadiness.

Liberation is possible through devotion that combines knowledge. By devotional practices, the hook that anchors the soul to *prakṛti* is disentangled and then bondage from *prakṛti* will never occur, because the soul is completely absorbed in God.

> It is the view of the wise men that the mind indeed is the cause of both, the bondage and liberation of embodied beings. If the mind is attached to *guṇa*s of *prakṛti* and other products, it leads to bondage; but when it begins to feel delight and attraction for God, it leads to liberation.[39]

---

39. *Kapila Upadeśa*, I.15.

9

Devotion as a Means to Self-realisation, Ātma-Jñāna

When all the powers of man's senses, which are ordinarily frittered away through external contacts, are purified through devotional practices and dedicated action, and they get naturally focused on Īśvara (the Supreme Lord) exclusively, without an extraneous and self-centred motivation, and with a firmness which no obstruction can overpower that state of mind is called *bhakti* or the highest form of devotion for the Lord. Such devotion is superior even to *mukti* (liberation).

— *Śrīmad Bhāgavata*, III.25.32-33

ACCORDING to traditional Hindu scriptures, *Brahman* (the Absolute) is the fountainhead of the creative cosmic energy, which is the primary cause of both animate and inanimate creation. *Brahman* is self-effulgent and self-evident. He exists as the stuff and substratum of all phenomena and can actually be experienced by any concentrated and pure mind and by an analysis of the three states of waking, dreaming and dreamless sleep. Such an examination shows that there is an inner witness of these three states generally termed as pure consciousness, which represents the soul (*ātmā*). The observer remains unchanged even in the midst of the changing states, and this alone can explain the fact of memory of the three states. This pure consciousness is the driving force even for the day-to-day knowledge; and this pure consciousness (*Saguṇa Brahman*, also termed as Absolute with attributes) constitutes the real essence of *sat*, the cause and support of the Universe.

Brahman and Our Consciousness

The Universal consciousness or life energy called *prāṇa* takes the form of physical and psychic manifestations, like intellect, ego, mind, emotion and feeling, on the one side and physical atoms and electrons on the other side. The conscious life principle or life force flows down through all individualised channels. That is to say, *Brahman* enters into these categories and causes them to intermingle in a way to form the various spheres and bodies of living beings. Thus, *Brahman* will be operative at every stage of evolution. There will always be a driving force for acquiring new capabilities and higher powers of action to know the all-powerful Universal Consciousness. The desire to know one's Self stimulates this driving force. New capabilities and higher powers of action accompany the knowledge gained through inspiration (or the inner voice).

First, it is necessary to know that every being has a soul or a Self. All traditional scriptures agree on this fundamental hypothesis. "The Self that is subtler than the subtle and greater than the great is lodged in the heart of every creature."[1] "The being (*puruṣa*) of the size of a thumb (the lotus of the heart is of the size of the thumb) resides in the body (in the space within the lotus of the heart)."[2] "*Puruṣa*, who is of the size of a thumb, is like a flame without smoke."[3]

The soul is the entity denoted by "I"[4] and as such, it creates the individual ego[5] by causing the delusion that the physical body itself is the soul. The ego grows running through thoughts, which manifest themselves in forms and objects through the perception of the universe, in which an infinite number of things appear and disappear. Consciousness is an attribute of the Self. When it is

1. *Kaṭha Upaniṣad*, I.2.20.
2. Ibid., II.1.12.
3. Ibid., II.1.13.
4. *Ahamārtha*.
5. *Ahaṁkāra*.

directed towards an object, it becomes objective but never gets separated from self-consciousness. It is the objective consciousness that varies and not the self-consciousness.

Consciousness is a particular mental activity, like the awareness of oneself, the awareness of who I am, where I am and the awareness of what I know, what I do not know and so on. The likes, the dislikes, the fears and the anguishes are in the depths of our objective consciousness. In other moments these do not appear.

Man has four states of consciousness: waking (*jāgrata*), dream (*svapna*), deep sleep (*suṣupti*) and the fourth (*turīya*).[6]

Both self-consciousness and objective consciousness are present in the waking state. Normally consciousness is only understood as objective consciousness. Man, though having the possibilities of four states of consciousness, lives in two states, that is, in sleep and in the waking state. Since dream experiences are invoked only in the waking state, they are included in this state.

Objective consciousness is a state, in which one comes into contact with the real world or the objective world, from which one is shut off by the senses, the dreams, imaginations and the subjective states of consciousness (perception of things by the mind, but not independent of the mind). In this state of objective consciousness, one is able to know the full truth of everything, that is, the universe as it is.

Self-consciousness is a state, in which one becomes objective towards oneself. The state of Self-awareness will reveal the real nature of one's Self or the soul. In this state, one can know the full truth about oneself. When one ascends above one's individual consciousness to the heights of universal consciousness, one will be able to know whatever one chooses to understand. The more one is involved in objective consciousness, the less one has the capacity to grasp the Self.

---

6. Also termed *samādhi*.

Yet, a full development of objective consciousness is only possible, when self-consciousness is well developed, as it is the basis for the former. In order to develop Self-consciousness the period of its awareness is to be prolonged, which is possible through concentration and contemplation.

To acquire and develop Self-awareness man has to work hard for a long period, controlling his emotional, sensorial and physical activities. The more one develops Self-consciousness, the easier it becomes to know the distinction between the Self and the Supreme. Moreover, this awareness provides for a perfect control over all other states of consciousness.

> From the awareness of the distinction between *sattva* (essence) and *puruṣa* (Universal psychic principle or the centre of divine consciousness) alone, arise supremacy over all states and forms of existence (omnipotence) and knowledge of everything (omniscience).[7]

Understanding and experiencing the differences between these two states is the base for the highest evolution of a living being, and this highest evolution in man is referred to as Self-realisation (*ātma-jñāna*). It is the full development of one's own capabilities. The soul (*ātmā* or *jīva*) pervades the body through consciousness.[8] The Supreme Self, *Paramātmā* is only known through Self-realisation. In this state opening before him, man sees new visions appearing in his consciousness.

Self-realisation

According to Hindu thoughts, man is not a completely developed being. His development comes to an end, when he realises the Supreme. Nature develops him to a certain point and then leaves him either to develop further by his own efforts and devices or to

---

7. *Pātañjala Yoga-Sūtra*, III.49.
8. *Ātmā = āpnoti iti ātmā*, that which pervades the body. It is also called the life principle.

deteriorate and lose his capacity for development. Self-realisation stands for the highest development of an individual in both the psychological and the spiritual spheres. The soul is an entity considered as the spiritual and immortal part of a person. Self-realisation means the full development of the soul, in its own nature.

Ancient Hindu psychology is the study of the soul. It believes in the cycle of births and the immortality of the living soul.

> The living soul is the master (rider), his physical body is his chariot, intellect (*buddhi*) is the charioteer, mind is the rein with which the senses (horses) are controlled, the sense attributes (such as perception, hearing, touch, taste and smell) are the pathways and the soul is thus the experiencer and enjoyer, so say the wise people (seers).[9]

Hindu psychological doctrines study man not only under the aspect of what he seems to be, but also in view of his highest possible evolution. Divine power takes its stand in the progressive spiritual evolution; this power is hidden in everyone.

Śvetāśvatara Upaniṣad describes the path of devotion in the quest of the Supreme as

> Practising the method of meditation (referring to *bhakti*) they (seers) realised that being, who is the God of religion, the Self of philosophy and the energy of science; who exists as the self-luminous power in everyone, who is the source of the intellect, emotion and will, who is one without a second, who presides over all the causes enumerated above, beginning with time and ending with the individual soul, and who had been incomprehensible because of the limitations of their own intellect.[10]

---

9. *Kaṭha Upaniṣad*, I.3.3-4.

10. *Śvetāśvatara Upaniṣad*, I.1.3. According to Sāṁkhya philosophy the cause of the limitations of the intellect is due to *ādhyātmika*, *ādhibhautika* and *ādhidaivika*. See Chapter 8 on "Fruits of Devotion".

Without man's conscious efforts, it is not possible to remove the limitations of one's intellect. Until then, full progress in man's psychological and spiritual evolution is impossible. On the path of self-development and evolution, a person becomes transformed. This development is only possible under certain definite conditions with special efforts on the part of man himself and guidance from those, who have already acquired practical knowledge.

Not all would accept evolution in their life and accept a change of their profile, either because they do not aspire for it or because they are ignorant. Unless man makes a sincere attempt for his own improvement, he cannot be transformed. Man's development depends on his understanding of what he must give for what he may get. "The Self (*ātman*) is not attained through discourses, nor through intellectuality, nor through much learning. Only he, who longs for it with the whole heart, gains it. For to such a one the Self reveals its true nature."[11] *Kaṭha Upaniṣad* reiterates,

> This Self cannot be known through much study, nor through the intellect, nor through much hearing. It can be known through the Self alone that the aspirant prays to; this Self of that seeker reveals Its true nature.[12]

Therefore, man is said to achieve his complete evolution, only when he realises his Self. Self-realisation (*ātma-jñāna*) aims at the union of the individual with the Universal Reality. This is the highest development, which is an evolutionary process of self-effort. Help in the form of grace and guidance of a spiritual master is an essential part in this study. All people feel that all worldly enjoyments and secular achievements fail to provide that peace of mind, which one really wants. One does not really know where to find that peace of mind. When the gap between the individual consciousness and the universal consciousness is bridged through

---

11. *Muṇḍaka Upaniṣad*, 3.2.3.
12. *Kaṭha Upaniṣad*, I.2.23.

methods like contemplation or meditation, one attains the peace, which is necessary to know the Supreme.

Christ said, "Knock the door and the door of heaven in thy heart shall be opened into thee." Existing in his own condition man will never get a proper response if he knocks at the door of heaven. He should acquire new qualities and powers that are appropriate to the transcendental state.

Man's movements, actions, words, emotions, moods and ideas are all influenced by some power that is beyond his normal perception. Seers found that this power is the power of the Supreme (*devātma śakti*), who is working behind the curtain, making man think, write, read, love, hate, fight and so on. Man cannot do anything on his own accord, though due to ignorance, he believes so.

The strong desire to know this power of Self-realisation gave birth to a variety of approaches by different schools of philosophy. Each school proposes its own method to elevate man's consciousness. Patañjali says that man can only reach the higher states of consciousness (subjective as well as objective) with the help of contemplation, unless he has already acquired the elevated consciousness. All the higher states of consciousness are attributes of the soul. Generally, man cannot go beyond sleep consciousness and in sleep consciousness, he is overcome by ignorance. So, the scriptures advise to approach men of higher states of consciousness. "Arise, awake, and learn by approaching the excellent ones. The wise ones describe that path to be as impassable as a razor's edge, which, when sharpened, is difficult to tread on."[13]

Since the object to be known is very subtle, it is hard to attain. Therefore, the different methods occupy a very important place in human development. Among them *bhakti-mārga*, the path of devotion is easier and a definite means in the attainment of Self-realisation (*ātma-jñāna*). Lord Kṛṣṇa, giving assurance to Arjuna, says,

13. *Kaṭha Upaniṣad*, I.3.14.

"Completely renouncing all *dharmas*, seek Me alone as refuge."[14]

Just like in human love, in divine love too both God and the devotee are eager to rush into each other's arms. The two aspects of love are God's love for man known as divine grace and man's love for God called devotion.

Patañjali also advocates devotion and self-surrender to God for attaining Self-realisation: "From Special Devotion to Īśvara also, Concentration becomes Imminent."[15] This has enabled many a man to reach the highest evolution in a short time.

Maitreya Upaniṣad says that one can attain Self-realisation (*ātma-sākṣātkāra*) within six months. It is the intensity that counts. Patañjali says, "*Yogins* with vehement intensity get concentration and the result thereof quickly."[16] A great intensity of earnestness polarises all the mental faculties and powers and thus helps greatly in the realisation of one's aims.

Devotion to the Supreme Power called God is one of the most popular and easiest means of defining one's attitude and relationship to the universe, human life and the power that is beyond one's knowledge. It is a widespread superstition that the Supreme is desperately fond of appeasement and gratification. Nevertheless, there are teachers, who tell us that God needs nothing from us, except devotion.

Hindus consider God as a Supreme Being, whose mercy is limitless. There are quite a few, to whom devotion is an end in itself. Devotion is an offering of all that one has to the Supreme Power without the least expectation of any earthly reward. This type of devotion expecting no personal gain but union with Him[17] is as profoundly moving as rare. Devotion to get desires materialised[18] is as common as the lily in the countryside.

14. *Bhagavad-Gītā*, XVIII.66.
15. *Pātañjala Yoga-Sūtra*, I.23.
16. Ibid., I.21.
17. *Niṣkāmya bhakti.*
18. *Kāmya bhakti.*

Innumerable are devotees or saints (all over the world), who attained Self-realisation during their lifetime through their profound devotion to God. Those, who were keen on the path of Self-knowledge, sacrificed all material comforts, went in search of a spiritual master or retreated to the forest, discarding all their worldly ties, to realise the great Truth. They shared their precious experience by giving us the means to realise, saving us from the hardships they underwent. Their instructions and initiation infuse devotion in us and accelerate our Self-realisation. With the guidance of a sincere spiritual master, our mind is irresistibly pulled higher and higher towards the centre of all attraction by something like spiritual gravitation. This influence may not be consciously felt in the beginning. But a person subjected to it cannot help becoming a devotee of the Lord in the end.

Different methods of initiations are given in the scriptures, out of which four are prominent:

- Initiation by the touch of the spiritual teacher's hand on the disciple's crown of the head.[19] *Garbha Upaniṣad* says, while describing the chronological growth of the foetus, that the soul, *jīva* (as *jñāna-śakti*) enters the child through the fontanel (*śīrṣa*). As *jīva* comes from above and works through the body, the head is given importance in initiation. The *guru* transfers his cosmic energy through his opening to infuse *bhakti* in the disciple.
- Initiation by touch.[20] The spiritual teacher touches with his right index finger certain vital points[21] like the base of the throat, the middle of the eyebrows, the shoulders.

19. *Hasta dīkṣā*.
20. *Sparśa dīkṣā*.
21. Vital points are the channels of communication between the dense and the subtle body (*sthūla śarīra* and *sūkṣma śarīra*). Even though there are many vital points, some of them are spiritually important.

- Initiation by mere look.[22] The spiritual teacher gazes at the eye of the pupil.
- Initiation by mere thought or will on the part of the *guru*.[23]

In all these types of initiations, the spiritual *guru* transfers his own cosmic energy to the devotee. It is to be kept in mind that this psychological transfer of energy cannot be demonstrated outside. This is a subjective experience between the Spiritual Master (*guru*) and his disciple (*śiṣya*).

Śaṅkara defines *bhakti* as the exploration of one's innermost being and contemplation on its significance.[24] Viśiṣṭādvaita, on the other hand, guarantees God and liberation to all finite beings, human, sub-human and celestial. It asserts that God is the inner life and soul of all beings. The idea of God as the soul of the world underlines the presence of God in all beings and the spiritual intimacy. The spiritual knowledge of the soul, *jīva* as different from the embodied Self and its attraction towards God leads to the high esteem of the infinite Self.

The idea that God is immanent in all religious beliefs for the purpose of cosmic redemption inspires the feeling that the God of all religions is ultimately one, though seers and sects may define Him differently. "All this is verily *Brahman*." "The sun cannot illumine that integral *Brahman* (God) nor can the moon, nor the stars, nor even this lightning shed its lustre on it. How then can this physical fire light it? For, all these reflect the light of *Brahman* alone when it shines and it is by the light of *Brahman* that all this is illumined."[25] The eternal abode of God is:

> Where the sun shines not, where winds blow not, where the moon sheds not her lustre, where stars twinkle not, where fire

---

22. *Cakṣuṣa dīkṣā.*
23. *Saṁkalpa dīkṣā.*
24. *Svarūpānusandhāna.*
25. *Kaṭha Upaniṣad*, II.2.15.

burns not, where death finds no access, where sorrows enter not and reaching where the *yogīs* return not, which is the goal of the *yogīs* and is hailed by gods; that is the supreme state, ever delightful, supreme, blissful, tranquil, eternal and ever blessed.[26]

Thereafter man should diligently seek for that supreme state, having attained to which he returns no more to this world; having fully resolved that he stands dedicated to that Primeval Being himself, from whom the flow of this beginningless creation has progressed, he should will and meditate on Him.[27]

Yoga-Vāsiṣṭha[28] brings out clearly the signs of the dawn of Self-realisation:

> *For a person who has made investigation (into the nature of the Self),*
> *who has a mind the movements of which are disappearing,*
> *who is giving up thinking (or imagination),*
> *whose mind is transformed to a certain degree having known the truth,*
> *who is completely giving up visible objects that are fit to be abandoned,*
> *who has attained to what is fit to be acquired,*
> *who is perceiving the seer and not perceiving the visible object which is not the seer,*
> *who is wakeful while living in the Highest Truth to which he ought to be awake,*
> *who is asleep to the way of the world full of dense ignorance (or confusion),*
> *who is indifferent to objects of enjoyment, agreeable or insipid,*
> *which are pleasing (only) until their enjoyment, on account of*
> *very great aversion to the limit (towards fleeting pleasures),*
> *and who is without desire, when the net of worldly desires is*

---

26. *Bṛhajjābala Upaniṣad*, VIII.

27. *Bhagavad-Gītā*, XV.4.

28. *Yoga-Vāsiṣṭha*, III.7.1-6. The Vision and the Way of Vasiṣṭha, tr. Samvid.

snapped off like a bird-net by a rat,
when the knot (of ignorance) of the heart is loosened by the force of asceticism,
then, the inherent nature of the person clears up (or becomes serene and happy) through the power of Knowledge (or Wisdom),

as water clears up having got the kataka or clearing-nut (whose powder clears up muddy water).

10

Meditation Techniques in Hinduism

The devotee who is full of wisdom and performs all acts in complete submission is blessed by the vivid and glorious vision of God.
To him the wide horizon of the universe is filled with the blazing glow of God.
Such a meditating mind is the noblest of all.

— *Ṛgveda*, 1.95.8

MEDITATION results in a gradual transformation of the aspirant's consciousness and makes him increasingly aware of a higher Reality. It ultimately leads to the awakening of the Self. This may be followed by a vision of the living image of the deity the aspirant had been meditating upon, illumined by the "uncreated light of *ātman*".[1] With the awakening of the inner Self, the old narrow egocentric self is reduced to a shadow. This newly awakened inner Self burns up the *saṁskāra* and orientates the whole personality to a higher Reality. This is the immediate goal of meditation. When it is attained, ordinary meditation fulfils itself. This does not mean the end of spiritual attainment. On the contrary, true spiritual life begins only with a direct experience of one's real Self. Ordinary meditation only leads the soul up to the door of the individual soul (*jīvātman*), and stops there. Beyond that lies the boundless realm of the Supreme Soul (*Paramātman*).

Literally, *upāsanā* means "sitting near" that is, mentally approaching an ideal. In Vedānta, *upāsanā* is a kind of mental

1. *Pātañjala Yoga-Sūtra*, 1.29 and 2.44.

process relating to the qualified (*Saguṇa*) *Brahman* such as, for instance, the Śāṇḍilya-Vidyā. Śaṅkara defines *upāsanā* as "mentally approaching the form of the deity or the like, as it is presented by the eulogistic portions of the Vedas relating to the object of meditation, and concentration on it, excluding conventional notions, till one is as completely identified with it as with one's body, conventionally regarded as one's self."[2]

So according to Śaṅkara, the object of meditation can be anything sanctioned by the authoritative texts, but it should not be something imaginary (that is, not according to one's fancy). Accordingly, *upāsanā* is either *vidyā* or *brahma upāsanā* or *pratīka upāsanā*.

Upāsanā, Vidyā

BRAHMA UPĀSANĀ OR BRAHMA-VIDYĀ

These formulas are devices to guide the mind from the symbol to Reality. The *vidyās* represent the highest form of *upāsanā*. *Vidyās* are analogical meditations. Āditya-Vidyā is meant for the expansion of the Self.

VIDYĀ

Vidyā is a technique of "grasping" the whole of *Saguṇa Brahman* by identifying one's inner Self with it. It is usually called *ahamgraha upāsanā*. *Ahamgraha* means "self-grasping", that is, self-identification. It is an attempt of the Self to identify itself with the Supreme Self. Here consciousness is not focused on anything; instead, it is simply allowed to expand. In actual practice, this means that the Self identifies itself with larger and larger dimensions of Reality. Here "identification" does not mean a subject-object relationship. It is an attempt of the Self to identify itself with the Supreme Self. As the Supreme Self is all-pervading, this meditation necessarily involves an awareness of higher divine

2. Śaṅkara on *Bṛhadāraṇyaka Upaniṣad*, 1.3.9.

immanence in creation. *Ahamgraha upāsanā*, thus, takes the form of a double meditation: Meditation on the Self as a part of God and meditation of God as present in all beings.

Here meditations are in no way connected to rituals, not even symbolically. They directly deal with *Brahman*. But *Brahman* is a transcendent principle which cannot be known through the ordinary senses and mind. So the great sages of the Upaniṣads used various familiar objects like the sun, *ākāśa*, *prāṇa*, *manas*, etc. to represent *Brahman*. These were not mere objects to be meditated upon. They connected each symbol to a certain framework of meaning, a spiritual formula. These formulae are devices to guide the mind from the symbol to Reality. When a purified mind meditates on such a formula, its true meaning, the ultimate Reality, is revealed to it. These meditation-formulae are called *vidyā*s. The *vidyā*s are keys to Upaniṣads and they represent the highest form of *upāsanā*. Śāṇḍilya-Vidyā, Dahara-Vidyā, Madhu-Vidyā, Pañca Agni-Vidyā are some of them. There are 32 *vidyā*s.

*Vidyā*s are analogical meditations. Here attention is directed towards certain attributes or qualities of the ultimate Reality with the help of an analogy. The *Bṛhadāraṇyaka Upaniṣad*[3] speaks of Āditya-Vidyā: "Of this Person in the solar orb, *bhū* is the head . . . , *bhuva* is the arms . . . , *sva* is the feet . . ." Here the sun stands for *virāṭ*, the Person is Hiraṇyagarbha.[4] Āditya-Vidyā is meant for the expansion of the Self.

3. *Bṛhadāraṇyaka Upaniṣad*, 5.5.3.

4. Golden Egg.

32 Vidyās of the Upaniṣads

Table 2: List of 32 Vidyās described in the Upaniṣads

Name of Vidyā	*Objective of Vidyā*	*Upaniṣad*
Ākāśa-Vidyā	*Brahman* as the Cosmic Ether	*Chāndogya Upaniṣad* (I.ix.1)
Akṣara-Vidyā	*Brahman* as the Imperishable	*Bṛhadāraṇyaka Upaniṣad* (III.viii.8)
Akṣarapara-Vidyā	Meditation on the Imperishable	*Muṇḍaka Upaniṣad* (I)
Akṣī-Vidyā	*Brahman* as being present within the Eye	*Chāndogya Upaniṣad* (IV.xv.1)
Ānandamaya-Vidyā	*Brahman* as the Self-consisting of Bliss	*Taittirīya Upaniṣad* (Ānanda Vallī)
Aṅguṣṭhamātra-Vidyā	*Brahman* as resident within the Heart, of the size of the Thumb	*Kaṭha Upaniṣad* (II.iv.12)
Antarāditya-Vidyā	*Brahman* as the Inner Controller of the Sun	*Chāndogya Upaniṣad* (I.vi.6)
Antaryāmī-Vidyā	*Brahman* as the Inner Controller	*Bṛhadāraṇyaka Upaniṣad* (III.vii)
Bālākī-Vidyā	Meditation as taught to Bālākī	*Kauṣītaki Upaniṣad* (IV)
Bhūma-Vidyā	*Brahman* as the Great One	*Chāndogya Upaniṣad* (VII)
Dahara-Vidyā	*Brahman* as the Imperceptible ether within the Heart	*Chāndogya Upaniṣad* (VIII)
Gāyatrī-Vidyā	*Brahman* as the Holy *Gāyatrī-Mantra*	*Chāndogya Upaniṣad* (III.xii)
Īśāvāsya-Vidyā	Meditation as taught in the *Īśāvāsya Upaniṣad*	*Īśāvāsya Upaniṣad*
Jyotiṣam Jyotir-Vidyā	*Brahman* as the Light of Lights	*Bṛhadāraṇyaka Upaniṣad* (IV.iv.16)
Madhu-Vidyā	*Brahman* as Honey	*Chāndogya Upaniṣad* (III.i)
Maitreyī-Vidyā	Meditation as taught by Yājñavalkya to his wife Maitreyī	*Bṛhadāraṇyaka Upaniṣad* (II.iv)

Naciketā-Vidyā	Meditation with the Naciketā fire	*Kaṭha Upaniṣad* (I.ii)
Nyāsa-Vidyā	Self-surrender	*Taittirīya Upaniṣad* (49-52)
Pañca Agni-Vidyā	The meditation of the five fires	*Chāndogya Upaniṣad* (V.iii to x)
Paramapuruṣa-Vidyā	*Brahman* as the Supreme person	*Kaṭha Upaniṣad,* (I.iii)
Paramjyoti-Vidyā	*Brahman* as the Supreme Splendour	*Chāndogya Upaniṣad* (III.xiii.7)
Paryaṅka-Vidyā	*Brahman* as the highest God seated in the Supreme Abode	*Kauṣītaki Upaniṣad* (I)
Prāṇa-Vidyā	*Brahman* as the Vital Breath	*Chāndogya Upaniṣad* (I.xi.5)
Pratardana-Vidyā	Meditation as taught to Pratardana by the God Indra	*Kauṣītaki Upaniṣad* (III)
Sad-Vidyā	*Brahman* as the ground of all being	*Chāndogya Upaniṣad* (VI)
Samvarga-Vidyā	*Brahman* as the All-Absorbing Being	*Chāndogya Upaniṣad* (IV.iii)
Śāṇḍilya-Vidyā	Meditation as taught by Śāṇḍilya	*Chāndogya Upaniṣad* (III.xiv.7)
Sarvāntarātma-Vidyā	*Brahman* as the Inner Self of All	*Bṛhadāraṇyaka Upaniṣad* (III.iv)
Satyakāma-Vidyā	Meditation as taught to Satyakāma	*Chāndogya Upaniṣad* (IV.iv)
Upakosala-Vidyā	Meditation as taught to Upakosala	*Chāndogya Upaniṣad* (IV.x)
Vāruṇi-Vidyā	Meditation as taught by the God Varuṇa	*Taittirīya Upaniṣad* (Bhṛgu Vallī)
Vaiśvānara-Vidyā	*Brahman* as the Universal Being	*Chāndogya Upaniṣad* (V.xi)

Ritual-bound Upāsanā (Aṅgava-Baddha)

This type of meditation evolved quite independent of sacrifices. There are two types: *sampad upāsanā* and *adhyāsa upāsanā*. *Sampad upāsanā* is a kind of *guṇa dhyāna*. But in *adhyāsa upāsanā,* the symbol chosen is itself a superior object and dominates the meditative field. Śaṅkara comments that *Brahman* is superimposed on the mind, on the sun, etc.[5]

In the Vedas, *upāsanā* first appears as a part of rituals in the Brāhmaṇa. The emphasis was on sacrificial rites (*yajña*). The sacrifice was regarded as most important and self-sufficient to produce the desired results. The meditation that was practised along with it was only an auxiliary part of it and had no independent existence. These meditations were supported neither by any *iṣṭa devatā* nor by any specific *mantra*. The purpose was to gain some additional merit and their omission in no way affected the sacrifice. They could just heighten the results of the rituals.

Svatantra

This type of meditation evolved quite independent of sacrifices. There are two types: *sampad upāsanā* and *adhyāsa upāsanā*.

When a symbol of a lower order is taken up and, by virtue of similarity, the qualities of a higher Reality are superimposed on it, it is meditation based on similarity (*sampad upāsanā*), through which the practitioner of meditation reflects not on the lower order of things, but on the higher ones, which the lower order things symbolise. In fact, the lower things are here raised through similarity to their higher correlates; here they find their fulfilment. The symbol is unimportant; the attributes of the higher Reality dominate the meditative field. For example, when a stone idol, a *śāligrāma* is worshipped as Viṣṇu, the worshipper forgets the stone and thinks only of the luminous splendour of Viṣṇu. "The mind is indeed infinite, and infinite are the Viśvadeva. So mind is the Viśvadeva."[6] *Sampad upāsanā* is a kind of *guṇa dhyāna*.

Upon this symbol, the attributes of the Reality are superimposed, but the symbol is as important as the attributes.[7]

5. Śaṅkara on *Brahma-Sūtra*, 1.1.4.
6. Ratnaprabha on *Bṛhadāraṇyaka Upaniṣad*, 3.16.
7. Ratnaprabha on Śaṅkara's *Brahma-Sūtra-Bhāṣya*, 1.1.4.

"The mind is to be meditated on as *Brahman*", "The sun is *Brahman*".[8] All that one has to do is to superimpose upon the sun the attributes of *Brahman*,[9] like infinity, consciousness, bliss, ultimate causality, etc.

Pratīka Upāsanā

Pratīka means a symbol (= going towards) upon which the mind is focused. *Pratīka* are of two types: *nāma* and *rūpa*. In it, a single thought current is directed towards a definite object which is invariably regarded as a symbol (*pratīka*) of *Brahman*. Since these symbols serve as frames of reference in understanding *Brahman*, they are also called *taṭastha upāsanā*.

Though *pratīka* are mainly used as aids to concentration, the purpose of this *upāsanā* is not mere concentration of mind, but the direct vision of the deity represented by the *pratīka*. It is a search for the soul's eternal Beloved. For this, a living image must first of all be implanted deep inside the heart. It is the continuous interior gazing at this living image in the depths of consciousness that really deserves to be called *pratīka upāsanā*. It is a process of converting imagination into reality. It is a technique for the transformation of consciousness.

Meditation on *OṀ* is one of the examples of this type of meditation. This meditation has given way to the images of gods and goddesses.

Post-Vedic *pratīka upāsanā* comes under two heads: *aṅgavabaddha* and *svatantra*. Apart from these, a third type of meditation developed called *guṇa dhyāna*, meditation on the divine qualities of the chosen deity, *iṣṭa devatā*.

This is mainly based on Vaiṣṇava, Śaiva and Śākta Āgamas. The Tantra made independent discoveries about *mantra*, *kuṇḍalinī*, etc. The harmony and synthesis effected by the Tantras opened a

8. *Chāndogya Upaniṣad*, 3.18.1.

9. Ibid., 3.19.1.

new era in the history of spirituality in India. The meditation techniques now prevalent show the strong influence of the Tantra.

One of the important changes that the Tantras introduced was in the field of symbols. The images of different gods and goddesses have completely replaced the Vedic images of fire, sun, air, etc. In the Vedic period, the approach to the ultimate Reality was direct. The Tantra made it indirect: the aspirant attains the vision of a God or Goddess and then through him or her realises the ultimate Reality. Symbols play an important part in human life. The Tantras have stressed them and regarding words they have shown that certain mystic words have an intrinsic power to produce changes in consciousness. The symbols can be divided into two groups: *rūpa* (form) and *nāma* (name). With these two groups came out two types of *upāsanā*: meditation on visual images, *pratīka upāsanā* and meditation on sound symbols, *nāma upāsanā*. They are based on the concept of chosen deity (*iṣṭa devatā*) and mystic syllables called *mantra*. Apart from these, a third type of meditation developed called *guṇa dhyāna*, meditation on the divine qualities of the chosen deity.

Subjective Meditation Techniques

In subjective meditation, the consciousness is focused back upon its own source, namely the Self. The process of enquiry into the nature of the Self (*ātma-vicāra*), meditation on *asmitā* (as in Patañjali), the *pratibodha* technique of *Kena Upaniṣad* are some of the examples.

Nididhyāsana, according to Śaṅkara, is determined meditation. *Pratibodha* is the constant Self-awareness.

Ātma-vicāra is an attempt to turn away from all objects and move backwards into the Self. In this technique the negation process of not this, not this (*neti, neti*) finds its most practical application. The Upaniṣadic sages first developed reflection, *vicāra* as a technique, Yājñavalkya being the most authoritative.[10] Enquiry

10. "How to know the knower?" Gārgī's question to Yājñavalkya. *Bṛhadāraṇyaka Upaniṣad*, 2.4.14.

into the nature of the Self, *ātma-vicāra,* contains three elements: *śravaṇa, manana,* and *nididhyāsana.*

Śravaṇa is usually translated as "hearing". It gives rise to the absolute knowledge of the Self for the aspirant who has got the right qualifications.

Manana is the application of the knowledge of scriptures in one's own life. *Manana* is always done on the basis of *śravaṇa.*[11]

Nididhyāsana, according to Śaṅkara, is determined meditation. According to Sureśvara Ācārya, it is the culmination of the process of the first two. Śaṅkara asserts that when these three are combined, only then is accomplished the true realisation of the unity of *Brahman,* not otherwise — not by hearing alone.[12]

Pratibodha is the constant Self-awareness. The *Kena Upaniṣad* says, "The Self is known when it is grasped as the witness of each state of consciousness."[13] This means that behind every thought and action there stands the silent, witnessing Self. By constantly holding on to this inner Witness, we can remain fully conscious and alert in the midst of all our activities.

Meditation in the Purāṇas

According to *Vāyu Purāṇa, dhyāna* is "unobstructed illumination". In *Kūrma Purāṇa,* Devī Durgā says, "I am attainable through meditation, *karma, yoga, bhakti* and *jñāna.* Millions of other types of work will not suffice." The *Viṣṇu Purāṇa* (4.4.27) defines *dhyāna* as "uninterrupted succession of perceiving consciousness, single-in-intent with regard to that object without desire for anything else." According to *Śiva Purāṇa* (29.52), the root *dhai* means to think and *dhyāna* means constant concentrated reflection on Śiva (*iṣṭa devatā*).

11. It is the logical process of *anvaya vyatireka,* by which one gains an indirect knowledge of one's own true nature as *Brahman* — Sureśvara's commentary on *Bṛhadāraṇyaka Upaniṣad.*
12. Śaṅkara on *Bṛhadāraṇyaka Upaniṣad,* 2.4.5.
13. *Kena Upaniṣad,* 2.4.

Śrīmad Bhāgavata provides a supreme, sublime Person as the object of meditation. Concentration is the essence of meditation. It is well known that the mind gets easily concentrated on matters of its liking. Objects of the senses are charming and the mind naturally flows towards them. The *Śrīmad Bhāgavata* provides innumerable forms of God for meditation, all sublime and enchanting. It becomes a spontaneous, smooth and incessant meditation. Ordinarily meditation is the despair of aspirants, for the mind does not relish any sort of restraint. But if the emotion is sweetened with devotion, meditation becomes sweet and spontaneous. When meditation is cultured in the emotion of love, it is easy, sweet and lovely. The Lord himself furnishes to Uddhava with the technique of meditation:[14] Śrī Kṛṣṇa tells Uddhava, "Do thou restrain by all means thy fickle mind, my son, by thy superior intelligence set steady on Me. This is the sum and substance of all *yoga*."[15] The *Śrīmad Bhāgavata* endows *Brahman* with the power of *māyā* to enable the mind to apprehend It. When *sat-cit-ānanda* is invested with a name and a form, the mind can grasp. Nārada instructs Vyāsa to sing the glories of the incarnations of God.

The *Śrīmad Bhāgavata* provides innumerable forms of God for meditation, all sublime and enchanting. It also allows free play to all human emotions. Emotions which are considered to be obstacles in spiritual life are to be shunned outright according to *jñāna-yoga*. Find an important place in *bhakti* to convert the whole of our life into a means for spiritual quest. The *Śrīmad Bhāgavata* approves of establishing any kind of emotional relation with divinity: paternal or maternal, fraternal or filial, erotic or esoteric all these relations to the Divine are adopted. Even an antagonistic way is recognised. All the demons of the *Śrīmad Bhāgavata* are deeply devoted to God.

The advantage in adopting an emotional and personal relation to God is that the mind dwells on Him constantly without

14. *Śrīmad Bhāgavata*, 11.14.37-41.

15. Ibid., 11.23.60.

cessation. It becomes a spontaneous, smooth and incessant meditation. The devotee dwells ever in the presence of God.

The normal haunts of the mind are the world of the senses. If something better and sweeter is given to it, it will take to it. Śrī Kṛṣṇa points this out to Uddhava: "The mind that dwells on sense objects gets stuck in them. The mind that remembers Me constantly, gets dissolved in Me."[16]

The Lord himself furnishes to Uddhava with the technique of meditation:[17]

> *One should meditate on this as inverted with the flower upwards and opened, and in the pericarp should think of the sun, moon, and fire, one within the other. In the fire, again, one should reflect on the following form of Mine which is good for Meditation;*
>
> *Symmetrical, serene, of a benign face, with four long and beautiful arms, with a well-formed and beautiful neck, beautiful cheeks, and graceful smile;*
>
> *With shining alligator-shaped pendants in the well-matched ears, with a golden cloth, dark-complexioned like a cloud, and with the peculiar marks known as śrīvatsa and Lakṣmī on the chest.*
>
> *Adorned with conch, disc, mace, lotus, and a garland of wild flowers, with the feet adorned with ringing anklets, and the chest resplendent with the gem kaustubha.*
>
> *Decked with a shining crown, bracelets, and a waistband, beautiful in every feature, appealing, with the face and eyes beaming with graciousness, and exquisitely tender.*

One should meditate on this form, concentrating the mind on all the features.

Meditation in Vaiṣṇavism

Meditation in Vaiṣṇavism is not different from *dhyāna* or *upāsanā*. The means of attaining God is worship with devotion. This *bhakti*

16. *Śrīmad Bhāgavata*, 11.14.27.
17. Ibid., 11.14.37-41.

is meditation or reverent concentration.[18] *Dhyāna* is not mere recollection, but continued recollection and concentration of the mind on a single object, a continuous process of mental concentration on the nature and form of *Brahman*. Vaiṣṇava *yoga* is the meditation on Lord Viṣṇu.

Among the authoritative opinions of Vaiṣṇava teachers, Rāmānuja's view is of special interest. According to him, Spiritual Experience (*vedanā*) is not a single act but a process which is to be repeated. It is not different from *dhyāna* or *upāsanā*. The means of attaining God is worship with *bhakti*. This *bhakti* is meditation or reverent concentration.[19] *Bhakti* is produced by representation (*dhyāna* being equivalent to memory, *smṛti*). The real value of the practice of ceaseless *dhyāna* lies in the recognition of the shortcomings of human endeavour and the reliance on divine grace as the only means to liberation, *mukti*. *Dhyāna* is a direct and immediate, distinct and precise vision which can be vastly extended by daily practice.[20] *Dhyāna* is not mere recollection, but continued recollection and concentration of the mind on a single object, a continuous process of mental concentration on the nature and form of *Brahman*. Rāmānuja emphasises that those places in the scriptures, which speak of seeing or knowing the Self,[21] teach that meditation is of the nature of "vision".[22]

Meditation in Śaivism

In Śaivism, *dhyāna* is a constant flow of an intellectual state (*buddhi*) towards the form of Śiva. So constant reflection on Śiva is *dhyāna*.[23] Śaivism holds *dhyāna* to be an unparalleled means of coming into contact with the Highest. There is nothing greater than that, and

18. In *Śvetāśvatara Upaniṣad*, 3.8, it is called Knowledge.
19. Ibid.
20. *Śrī Bhāṣya* of Rāmānuja, 4.26.
21. *Bṛhadāraṇyaka Upaniṣad*, 2.4.5; *Muṇḍaka Upaniṣad*, 2.2.8.
22. *Śrī Bhāṣya*, 1.1.29.
23. *Śiva Purāṇa*, 29.52.

those who apply themselves to *dhyāna* are dear to Śiva, not those who only perform rites. Here *dhyāna* is a constant flow of an intellectual state (*buddhi*) towards the form of Śiva. Meditation consists in picturing mentally before one's eyes the representation of the deity. According to *Śiva Purāṇa*, the root *dhyai* means to think. So constant reflection on Śiva is *dhyāna*.[24]

Meditation in Tantra, Tantra Dhyāna

A process of transmutation of the human soul into a divine soul is an integral part of all Tāntric meditation techniques. The identity of the divine inner Self of the worshipper with the Deity worshipped is another characteristic principle of Tantra *dhyāna*.

A special feature of the Tantra tradition is that only the man whose personality has been "deified" can succeed in his attempt to worship the Supreme Divinity.

Worship of God as the Divine Mother of the universe, Śakti is a distinct feature of Tantra *dhyāna*. The Mother is worshipped in various forms and names. Meditation is performed to invoke the particular deity in the image and also during the worship of the deity.

The *Mahānirvāṇa Tantra* says, "Through meditation is attained everything, through it, the *sādhaka* (the practitioner) identifies himself with Viṣṇu. The goal is reached by meditation; without its perfection in practice, *sādhanā* is an impossibility."[25] The *Kulārṇava Tantra* defines meditation as the process of thinking of one's chosen deity, *iṣṭa devatā* in the heart after having controlled all the activities of the senses.

Two types of meditation are found in the Tantras. Gross meditation is with form (*sarūpa*) while the subtle is without any form (*arūpa*). God with form is meditated upon in *sarūpa dhyāna*. *Arūpa dhyāna* is beyond the comprehension of mind and speech.

---

24. *Śiva Purāṇa*. 29.52.
25. *Mahānirvāṇa Tantra*, 5.137-39.

The Tantra classifies meditation in another way too: Gross, Effulgent and Subtle. Here the object of meditation is image, light, and *bindu*. According to *Mahānirvāṇa Tantra*, for grasping an idea, for attaining quick result, and to raise the power needed for meditation on subtle objects, meditation on a gross object is described.

11

Practical Exercises in Contemplation and Meditation

They who worship the Imperishable, Indescribable, Unmanifest, All-pervading, Inconceivable, Changeless, Immovable and Eternal, controlling well their senses, even-minded everywhere and devoted to the good of all beings (also) attain Me alone.

— *Bhagavad-Gītā* XII.3-4

Sages who are free from passion and anger, who have controlled their mind, and who have realised the Self, attain absorption in *Brahman* here and hereafter. — *Bhagavad-Gītā*, V.26

ŚRĪ KṚṢṆA warns the devotees, who do not believe or do not wish to follow the traditional devotional path (*bhakti-mārga*), but who choose the path of knowledge (*jñāna-mārga*) of the difficulties in following this path. "The trouble of those whose minds are attached to the Unmanifest is greater; for the way of the Unmanifest is attained with difficulty by the embodied soul."[1]

Yet, he appreciates and praises their approach:

Of these (followers of different paths of liberation), the man of knowledge who is constantly in communion and single-minded in his meditation excels. To the man of knowledge I am very dear indeed, and he is dear to Me.[2]

1. *Bhagavad-Gītā*, XII.5.
2. Ibid., VII.17.

> Even if you are the worst sinner amongst all sinners, (yet) you will cross all sin by the boat of knowledge alone.[3]

In the path of devotion (*bhakti*) the devotee can take refuge in the various practices of the cult, in Āgama rituals, or in different practices that the spiritual teachers like Rāmānuja, Madhva or Vallabha and even Śaṅkara have prescribed. On the other hand, the follower of the path of knowledge even if teachers like Śaṅkara or Buddha have given many indications has to rely on himself, because he cannot take refuge in rituals, in the practices of the cult nor in any scriptures. His only support and ultimate refuge would be the teachings of the great masters.

While taking refuge in God (*śaraṇāgati* or *prapatti*), having conviction in the true values of scriptural teachings of *bhakti*, the devotee gets freed from many obstacles like the fear of death, the attachment to the I-ness, the love for the body and so on, which is difficult for an aspirant of the path of knowledge. Such an aspirant will have to educate himself with repeated contemplation to overcome these and other obstacles.

Moreover, while devotees of the path of devotion (*bhakti-yoga*) have a set of pre-defined objects for their meditation which are inseparably linked to God, the objects of meditation of the path of knowledge (*jñāna-yoga*) are mainly based on virtues — the values they might consider as virtues from their point of view while they might not be so universally. A devotee will not be tempted to change the objects, whereas an aspirant of the path of knowledge will feel frequently tempted to shift his meditation from one object to another getting lost in a series of dispersions. In addition, an aspirant of the path of knowledge has to be continuously vigilant to avoid falling in the wrong way or getting caught in a dangerous trap.

Very often, the aspirant of the path of knowledge believes himself being his own master, a problem that would never arise

3. *Bhagavad-Gītā*, IV.36

in a devotee of the path of devotion, because he is already a servant of God.

Meditation is a method of acquainting man's mind with virtue. The more familiar man's mind is with virtue, the calmer and more peaceful it becomes. When the mind is peaceful man is free from worries and mental discomfort, and he experiences true happiness. If he trains his mind to become peaceful, he will be happy all the time even in the most adverse conditions; but if his mind is not peaceful, he will not be happy even if he has the most pleasant external conditions. That is why man should train his mind through meditation.

Man should first contemplate on the meaning of the virtuous instructions he has heard or read. By contemplating deeply on these teachings he will reach a conclusion and create a virtuous state of mind.

> He should then concentrate single-pointedly on a virtuous object for as long as possible to become deeply acquainted with it.

This is also called meditation (*dhyāna*).

In general, man can choose any virtuous object for meditation. If he discovers that by acquainting his mind with a particular object, his mind becomes more peaceful and virtuous, this object would be virtuous for him. Naturally, if the opposite happens, then it is not a virtuous object. A spiritual teacher can also indicate some virtuous objects for meditation.

> Man should first meditate on his precious human life to realise that he has a special opportunity to practise devotion. If he appreciates the great potential of this life, he will not waste it by engaging in meaningless activities.
>
> He also ought to meditate on death and impermanence to overcome procrastination. By meditating on a lower rebirth, taking refuge in the Supreme, avoiding non-virtue and practising virtue he will protect himself from downfalls and ensures an uplift conducive to devotional practices.

Man usually devotes much of his time and energy to mundane activities, such as seeking material and emotional security, enjoying the pleasures of the senses, or establishing a good reputation. Even if these activities make man happy, they are not everlasting and will lead to dissatisfaction in the end. Worldly pleasures incline to cause both physical and mental suffering by stimulating attachment, jealousy and frustration.

Happiness is a state of mind; therefore, the real source of happiness lies in the mind and not in external circumstances. If man's mind is pure and peaceful, he will be happy, regardless of external conditions, but if it is impure and without peace, he will never find happiness, whatever the external conditions might be.

The purpose of meditation and devotional practices is to cultivate those states of mind that are conducive to peace and well-being. Only man can seize this opportunity, because unlike animals he does not only have the capacity to enjoy food and sex, find homes, hoard wealth, subdue his enemies and protect his family, but also the capacity to eliminate suffering and attain lasting happiness. It would be a great loss to man if he was to use his precious human life to achieve merely what animals can achieve. He should therefore fulfil the real purpose of being born as a human and devote himself to devotional practices.

Every action man performs leaves an imprint on his very subtle mind; and each imprint eventually gives rise to its own effect. Man's mind is like a field, and performing actions is like sowing seeds in that field. Virtuous actions sow seeds of future happiness and non-virtuous actions sow seeds of future suffering. The seeds man has sown in the past remain dormant until the conditions needed for their germination set in. The seeds that ripen when man dies are very important, as they determine the kind of rebirth he will take. Which particular seed ripens at death depends upon the state of mind in which man dies. If he dies with a peaceful mind, this will stimulate a virtuous seed and he will experience a fortunate birth; but if he dies with an uneasy mind, this will stimulate a non-virtuous rebirth. This is comparable to the way in which nightmares are touched off: the mind has been in an agitated state just before falling asleep.

Five Steps to Meditation

A devotional practice consists of five parts: preparation, contemplation, meditation, dedication and practice.

PREPARATORY PRACTICES

Preparatory practices purify man's mind from hindrances caused by his previous negative actions so that meditation is successful, empower his mind to merits, and inspire it with the blessings of spiritual teachers.

> These practices correspond to the prayers to God and the spiritual teachers in devotional practices, when the devotee believes in God, and should be performed at the beginning of each meditation session.
>
> If the devotee feels that his meditation is not progressing, he should repeatedly follow these preparatory practices till he feels his mind purified of negative actions.

CONTEMPLATION

The purpose of contemplation is to establish the object of meditation in the mind; this is done by reasoning and reflecting on the instructions of the scriptures.

> The devotee should supplement and enrich the instructions through further study of scriptures or by following the instructions of spiritual masters.
>
> At the end of the contemplation, the devotee should invoke or concentrate on a virtuous object, which helps in developing and maintaining a peaceful mental state, immediately and in future, and examine whether it sets up clearly in his mind without the presence of non-virtuous values.

This enables the devotee to attain the third stage of practice.

MEDITATION

> At the beginning of meditation, the devotee might be distracted; he might lose the object of meditation. He should then revert to the contemplation practices and practise them repeatedly. He should be aware of the fact that getting down the ladder is not a loss of spiritual practice but only a concrete establishment of his meditation. Every time the mind swerves to non-meditative objects, he should go back to contemplation and try his meditation again. The devotee should choose different virtuous objects, without losing the intrinsic value of the previous virtuous object, as he will be forced to recall to mind the previous objects used in meditation.

The more familiar the devotee is with such virtuous objects, the more peaceful his mind becomes, and eventually he will be able to maintain a peaceful mind continuously.

DEDICATION

> Dedicating the benefits of meditation to humanity in general, free from bias, is a very important step in this type of meditation.

It is a stepping-stone to the attainment of the highest spiritual transcendence. Dedicating the benefits of meditation is more efficacious than material gifts. Moreover, it makes man learn to be compassionate towards others. Man should dedicate the benefits of his meditation not only to his kith and kin but also to those who do not have the chance of performing meditation, whatever the reason behind their absence from meditation may be.

PRACTICE

Practice is the application of meditative principles in daily life. It is important to remember that the spiritual practice is not confined to man's activities during his meditative sessions. It should permeate his daily life. His meditation is crowned with success when he is able to reduce the gulf between the state of mind obtained from meditation and the state of mind in his daily life.

> Man should keep a watch on his mind at all times by applying mindfulness, alertness and conscientiousness; he should make an effort to avoid and abandon the non-virtuous habits he may have.

The devotee should not be impatient, as the deep experience of this type of meditation is the result of a practical training over a long period of time, both, in and out of meditation.

Preparatory practices are like the preparing of the field by removing the obstacles caused by past negative actions, making it fertile with merit and watering it with the blessings of spiritual masters. Contemplation and meditation are like sowing good seeds, while dedication and the subsequent practice are the methods for ripening the harvest of Realisation.

Preparatory Practices

The three essential preparations for successful meditation are purifying negative tendencies, accumulating merits and receiving blessings.

1. Before sitting down for meditation, it is necessary to make sure that the place is clean. Since the devotee invites the spiritual masters to bless him, it is important that the place is conducive to receive them. Moreover, a clean place protects the devotee's mind from negative thoughts. It is advisable to have an image of a spiritual master and of his chosen deity, keeping in front of him some offerings like flowers and fruits or even a bowl of water. As far as possible, the devotee should sit cross-legged or kneel down; sitting on the heels, failing which he should sit on a chair. In any case, he should take care that he does not show his feet to the spiritual master. It is most important to have a straight back and to keep the mind alert. His

hands are to be placed on the knees with the palms turned upward.

2. Thus established, the devotee should do some deep breaths keeping himself away from the physical sensation of his breathing and imagining that he receives the blessings of the holy beings during inhalation and that he expels all his negative and distracting thoughts during exhalation. This can be done following the technique of *prāṇāyāma*.[4]

3. After these breaths, the devotee should cultivate strong faith in the spiritual values of the scriptures and the conviction that his meditation will save him from the cycle of rebirths.

4. Now the devotee should develop love, compassion, joy and equanimity: Wishing happiness to all beings, human, animal, divine, known, unknown, liked or disliked; wishing all beings to be free from suffering; wishing all beings to attain liberation and promising an even attitude towards all beings.

5. The devotee should invoke his ancestors, visualise holy beings or liberated souls, invite them in his meditation place, make prostrations, offer flowers and fruits and seek their presence and blessings.

6. Now that the devotee is purified in mind and that he

---

4. The general technique of *prāṇāyāma* is: Facing east, sit cross-legged with an erect back. Fold the index and the middle finger of the right hand. Bend the right arm to bring the right hand in front of the nose. Then close the right nostril with the thumb and inhale through the left nostril. At the end of the inhalation, hold the breath for 5 or 10 seconds according to your capacity. Close the left nostril with the ring and the little finger. Open the right nostril and exhale through the right nostril. Keeping the left nostril closed inhale through the right nostril. Again, hold the breath for 5 or 10 seconds according to your capacity. Then close the right nostril, open the left nostril and exhale through the left nostril. This forms one cycle.

accumulated the merit of positive actions and received blessings, he is ready to begin his contemplation and meditation. If his mind becomes dull or meets mental obstacles during the course of meditation, he should interrupt and say prayers to the holy beings by invoking them again and keeping their image in his mind as long as the obstacles do not vanish, before resuming the contemplation and meditation.

7. At the end of the meditation, the devotee should dedicate the benefits of his meditation to all beings: human, divine and animal.
8. Finally, before leaving the place of meditation the devotee should stay in silence for a few minutes.

Contemplation

CONFIDENCE IN A SPIRITUAL TEACHER

Relying on a qualified Spiritual Teacher is the foundation of all spiritual attainments, whether one believes in God or not, whether one adheres to a religion or not. A spiritual master is like man's parents or school teachers who taught him to sit and walk, to eat and talk, to read and write and so on. Just as he obtained many benefits from his parents and teachers, whom he might have forgotten, so too, through the guidance of a spiritual master he will obtain many benefits that will help him climb the path of realisation and liberation.

The devotee should constantly think that his spiritual guide would lead him along the spiritual path, which alone gives significance to the devotee's life. Moreover, contemplating on the spiritual master will assure the devotee of a better birth in his future lives.

> A devotee should contemplate on the various benefits he will get until he firmly relies on the Spiritual Master with strong faith.

PRECIOUS HUMAN LIFE

Human life is very precious, because it provides the special opportunity to obtain liberation. According to the theory of *karma*, countless living beings take rebirth as animals, hungry ghosts and demonic beings. Unfortunately, none of them has the opportunity to keep to spiritual practices. Even amongst men millions live in countries where spiritual practices are not tolerated, many are physically or mentally disabled, others are caught up in extreme misery, natural or war disasters. A devotee should think and realise that he has the blessed opportunity to follow spiritual practices and even obtain liberation which many others might never obtain.

> Contemplating on this uniqueness, the devotee generates a feeling of deep appreciation for his fortunate life; he should meditate on this feeling single-mindedly.

He thus develops contentment and compassion. By repeated meditations, he will discard laziness or despair and will stop wasting time on negative thoughts.

DEATH CONSCIOUSNESS

"For one who is born, death is certain, and to one who dies, rebirth is certain."[5]

This human life only becomes significant when it is appropriately used to attain its goal: Liberation from rebirth and freedom from the entanglement of births and deaths (*saṁsāra*). But man is so much attached to worldly activities that he does not have a strong wish to practise spiritual disciplines which is a major obstacle by itself. The only way to overcome this obstacle is to contemplate on death.

Even though man knows that his life is not permanent, that death is at his doorstep, he continues to live as if death did not

5. *Bhagavad-Gītā*, II.27.

exist. He creates an artificial wall by getting more and more attached to worldly activities. Yet, there is no way to prevent his body from decaying and his life from slipping away. He does not have the faintest idea when he will die; the time of death is unknown. Death will stop at nothing, neither at health nor at richness or poverty. Some die young, some die old, some die in accidents, others die in war or calamities and so on. No one has escaped death, even if modern sciences try to prolong life.

> A devotee should repeatedly reflect and contemplate on his death: he may die today, tomorrow is not certain.

Since he will have to depart one day or the other, there is no sense in his becoming attached to worldly enjoyments. Instead, he should devote his life to spiritual practices so that he will not die without accomplishing the goal for which he was born a human being.

> During this contemplation, the devotee should be watchful in not getting attracted towards the images of this worldly life.
> If they appear, he should invoke his Spiritual Master and then contemplate on the impermanence of life.

THE RISK OF A DOWNGRADED LIFE

If the *karma* that matures is negative when man dies, he will be reborn in one of the lower realms. By meditating on this danger, he will avoid accumulating negative *karma*. Man has no influence on his existence here and no choice about where to go, because he is blown to the place of his next birth by the winds of *karma*. Only if the *karma* that ripens is virtuous, he will either be liberated or be born in a higher realm where he can evolve in the path of liberation.

Whereas it is very easy to commit non-virtuous actions, great care and attention is needed to do virtuous actions. The aspirant should frequently ask himself the question "Where would I be born in the next life, if I died now?"

By contemplating on the sufferings and the disadvantages of lower realms, he will realise the necessity to act now in such a way to obtain either liberation or a better life to avail himself of the opportunities of that life for liberation.

KARMA AND ITS EFFECTS

The devotee should learn to observe the laws of *karma* by reducing and finally abandoning all non-virtuous actions and practising only virtuous actions. This will not only protect him from rebirth in lower realms but will also constitute the basis for liberation.

All suffering man experiences in this life such as sickness, poverty, conflict, accidents, etc. is the result of his own past *karma*. Conversely, his precious human life, all the comforts and happiness that he experiences is due to the virtuous *karma* of previous lives.

This mutual relationship between actions and their effects is one of the teachings of the Veda and taught by all spiritual teachers from the Vedic times to date.

By contemplating on this law, man develops conviction in the truth of *karma*, abandons non-virtuous actions and increases his virtuous actions.

As a subsequent practice, man should avoid even small negative actions immediately after his meditation sessions. The best way to avoid any non-virtuous actions to bounce is performing deliberately virtuous actions.

DEVELOPING RENUNCIATION

Man is imprisoned in the chain of birth and death (*saṁsāra*). The more he is attached to the enjoyments of the worldly life, the stronger his chain of birth and death will be. As long as he is attached to this chain, he will not succeed in his goal of liberation — he has to get detached from this chain. One of the ways to become unchained is renunciation from the enjoyments of the worldly life.

Since the root cause of *saṁsāra* is attachment to the worldly life, the devotee should reflect on the faults of the worldly life and the consequences of birth.

> He should contemplate on the acceptance of unavoidable situations of life — birth, ageing, sickness and death — and reflect on the possibility of committing non-virtuous actions done out of jealousy and envy, because those who are younger than us enjoy more than we do.

Even though man is already born, he will find every means to find fault in his parents for not having obtained a better life. He will even hold them responsible for his sicknesses and sufferings. If he has brothers and sisters, he will constantly compare what he has obtained as enjoyment with what they obtained from his parents. As he grows old, his youthful vitality diminishes, his senses become weaker and he does not obtain the same enjoyment from the things he used to enjoy, such as food, drink and sex. He is tired to play games, memory fails him and he is weak and incapable of worldly activities. His intellect has lost sharpness, and he is slow in understanding. He feels useless to the family and to society. He is often neglected by his own children and his fear of death increases every time he hears about the death of his friends or contemporaries. Loneliness deepens in his life worsening his misery.

Practising spiritual disciplines from youth or when the opportunity arose, he would have avoided these consequences, even if he were aged. He would have gradually given more time and energy to spiritual practices, he would have less fear of death and above all he would have minimised his attachment to worldly life.

It is almost impossible to be free from sickness, since the causes are many: man's way of living, his food, his activities, his environment and so on. Very often, abusing his sense activities, becoming a slave to sex experiences, he contracts long-lasting diseases. Even if he is relieved from incurable degenerative diseases, he is not completely eased as deterioration establishes slowly but surely. As long as man lives in this cycle of birth and death, he will never be free from sickness which is also caused by unhappiness, dejection, despair, anger and jealousy. Following a spiritual discipline, practising virtuous actions, and contemplating on the impermanency of a healthy life the devotee will protect himself against further mishaps by avoiding the factors bringing on sickness.

During his life man worked hard to acquire possessions (life-partner, children, pets, wealth and power); he naturally becomes very much attached to them and experiences great suffering when he is separated from them. At the time of death, this separation becomes unavoidable. When he dies, he is left alone by his own life-partner, children, pets, wealth and so on. When death approaches, he realises that all his acquisitions, all his efforts and all his love for his family will not help him to escape from the clutches of death, and he becomes miserable. He will start becoming angry against his family surroundings because he is left alone; he will be jealous, because all his wealth will be enjoyed by others; he will be envious, because others will continue to live while he will die. His mind is filled with non-virtuous thoughts while he tries to grip life. His next life will definitely be in a lower realm.

Contemplating on the stronghold of *saṁsāra*, on the impermanence of life as also on the inevitable death the aspirant will not only free himself from the clutches of these attachments but he will also accept death with happiness and peace.

He will leave this world with virtuous thoughts which will lead him either to liberation or to a birth in a better world to complete his task of liberation.

DEVELOPING EQUANIMITY

"He who considers Me residing in all beings in a spirit of unity, becomes a *yogī* and, whatever his mode of life, lives in Me."[6]

6. *Bhagavad-Gītā*,, VI.31.

Man's attitudes towards others are unbalanced and unpredictable. When he sees a friend or someone attractive, he feels pleased; when he sees an enemy or an unattractive person, he feels displeased. In the absence of personal affection, he becomes indifferent. Moreover, he changes his likings: one who was a friend, one who had many values to share becomes all on a sudden one to dislike and one with whom there is nothing to share. This happens even to couples who loved each other ardently. These unbalanced attitudes merely develop a biased love and passion in him.

> The devotee should contemplate on the ever-changing attitudes he has developed all through his life in order to rectify them and to cultivate and develop a balanced attitude towards one and all, so that a genuine equanimity is sown and cultivated.

He should think that a friend in this life might have been an enemy in a previous life and an enemy in this life might have been a friend in a past life. He should also consider that even during this span of life there is no certainty that friends will remain so all one's life and that his love to the partner is permanent.

RECOGNISING THE KINDNESS OF ALL BEINGS

Every man received and continues to receive kindness from the world that surrounds him.

> He should constantly remember and contemplate on the immense kindness he received, the kindness both the known and the unknown have and are showing to him so that he lives a comfortable life.

First of all, his mother carried him during the entire period of pregnancy; he should think of the sacrifice she did and the suffering she underwent to give him life and space in this world. During childhood, she gave him her loving care and attention day and night, regarded him more important than herself. She probably saved his life many times and maybe she lost her own love and family life. She ensured his good education. She gave him the opportunity to practise spiritual disciplines and to attain liberation mainly through her kindness.

So too, the trees give him flowers, fruits and shade; the animals give him milk and meat; and many fellow human beings worked for his comfort. Everything he enjoys has been provided by the generosity of other beings. Many have sacrificed their lives so that man can enjoy a comfortable journey by road, train or air. Many animals suffer and are tortured only to be food for man.

Even man's spiritual education derives from the kindness of spiritual masters who transmitted their knowledge to humanity out of benevolence, despite the hardships and sacrifices they might have undergone, so that everyone in this world attains liberation without undergoing the same hardship as they did.

As a part of contemplation, man should come to realise that all beings are kind to him. This will prevent him from getting involved in arguments and criticisms which are themselves non-virtuous acts. This type of contemplation paves the way for love, compassion and peace.

CHERISHING OTHERS EQUALLY

It is man's nature to esteem himself. However, he should develop and cultivate the attitude of cherishing all living beings as he cherishes himself. Usually he regards himself as precious, and he feels that his happiness is most important. This attitude is a great obstacle to develop compassion and peace.

To cultivate respect towards other living beings a devotee should reflect and contemplate on the following: All living beings have shown him great kindness in this and in previous lives; all living beings wish to be free from suffering and wish to experience happiness and obtain peace like him; since he is not alone in this world and his self-esteem depends mainly on others, it will have no value, unless he esteems others. Moreover, others would also like to be cherished, so he should engage in cherishing others before he cherishes himself. After this contemplation, the devotee should remember the engagement he took whenever he meets someone, so that he feels affectionate and happy towards all living beings.

COMPASSION

> After having developed cherishing love for all living beings, the devotee should contemplate on the suffering of the living beings.

When he is conscious that all creatures make an effort and sacrifice their life for his well-being, contemplation on their suffering generates compassion for them. All living beings around him suffer in one way or the other. They all long to be free, but ignore the means of escape. Like the devotee, they too suffer from birth, ageing, sickness and death. Moreover, they are very often victims of man's desires.

> Repeated contemplation makes him realise that his suffering is more bearable than that of others: fellow beings and animals. This helps to develop non-violence in him which in turn promotes compassion towards all beings.

Meditation

Having developed a good heart towards all living beings, the devotee should engage in the path of realisation. To attain this, he has to climb another ladder of four steps: peaceful mind, visions of the Self, renunciation of I-ness and refuting the permanence of the body.

PEACEFUL MIND

Man can abandon his attitude of self-centredness, which is the root of all delusions; he should maintain a peaceful mind. Man's mind is like a candle flame exposed to the wind, always flickering, never showing its light constantly on any object.

All previous contemplations will help the devotee to exercise pure concentration on any object with a stable mind, free from distractions. He should make every effort to train his mind to keep this peaceful and tranquil state for a long time; unless this mental state is not maintained uninterruptedly for a long time, the winds of distraction will make the mind flicker just like a candle flame exposed to the wind.

To train the mind for peace and tranquillity the devotee should guard against laziness, forgetfulness, deception, despair and excitement. He should also protect himself against physical and mental sickness, languor, doubt, carelessness, addiction to the sense objects, erroneous perception, and failure to attain any stage of contemplation. Instead, he should care for a firm cultivation of faith, aspiration, effort, suppleness, alertness and application.

> The man of faith, zeal, and self-control attains knowledge: having attained knowledge, he immediately attains Supreme Peace.[7]

> When the object fades during his meditation, the devotee should return to contemplations to bring the object back to his mind. In the beginning, he will have to alternate between contemplation and meditation till his meditation becomes well established.

> When there is an interruption or doubt, he should reflect on the benefits of attaining a tranquil state of mind.

VISION OF THE SELF

Shutting out external sense-objects, fixing the gaze between the eyebrows, controlling the outgoing and incoming breaths that move through the nostrils, with the senses, mind and intellect restrained, and free from desire, fear and anger, the sage who has liberation as his highest goal is indeed ever free.[8]

> When there is love and compassion in the heart coming from previous contemplations and when his mind is peaceful and

---

7. *Bhagavad-Gītā*, IV.39.

8. Ibid., V.27-28.

tranquil, the devotee will be able to realise his soul free from all entanglements.

During this ultimate meditation, the devotee's phenomenal existence is projected by his mind. It will appear to be inherently existent. As long as the devotee is not concerned in these appearances, he will maintain the acquired state of peace and tranquillity and remain in it.

The devotee needs a twofold contemplation during this meditation of the Supreme Self: First, he should realise how he used to identify the way this phenomenal world appears to his mind and how he believed in the reality of this phenomenon, in the second stage he should realise the impermanency of this phenomenon and refute its existence in his mind.

When the devotee succeeds in this contemplation and continues to maintain his peaceful and tranquil mind free from all negative thoughts and feelings, feeding constantly love and compassion, he will have the vision of his Self.

At this stage of Self-awareness or the Vision of the Self, the devotee needs to contemplate intensively on the emptiness of the I-sense and the impermanency of the body, so that he will be led to the Vision of the Supreme.

RENUNCIATION OF THE I-NESS

Man continuously grasps the inherent existent I, even if he is unable to identify it clearly. The devotee should begin attaining a clear image of the I by allowing the I to manifest strongly, contemplating on such situations in which he has already exaggerated his sense of the I, such as when he was ashamed, indignant, criticised, despised or offended.

Without making any analysis or comment, he should attain a clear mental image of how naturally the I appears.

The devotee will certainly need many sessions before he will arrive at a clear image.[9] Eventually he will realise that the I appears to be very solid and real, existing independent of his body and mind. It is the I that he defends when he is criticised; and it is the I that he is proud of when he is praised.

> He should try to identify his I by observing it when he meditates to discover how it appears to his mind. Once again, he might need many sessions before he will attain a clear image. Eventually he will realise that his I is less inflated in this case, even if it appears to be inherently existent, existing without dependence on the body or the mind.
>
> He should contemplate to analyse whether the I exists as the body, as the mind, as the body and mind, or as something separate from the body and the mind in reality.
>
> The devotee should continue this contemplation until he is convinced that the I, to which he is so much attached, does not really exist.

Where an inherently existent I appeared previously, there now appears an absence of that I indeed. It is at this stage of meditation that the devotee gets renounced from the I; and this is the first step towards the Ultimate Truth.

> The devotee should remember that the object of meditation is the Ultimate Supreme Self and not the I. He should occasionally verify that his object is not deviated towards the I, in which case he should return to the contemplations to clear the mind of this delusion.

Great courage and extreme vigilance are required to avoid being caught in the trap of fearing to lose the I. When such a situation arises, the devotee should take shelter in the teachings of his spiritual master.

---

9. "When practised for a long time uninterruptedly and with devotion, it becomes firmly grounded." *Pātañjala Yoga-Sūtra*, I.14.

REFUTING THE PERMANENCE OF THE BODY

The way to realise the impermanence of the body is similar to the way the devotee is advised to renounce the I-ness.

When man thinks of "my body", he mentally forms an image of a body or parts of it, existing apart from the body he thinks to be his own. This amounts to having two bodies. Yet, in spite of accepting the mental image, he refutes it, for otherwise he would be outside his own body. If he accepts the mental image as his body, then he will refute the inherent physical body which he thought was his body. Further, the mental image of "my body" is either in parts or a collection of parts, like arms, legs, trunk and so on but not the entire body. This image will not reflect the flesh, the blood, the bones and so on.

> The devotee should also recall how his body appears to him when it is praised or insulted.
>
> The devotee should contemplate on the reasoning that the collection of the parts of the body is an aggregation of many distinct elements that function together; it may be thought of as a unit, but that unit itself has no existence independent of its constituent parts.

The devotee should repeatedly contemplate on these factors, until he realises what appeared as inherently existent body, the real nature of the body can reveal itself: its non-existence. At this stage of meditation, the devotee gets renounced from the body, and his fear of death vanishes. This is the second step towards the Ultimate Truth.

Once again, at this stage, the devotee should remember that the object of meditation is the Ultimate Supreme Self and not the body. As said above he should occasionally verify that his object is not deviated towards his body or his I, in which case he should return to the contemplations to clear the mind of these delusions.

Great courage and extreme vigilance are needed to avoid being trapped in the fear of death. When such a situation arises, the devotee should take shelter in the teachings of his spiritual master.

Vision of the Ultimate

Once the devotee is freed from these two great attachments, he should meditate on the objects of the phenomenal world applying the same principles he used for the renunciation of his body.

> Repeated meditation will make him realise that all objects including the virtuous ones are nothing but a collection of parts and not separate from the parts. In this way, he realises the impermanency of the phenomenal world.
>
> It is very important to meditate on the true nature of the phenomenal objects that cause strong delusions in man such as desire, attachment or anger.

By contemplative analysis, he realises that the object he desires, or the object that he dislikes does not exist as such, and that all attributes are simply imputed to his mind devoid of peace and Self-awareness. The more he contemplates in this way, the more steadfast his Self-awareness will be. With the permanent presence of compassion, love and equanimity the vision of the Self continues to shine unhindered, just like the smooth flow of a viscid oil, or a candle light protected from wind. The devotee will obtain the vision of Light — the Light that is motionless, constant, unchanging, existing and non-existing, because it is formless.

> When this vision is well established, the devotee will be blessed with the Superior Vision: the Vision of the Ultimate.

Dedication of Meditation

While in devotional practices — for one who believes in God or the Supreme Being — all fruits of the devotee are offered to God or to the Supreme Being, in case of meditation where devotees do not believe in God or the Supreme Being, all the fruits of meditation are dedicated to all living beings: human or animal, liked or disliked, known or unknown.

I now realise the presence of the
Almighty Lord, the universal entity
The one who is self-illuminated and
Radiant like the sun.
He is beyond all darkness;
With the realisation,
Now I fear not even death.
I proclaim, this is the path, the only path to salvation,
To the goal of life, the eternal bliss.

— *Yajurveda*, 31.18

sarvejanāḥ sukhino bhavantu,
sanmaṅgalāni bhavantu.

Let all beings be happy and peaceful;
Let auspiciousness be in all.

Glossary

abhiniveśa	Determination. Fear of death or of the non-existence of the self which is really immortal, a type of affliction (*kleśa*).
Acyuta	One of the names of Viṣṇu.
adbhuta	Wonder.
adharma	Unrighteousness, wickedness, sinful actions.
ādhyātmika	Miseries or sufferings related to the body and the mind.
ādhibhautika	Miseries or sufferings caused by living beings, relating to animate objects.
ādhidaivika	Miseries brought by Nature.
adhyāsa upāsanā	Meditation on the symbol of a superior object on which the attributes of the Reality are superimposed. Meditation on the sun is an example.
adhyātma bhāva or *ādhyātmika bhāva*	The Self-aspect of God or the Creator.
Āditya-vidyā	One of the meditations on Sun.
Advaita	Non-dualism. Associated with the philosophy of non-dualism of Śaṅkara.
Āgama	Revealed scripture, the treatises dealing with the modes of worship of God and matters relating to temples. To join, to reach, to come to (the goal).

āgama karma	Future actions.
Agni	Fire, consecrated fire.
aham brahmāsmi	"I am *Brahman*". One of the "great sayings" or *mahāvākyas*.
ahamgraha upāsanā	Technique of meditation in which the individual Self is identified with the Supreme Self.
ahaṁkāra	The ego. The process of individuation. An evolute of cosmic matter.
aindra	Name of a deadly arrow Lakṣmaṇa used to slay Indrajit, Rāvaṇa's son.
ajñāna	Ignorance, absence of knowledge.
ākāśa	Ether, space.
akṣara	Imperishable, immutable, a syllable letter.
ālambana vibhāva	Supporting cause.
Āḻvār	One who is deeply immersed in God's experience. A Vaiṣṇava saint of south India.
ambhas	Waters.
aṁśa	A part.
ānanda	Bliss, blissful, an essential attribute of *Brahman*.
ānanda rasa	Essence of pure love. Nectar from the Divine is Divine bliss.
ānandatva	Blissfulness.
anantatva	Infinity.
anapāyinī	One who never keeps away from the Lord. Attribute of Goddess Śrī.
anātman	Non-Self.
aṅgava baddha	Ritual bound (a type of meditation).
Aṅgīras	Name of a Vedic Sage.

antarātmā	The indwelling Self, the *Paramātman* who is immanent in all beings.
antaryāmin	The inner controller, the immanent Supreme Self.
aṇu	Atom.
anurāga	Affection, attachment, passion.
apāna	Breathing out, one of the five vital airs.
aparādha	Sinful, immoral acts.
artha	Meaning. Object denoted by words. Acquisition of wealth.
Aruṇaketu	Created from Prajāpati's flesh to take over the task of the creation.
arūpa dhyāna	Meditation independent of thoughts and forms.
āsana	Seat. One of the eightfold *yoga* disciplines.
asat	Non-existence.
āśraya	Locus, basis.
Aṣṭākṣara	Another name for *Nārāyaṇa-Mantra* as it contains eight letters.
aṣṭāṅga yoga	The eightfold discipline of *yoga*: *yama, niyama, āsana, prāṇāyāma, pratyāhāra, dhāraṇā, dhyāna* and *samādhi.*
aśvattha	The Indian fig tree.
asmitā	Egoism (different from *ahaṁkāra*, the second evolute of *prakṛti*). It is the individual aspect with all its concomitant troubles.
asura	Demons.
ātmā	Soul.
ātma-jñāna	Knowledge of the Soul or the Self.

ātma-sākṣātkāra	Self-realisation.
ātma-vicāra	Enquiry into the nature of the soul.
Ātman	The Self, the individual soul.
Ātmāvalokana	Direct vision of the Self, Self-realisation.
āvaraṇa śakti	Veiling power.
avatāra	Descent of God, incarnation of God.
avidyā	Ignorance, the cosmic principle that is the cause of the worldly illusion. Knowledge that is opposed to true knowledge.
avyakta	Unmanifest.
ayamātma brahma	This *Ātman* is *Brahman*, one of the four great sayings (*mahāvākya*s).
Āyurveda	The Science of Indian Medicine.
bhaga	Good fortune. Name of feminine divinities.
Bhagavān	The Supreme Being endowed with six principal attributes, Viṣṇu.
Bhagavatī	The Supreme Goddess.
bhakti	Devotion to God, loving meditation on God.
bhakti-mārga	Path of devotion.
bhakti rasa	Joy kindled from the experience of divine love.
bhakti-yoga	Observance of unceasing meditation on God as a means to liberation (*mokṣa*).
bhāva	Emotional expressions.
bhaya	Fear.
bhayānaka	Fearful.
bībhatsa	Wonder.
bhoktā	One who has the experience.
bhūta bhāva	The creative aspect of God or creator.

bhūta sūkṣma	Subtle matter.
brahma bhūta	State of *Brahman*.
brahma-jijñāsā	Enquiry into the nature of *Brahman*.
brahma nirvāṇa	Bliss of *Brahman*.
Brahma-Sūtra	Another name for *Vedānta-Sūtra*.
brahma upāsanā	Meditation on *Brahman*.
brahma-vidyā	Knowledge of the soul, also *ātma-vidyā*. Meditation on *Brahman*.
brahmāgni	The Fire of *Brahman*.
Brahman	The Absolute of philosophy, the ultimate Reality, the personal God according to Viśiṣṭādvaita.
Brahmaṇaspati	The Lord of prayer. *Brahman*.
brahmāṇḍa	The bliss of the *Brahman*. A solar system.
brahmano mukhe	For the attainment of *Brahman*.
Bṛhaspati	Priest of the Gods. *Brahman*.
bṛhatva	Having the quality of greatness.
buddhi	Intellect, intelligence. The third of the twenty-five principles of the Sāṁkhya philosophy, internal organ, one of the *antaḥkaraṇa*.
buddhi-vadha	Injuries of the intellect or defects of the intellect.
cakra	Discus, wheel.
cakṣuṣ dīkṣā	Initiation by mere look of a spiritual master. The spiritual teacher gazes at the eye of the pupil.
Caraka	Author of *Caraka Saṁhitā*, a medical treatise on Āyurveda.
cidākāśa	*Brahman* in Its aspect as limitless knowledge, unbounded intelligence. This is a familiar

	concept of the Upaniṣad. It is not meant that the physical ether is consciousness. The Pure Consciousness is like the ether (*ākāśa*), an all-pervading continuum.
cit	Sentient being, individual self. The Spirit, *Brahman*.
citta	Consciousness. Mind looked upon as the thinking principle. The intellect (*buddhi*), ego (*ahaṁkāra*) and senses (*indriya*) as one internal organ (*antaḥkaraṇa*).
citta vimukti	Liberation as spiritual freedom.
Dahara-vidyā	One of the meditations (*upāsanā*).
Dakṣa	One of the ten progenitors.
ḍamaru	The percussion instrument of Lord Śiva. It symbolises the origin of sound and space.
dāna	Giving away as charity.
dayā	Divine mercy.
deva	God, Divine.
devātmā śakti	Power of the Supreme.
Devī Durgā	Goddess Durgā.
dhāraṇā	Concentration.
dharma	A quality of a substance, an attribute, righteousness, religious duty. Merit earned by the performance of duties allotted to each person's *dharma*.
dhyāna	Contemplation, meditation. A term used in the Upaniṣads to mean *bhakti*.
Duryodhana	The eldest of the Kaurava brothers.
Dvaita	Dual. A system of Vedānta founded by Madhva.

Dvaya	A Vaiṣṇava *mantra* comprising two sentences referring to self-surrender (*śaraṇāgati*).
dveṣa	Hatred, aversion. Different forms of aversion are: Anger, ill-will which is a deep-seated inclination, resentment, jealousy and indignation.
Garuḍa	The Divine eagle. King of birds. Son of Kaśyapa, himself grandson of Brahmā.
Gauḍapāda	Expounder of early Advaita Vedānta.
guṇa	Quality, property, thread, three attributes of *prakṛti* (*sattva, rajas* and *tamas*).
guṇa dhyāna	Meditation on the divine qualities of a chosen deity.
guṇa vṛtti	Interaction of *guṇa*.
guru	Preceptor imparting spiritual knowledge.
Hari	Another name of Viṣṇu.
hasta dīkṣā	Initiation by the touch of the spiritual teacher's hand on the disciple's crown of the head.
hāsya	Comic.
Hayagrīva	God of knowledge and wisdom.
Hiraṇyagarbha	The Golden Egg. The Vedic deity entrusted with the function of cosmic creation, Brahmā, name of Viṣṇu.
Indra	A Vedic God.
Indrajit	Son of Rāvaṇa — a character in *Rāmāyaṇa*.
īṣṭa devatā	Chosen deity.
Īśvara	God, the Supreme Being as the controller of all beings.
jaḍa	Non-sentient, inert object.

jāgrata	Waking.
jāgrata avasthā	Waking state.
Janārdana	One who protects all. The Supreme Lord.
jīva	Individual self.
jīvan mukta	One purified by true knowledge while still living and therefore freed from the cycle of births.
jivātmā	The soul residing in a living body.
jīvātman	Individual self as distinct from *Paramātman*.
jñāna	Knowledge. Usually, the knowledge of the Truth, of the Supreme.
jñāna-kāṇḍa	The philosophical portion of the Vedas.
jñāna karma samuccaya	Maintaining harmony between knowledge and action.
jñāna-mārga	Path of Knowledge.
jñāna śakti	Power of Knowledge.
jñāna-yoga	Path of Knowledge.
Kailāsa	The Mount Everest, the abode of Lord Śiva.
kaivalya	The state of existence of the Self in its true form as free from bondage, a state of liberation (*mokṣa*).
Kakṣīvat	A Vedic *ṛṣi*. Son of Uśij.
kāla	Time. The Great Time, name of a Hindu Deity.
kalpa	Period of one creation .
Kāma	Passion, attachment, desire. The desire for a thing that one has not yet attained. All desires should be an act of service to God, to uplift society. The secret to keep away from sin is to perform all acts with a selfless motive.
kāmya karma	Religious observances prompted by desire for

	specific results.
Kapila	Author of *Sāṁkhya-Sūtra*. Considered as an incarnation of Mahā-Viṣṇu.
kāraṇa śarīra	The causal body. It is the cause of the two other bodies (*sūkṣma śarīra* and *sthūla śarīra*) comprising the soul and ignorance (*avidyā*).
karma	Action both mental and physical, rituals, past deeds and their results in the form of merit and sin.
karma indriya	Motor organs.
karma-kāṇḍa	The earlier part of the Vedas dealing primarily with the rituals.
karma-mārga	Path of *karma*.
karma-yoga	Observance of religious acts as a means for self-realisation, *yoga* of action.
karmāśaya	Latent impression of action which will eventually fructify.
karttā	The doer.
karuṇā	Pathetic.
kārya Brahman	"Effected *Brahman*" or Hiraṇyagarbha.
Kausalyā	Mother of Śrī Rāma.
kevala	To be alone, general, simple, unalloyed.
kleśa	Pain, anguish, distress, worry. Affliction. Psychic misconceptions which act as hindrances (*avidyā, asmitā, rāga, dveṣa* and *abhiniveśa*).
Kratu	One of the ten primeval progenitors.
kṛpā	Love and tenderness.
Krishnama-charya, T.	Authors' father and spiritual master.
kriyā-yoga	One of the practical ways to attenuate afflictions.

kriyamāna karma	*Karma* that are sown in this life.
krodha	Fury, anger.
kṣetra	A field, the body as field of action.
kṣetrajña	The knower of the body, the individual Self.
kṣīra sāgara	The milky ocean.
kṣirābdhi	The milky ocean.
kṣīrodbhava	Emanated from the ocean of milk .
kuṇḍalinī śakti	The Serpent Power.
Kuraḷ	A poetical ethical, moral and philosophical work in Tamil by Thiruvalluvar. Also called *Tirukkuraḷ*.
Lakṣmaṇa	Śrī Rāma's brother.
Lakṣmī	Name of Goddess who is the consort of Viṣṇu.
Lakṣmī Nārāyaṇa	Name of Lord Viṣṇu with his consort Lakṣmī.
liṅga	Identity mark, the symbolic representation of Śiva.
liṅga śarīra	The subtle body also called *sūkṣma śarīra* comprises the mind, the intellect, the ego, the five sense-elements of sound, touch, colour or form, taste and odour, and their sensory functions.
lobha	Greed.
madhu-vidyā	A type of meditation.
Mahābhārata	One of the two great Hindu Epics, the other being the *Rāmāyaṇa*.
mahat tattva	The great principle.
*mahāvākya*s	The great sayings of the Upaniṣads. Consciousness is *Brahman* (*prajñānam brahma*), I am *Brahman* (*aham Brahma asmi*), Thou art That

	(*tat tvam asi*) and This *ātmā* is *Brahman* (*ayam ātmā Brahma*).
manana	Logical reflection.
manas	Mind.
Mānasa Sarovara	Name of a lake in the Himālayan ranges.
mantra	Sanskrit language syllables or words signifying spiritual ideas, a Vedic hymn.
Manu	The first man. Father of the race and guide to humanity. Author of *Manu-Smṛti* (Dharmaśāstra). Dharmaśāstra is the oldest code of conduct which is followed in Hinduism.
Marīci	A Vedic sage. One of the ten primeval progenitors.
māyā	Cosmic principle which gives rise to the worldly illusion, the phenomenal character of the universe, the primordial matter (*prakṛti*).
mokṣa	Liberation of the soul from bondage, a complete and comprehensive experience of *Brahman*, attainment of *Brahman*.
mukti	Immortal freedom or Liberation.
Mukundamālā	Vaiṣṇava Devotional hymns of Kulaśekhara Āḻvār.
Naciketā	A young philosopher of the *Kaṭha Upaniṣad*.
Nammāḻvār	One of the important Vaiṣṇava saints of south India.
Nārada	A divine sage, author of *Nārada Bhakti-Sūtra*.
Nārāyaṇa	The Supreme Being who is the ground of all sentient and non-sentient entities in the universe and also immanent in them.
Nātha Muni	One of the Vaiṣṇava saints of south India.

Nāthan	The Lord.
nava rasa	The nine emotions.
neti	Negation. Not this.
nididhyāsana	Steadfast meditation.
niṣkāma karma	Actions that are free from desire for any results.
niṣkāmya bhakti	Devotion without expecting any personal gain but union with God.
niyama	Observance as an accessory to *yoga* comprising cleanliness, contentment, austerities, study of scriptures and devotion to God.
Padmanābha	Name of Viṣṇu.
Pañca Agni-Vidyā	A technique of meditation.
Pāñcarātra Āgama	The religious treatises dealing with the modes of worship of God and matters relating to temples, particularly of Viṣṇu.
Pāṇḍavas	The five cousin brothers of Kaurava.
pāpa	Sin accrued as a result of the performance of evil deeds. Unfavourable disposition of God.
pāpa karma	Sinful, wicked acts.
Para Brahma	The ultimate metaphysical Reality, the supreme personal God.
Parā jyoti	Name of Lord Nārāyaṇa.
parā tattva	Ultimate principle.
parama bhāva	The absolute aspect (*Brahman*).
paramahaṁsa	One who has controlled and subdued all his senses by meditation.
paramātmā	The Supreme Soul.
Parameśvara	The Supreme God.

Parāśara or	Father of Vyāsa, the author of *Mahābhārata*.
Parāśara Bhaṭṭa	Author of *Parāśara Smṛti*.
pariṇāma	Modification.
pāśa	Bondage.
Paśupati	Lord of individual souls. Lord Śiva.
Patañjali	Author of *Pātañjala Yoga-Sūtra*.
Peria Tirumoḻi	A Tamil composition of devotional verses.
prabandha	A composition of Tamil hymns by Āḻvārs.
prādurbhāva	Manifestation of God.
Prahlāda	The child devotee of *Śrīmad Bhāgavata Purāṇa*.
Prajāpati	A personification of Brahmā.
prajñāparādha	Misuse of intelligence.
prakṛti	Primordial matter.
pralaya	Dissolution of the universe
prāṇa	Vital breath, also applicable to *Brahman*.
prāṇāyāma	Breath control, one of the eight accessories conducive to *yoga*.
prapatti	Total self-surrender to God as the sole refuge.
prārabdha karma	*Karma* which has already begun to give result.
pratibodha	Constant self-awareness.
pratīka	Form or image.
pratīka upāsanā	Meditation on a particular form or image.
pratyāhāra	The withdrawal of senses from external objects.
prema rasa	Emotion of love.
Pulaha	One of the ten primeval progenitors.
Pulastya	One of the ten primeval progenitors.
puṇya	Merit, good deed. Merit accrued as a result of the performance of good deeds.

puṇya karma	Virtuous or meritorious deeds.
pūrṇa	Complete, Full.
puruṣa	The Supreme Soul. Absolute Awareness. The first of the twenty-five principles of Sāṁkhya philosophy. Man.
Puruṣa-Sūkta	A Vedic hymn to the Creator.
Puruṣottama	The Supreme Lord.
rāga	Attachment. Passion, that which dwells upon pleasure.
rajas	One of the three attributes of *prakṛti* (*sattva, tamas*): the quality which causes suffering, passions, etc.
rājasika	That which is of the nature of *rajas*.
Rāmāyaṇa	One of the two important Hindu epics, the other being the *Mahābhārata*.
rasa	Quality of deliciousness. That which something really is. Sentiment. Commonly translated as chyle or, blood plasma. It is in fact the nutritive element resulting from the digestive processes in the alimentary canal. This nutritive element is required for all the tissues.
raudra	Furious.
Rāvaṇa	The Demon king that Rāma killed.
Rudra Gāyatrī	Name of Vedic *mantra*.
Rudra Mahādeva	Name of Śiva.
Sadasaspati	The Lord of the assembly at a sacrifice. Personification of *Brahman*.
sadeha mukti	Liberation in this mortal existence.
sādhanā saptaka	Sevenfold practice.

saguṇa	Endowed with attribute.
Saguṇa Brahman	*Brahman* endowed with attributes.
sahasrāra	With thousand petals. One of the *cakra*s.
samādhi	Final stage of the eightfold Yoga discipline. The concentrated attention and mental realisation.
sāman	Method of chanting Veda.
saṁkalpa dīkṣā	Initiation by mere thought or will on the part of the spiritual teacher.
Saṅkarṣana	Divine manifestation of Viṣṇu. The spiritual form created through the function of True Knowledge and strength.
Sāṁkhya	Name of a Hindu philosophical system.
sampad upāsanā	Meditation on the divine qualities of a chosen deity.
saṁsāra	Life cycles of births and deaths.
saṁskāra	The subliminal impressions which lie latent in the mind.
saṁyama	Combined practice of *dhāraṇā, dhyāna* and *samādhi.*
Sanātana Dharma	Traditional name for Hinduism.
Sanatkumāra	Name of Vedic Sage.
sarūpa dhyāna	Meditation on God with form.
Sarveśvara	Lord of all.
sat	Existence, that which always exists.
sat-cit-ānanda	Existence-Consciousness-Bliss.
sattva	One of the three attributes of *prakṛti* (*sattva, rajas* and *tamas*), the quality which represents whatever is fine or light.
sāttvika	Pertaining to or characterised by *sattva guṇa.*

sāttvika prajñā	Pure intellectual illumination.
satya	True, truth.
sāyujya	The state of *mokṣa* in which the individual self enjoys equal status with *Brahman*.
śakti	The power. The active power of a deity. The Female power in Śaivism.
śama	Calmness, tranquillity, mental calmness.
Śaṁbhū	Giver of happiness and prosperity. Name of Śiva.
Śāṇḍilya	The author of *Śāṇḍilya Bhakti-Sūtra*. Śāṇḍilya, name of a sage, author of a law book, an Upaniṣad is named after him: *Śāṇḍilya Upaniṣad*.
Śāṇḍilya Bhakti-Sūtra	Śāṇḍilya's aphorisms on Devotion.
Śāṇḍilya vidyā	Name of a meditation.
Śaṅkara	Propounder of Advaita Vedānta. Name of Śiva.
śānta	Peaceful, serene.
śānta rasa	Emotional expression of peace and calmness of mind.
Śaraṇāgati	Surrendering to God as the sole refuge.
Śaraṇāgati Gadya	One of the three devotional works of Rāmānuja.
śarīra	Body, that which is necessarily supported by the Self, controlled by it and subserves its purpose.
Śāstra	Sacred texts.
Śeṣa	One who exists for the purpose of the Lord, individual Self as *śeṣa* of God, the dependent.
śīrṣa	The fontanel.

Śiva	Name of the Supreme Deity of Śaivism. Auspiciousness. Viṣṇu.
Śiva-liṅga	One of the two aspects of *Prāṇa-liṅga* (*Cara-liṅga* and Śiva-liṅga). The symbolic representation of Śiva. The Sanskrit word *liṅgam* means symbol, so Śiva-liṅga means symbol of Śiva. It is considered the foremost sacred symbol for Śaivaites and has been worshipped for ages. Śiva-liṅga represents the infinite column of flame.
Śiva-Śakti	The power of Śiva.
śravaṇa	Hearing, comprehending what is taught by the teacher.
śuddha sattva	Pure unalloyed *sattva* quality, transcendental spiritual matter.
śūnya	Void.
Skanda Purāṇa	One of the Purāṇas.
soma	Name of a plant. The most important ingredient in Vedic sacrificial offerings. Nectar. Beverage of the Gods. Name of Śiva (Vahni, Arka and Soma).
sparśa dīkṣā	Initiation by touch. The spiritual teacher touches the disciple with his right index finger certain vital points like the base of the throat, the middle of the eyebrows, the shoulders.
Śrī	The name of Goddess Lakṣmī, the consort of Viṣṇu, a prefix indicating veneration. Also called Śrī Lakṣmī.
Śrī Vaiṣṇava	Worshippers of Viṣṇu and Śrī Lakṣmī.
śṛṅgāra	Marvel and peace.

śṛṅgāra rasa	Sentiment that gives pleasure and delight.
Śriyaḥpati	Lord of Śrī (the Goddess). Name of Nārāyaṇa.
sthitaprajña	One who has acquired perfect mental tranquillity through *karma-yoga*.
sthūla śarīra	The gross body.
Stotra Ratna	Devotional hymns of Yāmunācārya.
subhage	"O! Graceful one!" A courteous way of addressing a goddess or a woman.
sudarśana	Good looking, beautiful.
sudarśana cakra	The discus of Viṣṇu.
sūkṣma śarīra	The subtle body also called *liṅga śarīra*, comprises the mind, the intellect, the ego, the five sense-elements of sound, touch, colour or form, taste and odour, and their sensory functions.
suṣupta avasthā	State of deep sleep.
suṣupti	Deep sleep.
svabhāva	Nature.
svapna	Dream.
svapna avasthā	Dream state.
svarūpa anusandhāna	Devotion as the exploration of one's inner-most being and contemplation on its significance.
svatantra	Independent.
tāṇḍava	A kind of dance. The dance of Śiva.
tantra dhyāna	A type of meditation used in Tantra.
tapas	Austerity.
taṭastha upāsanā	A kind of meditation in which symbols serve as frames of reference in understanding *Brahman*.

tālī	A symbolic representation of *liṅga* made out of the mountain palm leaves.
tamas	Quality of causing lethargy, darkness; One of the three *guṇa*s (*sattva, rajas* and *tamas*).
tāmasika	Having the characteristics of *tamas*.
tattva	Ultimate Reality. Metaphysical category.
Thirumoḻi	One of the two devotional compositions of Āṇḍāḷ, a Śrī Vaiṣṇava woman saint.
Thiruvalluvar	A great Tamil poet. Author of *Kuraḷ* or *Tirukkuraḷ*.
trimūrti	Three-faced: Brahmā, Viṣṇu and Īśvara.
turīya	The fourth.
turīya avasthā	The fourth state, the transcendental state.
Tyāgarāja	A saint composer of Karnatic Music. One of the most important music composers of India.
udgīta	The sacred syllable *oṁ*.
Upaniṣad	The philosophical portion of the Veda.
upāsanā	Meditation. A term used in the Upaniṣads to mean *bhakti*.
Uśij	A female servant of queen of Kaliṅga. Mother of Kakṣīvat.
Vaiṣṇava	A devotee of Viṣṇu.
vaiśvānarāgni	The digestive fire.
Varuṇa	Vedic God of rain.
vāsanā	Subliminal imprint of an experience but not producing direct results.
Vasiṣṭha	A great Vedic Sage.
Vāsudeva	The Supreme Being as described in the Pāñca-rātra system. Viṣṇu.

vātsalya	Tender affection, an attribute of God.
Vāyu	Vedic God of Air. The Air element.
vedanā	Knowledge of *Brahman*. Meditation on *Brahman* according to Rāmānuja.
Vedānta	End of Veda. A system of Hindu philosophy. A term used in the Upaniṣads to mean devotion.
Vibhu	All-pervasive. The Supreme God.
vikṛti	An evolute of *prakṛti* which does not serve as a cause of another evolute.
vikṣepa śakti	Transforming power.
viparyāya	The five modes of ignorance. Ignorance (*tamas*), delusion (*moha*), great delusion (*mahā-moha*), blindness (*tāmiśra*) and extreme blindness (*andhatāmiśra*).
vīra	Heroism.
visarga bhāva	The creation.
viśiṣṭa	That which is qualified, a characterised entity.
Viśiṣṭādvaita	Non-dualism in the sense of organic unity, a system of Vedānta expounded by Rāmānuja.
Viṣṇu	The Supreme Deity of Vaiṣṇavism, the all-pervasive God.
viveka	Discriminatory knowledge.
Viveka-Cūḍāmaṇi	A philosophical work by Śaṅkara.
Vyāsa	Compiler of Veda. Author of another great epic, *Mahābhārata*.
yajña	Offering of sacrifice in the consecrated fire. A ritual prescribed by sacred texts. Vedic ritual of offering libations into the sacrificial fire.
Yājñavalkya	A Vedic Seer.

Yama	The Vedic God of Death. Five moral disciplines.
Yamunā	Name of a river in north India.
Yāmuna Ācārya	Preceptor of Rāmānuja.
Yogīśvara	Attribute of Śiva.
Yudhiṣṭhira	The eldest of the Pāṇḍavas.

Bibliography

Adidevananda, Svami (tr.), *Yatīndramatadīpika of Śrīnivāsadāsa*, Chennai: Sri Ramakrishna Math.

Agarwal, Madan Mohan, *Six Systems of Hindu Philosophy*, Delhi: Chaukhamba Sanskrit Pratishthan.

Aiyangar, S.K., *History of Vaishnavism in South India*, Oxford University Press.

Anantha Rangacharya, N.S. (tr.), *Principal Upanishads* (2 vols.), Text, English Translation and Brief notes according to Sri Ranga Ramanujamuni, Bangalore: N.S. Anantha Rangacharya.

Apte, Vaman Shivram, *The Practical Sanskrit-English Dictionary*, Delhi: Motilal Banarsidass.

Aranya, Hariharananda, Rendered into English by P.N. Mukerji, *Yoga Philosophy of Patanjali*, University of Calcutta.

Atreya, B.L. (tr. by Samvid), *The Vision and the Way of Vasistha*, Madras: Indian Heritage Trust.

Ayyangar, Narasimha, *Vedāntasāra of Bhagavad Rāmānuja* (tr.), The Adyar Library and Research Centre.

Bhandarkar, R.G., *Vaiṣṇavism, Śaivism and Minor Religious Systems*, Varanasi: Indological Book House.

Bhat, G.P. (tr.), *Skanda Purāṇa*, Delhi: Motilal Banarsidass.

Bhattacharya, Haridas (ed.), *The Cultural Heritage of India* (6 vols.), Calcutta: The Ramakrishna Mission.

Bhishagrathna, K.K. (tr.), *Suśruta Saṁhitā*, Text with translation (3 vols), Varanasi: Chowkhamba Sanskrit Series Office.

Bhumanand Sarasvati, Svami, *Anthology of Vedic Hymns*, Calcutta: Savitri Devi Bagaria Trust.

Caland, W. (tr.), *Vaikhānasasmārtasūtram*, Delhi: Ramanand Vidya Bhawan.

Chand, Devi, *The Yajurveda*, Sanskrit Text with English Translation, Delhi: Munshiram Manoharlal.

Chari, S.M.S., *Philosophy and Theistic Mysticism of the Āḻvārs*, Delhi: Motilal Banarsidass.

Chennakesavan, Sarasvati, *Concept of Mind in Hindu Philosophy*, Delhi: Motilal Banarsidass.

Coburn, T.B., *Devī Māhātmya: The Crystallization of the Goddess Tradition*, Delhi: Motilal Banarsidass.

Comans, Michael, *The Method of Early Advaita Vedānta*, Delhi: Motilal Banarsidass.

Cowel, E.B. and A.E. Gough (tr.), *The Sarva-Darśana Saṁgraha of Madhvācārya*, Delhi: Motilal Banarsidass.

Cowell, E.B., The *Kauṣītaki-Brāhmaṇa-Upaniṣad*, Varanasi: Chowkhamba Publication.

Dasgupta, S.N., *Hindu Mysticism*, Delhi: Motilal Banarsidass.

Dasgupta, Surendranath, *A History of Hindu Philosophy* (5 vols.), Delhi: Motilal Banarsidass.

De Nicolas Antonio T., *Meditations through the Ṛgveda*, Shambhala Boulder and London.

Deshpande, N.A. (tr.), *Padma Purāṇa*, Delhi: Motilal Banarsidass.

Deussen, Paul V.M. Bedekar, G.B. Palsule (tr.), *Sixty Upaniṣads of the Veda* (2 vols.), Delhi: Motilal Banarsidass.

Dhananjayan, V.P., *A Dancer on Dance*, Chennai: Bharata Kalanjali.

Dutt, Manmath Nath (tr.), *The Dharmashastra, Hindu Religious Codes*, Delhi: Cosmo Publications.

Gambhīrānanda, Swāmī, *Eight Upaniṣads with the Commentary of Śaṅkarācārya* (tr.) (2 vols.), Kolkata: Advaita Ashrama.

———, (tr.), *Brahma-Sūtra Bhāṣya of Śaṅkarācārya*, Calcutta: Advaita Ashram.

Gandhi, M.K., *Songs From Prison*, Macmillan.

Ganguli, Kisari Mohan (tr.), *The Mahābhārata* (12 vols.), Delhi: Munshiram Manoharlal.

Goswami, C.L., *Śrīmad Bhāgavata Mahāpurāṇa* with Sanskrit Text and English Translation, Gorakhpur: Motilal Jalan.

Griffith, Ralph T.H., *The Texts of the White Yajurveda or Vājasaneyī Saṁhitā*, Delhi: Munshiram Manoharlal.

———, (tr.), *The Hymns of the Ṛgveda*, Delhi: Motilal Banarsidass.

———, *Sāmaveda Saṁhitā*, Delhi: Motilal Banarsidass.

Harshananda, Swami, *Śāṇḍilya Bhakti-Sūtra*, Mysore: Prasaranga, University of Mysore.

Hume, R.E. (tr.), *The Thirteen Principal Upanishads*, Madras: Oxford University Press.

Sinha, Jadunath, *Hindu Philosophy by Jadunath Sinha* (3 vols.), Delhi: Motilal Banarsidass.

Jagannatha Pandita, *Rasa Gandhāra*, Asiatic Society.

Kale, Moreshwar Ramachandra, *Kumārasambhava by Kālidāsa*, Motilal Banarsidass.

Keith, A.B., *The Religion and Philosophy of the Veda and Upaniṣads* (2 vols.), Delhi: Motilal Banarsidass.

Krishna Warrier, A.G. (tr.), *The Sāmānya Vedānta Upaniṣads*, Madras: The Adyar Library and Research Centre.

Lester, Robert C., *Rāmānuja on the Yoga*, Madras: The Adyar Library and Research Centre.

Macdonnel, A.A. and A.B. Keith, *Vedic Index of Names and Subjects* (2 vols.), Delhi: Motilal Banarsidass.

Mādhavānanda, Swāmī, The *Bṛhadāraṇyaka Upaniṣad* with the commentary of Śaṅkarācārya (tr.), Calcutta: Advaita Ashram.

Mahadeva Sastry, Alladi (tr.), *The Bhagavad Gītā* with the Commentary of Ādi Śrī Saṅkarācārya, Madras: Samata Books.

———, (tr.), The Taittirīya *Upaniṣad* with the Commentaries of Śrī Śaṅkarācārya, Śrī Sureśvarācārya, Śrī Vidyāraṇya, Madras: Samata Books.

Manmatha Nath Dutt (tr.), *Viṣṇu Purāṇa: Prose English Translation*, Varanasi: Chowkhamba Publication.

Max Müller, *Vedānta-Sūtras with Rāmānuja's Commentary*, Delhi: Motilal Banarsidass.

Meppathur Narayana Bhattatiri, tr. Swami Tapasyananda, *Nārāyaṇīyam*, Chennai: Sri Ramakrishna Matha.

Narasimhachary, M., *Contribution of Yāmunācārya to Viśiṣṭādvaita*, Hyderabad: Sri Jayalakshmi Publications.

Narayanaswami Aiyar, K., *Thirty Minor Upaniṣads* (Sanskrit text with English translation), Delhi: Parimal Publications.

———, (tr.), *Laghu-Yoga-Vāsiṣṭha*, The Adyar Library and Research Centre.

Nicholson, R.R., *A Literary History of the Arabs*, Cambridge University Press.

Nikhilananda, Swami, *Vedāntasāra of Sadānanda Yogīndra* (Sanskrit text and translation), Calcutta: Advaita Ashram.

O'Flaherty, W.D., *The Origins of Evil in Hindu Mythology*, Delhi: Motilal Banarsidass.

———, *Karma and Rebirth in Classical Indian Traditions*, Delhi: Motilal Banarsidass.

Olivelle, Patrick (tr.), *Dharmasūtras* (The Law Codes of Āpastamba, Gautama, Baudhāyana, and Vasiṣṭha), Delhi: Motilal Banarsidass.

Pandurangi, K.T., *Aitareyopaniṣad*, with English Translation and Notes according to Śrī Madhvācārya's Bhāṣya, Śrīman Madhva Siddhantonnahni Sabha, Chirtanur (near Tirupati).

———, *Bṛhadāraṇyakopaniṣad* with English Translation and Notes according to Śrī Madhvācārya's Bhāṣya, Śrīman Madhva Siddhantonnahni Sabha, Chirtanur (near Tirupati).

Panikkar, Raimundo, *The Vedic Experience, Mantramanjarī: An Anthology of the Vedas for Modern Man and Contemporary Celebration*, Delhi: Motilal Banarsidass.

Prabhañjanācārya, V. (Kannada Translation), *Harikathāmṛtasāra of Śrī Jangannātha Dāsa*, Bangalore: Aitareya Prakashana Vyasanakere.

Prabhavananda, Swami, *Nārada's Way of Divine Love (Nārada Bhakti-Sūtras)*, Chennai: Sri Ramakrishna Matha.

Radhakrishnan, S., *Bhagavad-Gītā*, Delhi: Motilal Banarsidass.

———, *Hindu Philosophy* (2 vols.), Madras: Oxford University Press.

Ragavachar, S.S. (tr.), *Vedārtha-Saṁgraha of Śrī Rāmānujācārya*, Mysore: Sri Ramakrishna Ashram.

Raghunathan, N. (tr.), *Śrīmad Bhāgavatam* (2 vols.), Madras: Vighneswara Publishing House.

Rajagopalachari, C. (tr. and commentary), *Bhaja Govindam of Śrī Saṅkara*, Bombay: Bharatiya Vidya Bhavan.

———, (tr.), *Kuraḷ: The Great Book of Thiruvalluvar*, Bombay: Bhavan's Book University.

Ramakrishna Bhat, M. (tr.), *Varāhamihira's Bṛhat Saṁhitā*, Delhi. Motilal Banarsidass.

Ramanathan, A.A. (tr.), *The Saṁnyāsa Upaniṣads*, Madras: The Adyar Library and Research Centre.

Ramanujachari, C., *Spiritual Heritage of Tyāgarāja*, Chennai: Sri Ramakrishna Math.

Rangacharya, M. and M.B. Varadaraja Iyengar, (tr.), *The Vedānta Sūtra with Śrībhāṣya of Rāmānuja* (3 vols.), Delhi: Munshiram Manoharlal.

Rangacharya, M., *The Philosophy of Conduct: Lectures on the Bhagavadgītā* (3 vols.), Delhi: Munshiram Manoharlal.

Rukmini, R.S., *Yogasūtrabhāṣyavivaraṇa of Śaṅkara*, Vivaraṇa Text with English translation and critical notes along with text and English translation of *Pātanjala Yoga-Sūtras* and *Vyāsabhāṣya* (2 vols.), Delhi: Munshiram Manoharlal.

———, *Yogavārttika of Vijñānabhikṣu*, Text with English Translation and critical notes along with the text and English translation of *Pātanjala Yoga-Sūtras* and *Vyāsabhāṣya* (4 vols.), Delhi: Munshiram Manoharlal.

Sampatkumaran, M.R. (tr.), *The Gītābhāṣya of Rāmānuja*, Bombay: Ananthacharya Indological Research Institute.

Sanjukta Gupta, *Laksmi Tantra: A Pāñcarātra Text*, Delhi: Motilal Banarsidass.

Sarasvati, Svami Satya Prakash (tr.), *Atharvaveda Saṁhitā* (3 vols.), Delhi: Veda Pratishthana.

Sarvananda, Swami, *Īśavāsyopaniṣad*, Including the Original Verses, Construed

Text with a Literal Word by Word Translation, Madras: Sri Ramakrishna Math.

Sharma, B.N.K., *Madhva's Teachings in His Own Words*, Bombay: Bharatiya Vidya Bhavan.

Sharma, P.V., *Caraka Saṁhitā*, Text with translation (3 vols.), Varanasi: Chaukhambha Oritentalia.

Shastri, Hari Prasad (tr.), *The Rāmāyaṇa of Vālmīki* (3 vols.), London: Shanti Sadan.

Shastri, J.L. (tr.), *Liṅga Purāṇa*, Delhi: Motilal Banarsidass.

———, *Śiva Purāṇa*, Delhi: Motilal Banarsidass.

Shinga Bhupala, *Rasārṇava Sudhākara*, Trivandrum Sanskrit Series.

Shingy, R.K. and Prem Lata Sharma, *Saṅgītaratnākara of Śārṅgadeva* (2 vols.) (Sanskrit Text and English Translation with comments and notes), Delhi: Munshiram Manoharlal.

Shrama, B.N.K., *Philosophy of Śrī Madhvācārya*, Delhi: Motilal Banarsidass.

Sinha, Jadunath, *The Indian Psychology* (3 vols.), Calcutta: Sinha Publishing House.

Srikantha Murthi, K.R., *Vāgbhata's Aṣṭāṅga Hṛdayam*, Text with English translations, notes (3 vols.), Varanasi: Krishnadas Academy.

Srila Visvanatha Cakravarti Thakura, *Rasāmṛta Sindhu*, ISKCON.

Srinivasa Gopalacharya (compiled and ed.), *Śabdārtha Kaustubha* (Sanskrit-Kannada Dictionary) (6 vols.).

Srinivasa Iyengar, *Haṭha-Yoga-Pradīpikā of Svātmārāma Svāmin* (Text in Devanāgarī and English Translation), Madras: Theosophical Publishing House.

Srinivasachari, S.M., *Advaita and Viśiṣṭādvaita*, Delhi: Motilal Banarsidass.

———, *Fundamentals of Viśiṣṭādvaita Vedānta Based on Vedānta Desika's Tattva Mukta Kalāpa*, Delhi: Motilal Banarsidass.

———, *Vaiṣṇavism: Its Philosophy, Theology And Religious Discipline*, Delhi: Motilal Banarsidass.

Suryanarayana Sastri, S.S. (tr.), *The Sāṁkhyakārikā of Īśvara Kṛṣna*, Chennai: University of Madras.

———, *Vedāntaparibhāṣā*, The Adyar Library and Research Centre.

Suzuki, D.T., *Studies in the Lankavatara Sutra*, London: Routledge and Kegan Paul Ltd.

Swāhānanda, Swami, The *Chāndogya Upaniṣad*, containing the original text with word-by-word meaning, notes, Madras: Sri Ramakrishna Math.

Tagare, G.V. (tr.), *Kūrma Purāṇa*, Delhi: Motilal Banarsidass.

——— (tr.), *Śrīmad Bhāgavata Purāṇa*, Delhi: Motilal Banarsidass.

——— (tr.), *Vāyu Purāna*, Delhi: Motilal Banarsidass.

Taimini, I.K., *The Science of Yoga*, Madras: The Theosophical Publishing House.

Tapasyananda, Swami (tr.), *Śrīmad Bhāgavata* (4 vols.), Madras: Sri Ramakrishna Math.

———, *Svetāśvatara Upaniṣad*, Madras: Sri Ramakrishna Math.

———, *Nārada Bhakti-Sūtra*, Madras: Sri Ramakrishna Math.

Vasu, Rai Bahadur Srisa Chandra, *The Śiva Saṁhitā* (tr.), Delhi: Oriental Books Reprint Corporation.

Vedānta Deśika *Tamil Prabandham*, Āhāra Niyamam.

Venkitasubramania Iyer, S. (tr.), *Varāha Purāṇa*, Delhi: Motilal Banarsidass.

Vidyalankar, Pandit Satyakam, *The Holy Vedas*, Delhi: Clarion Book.

Vijayananda, Swami (tr.), *Nārada Pāñcarātram*, Delhi: Parimal Publications.

Vimalananda, Swami, *Mahā Nārāyaṇa Upaniṣad*, Introduction, Translation, Interpretation, Madras: Sri Ramakrishna Math.

Vireswarananda, Swami and Swami Adidevananda, *Brahma-Sūtras Śrī-Bhāṣya with Text and English Rendering of the Sūtras, Comments*, Calcutta: Advaita Ashram.

Vivekananda, Swami, *Religion of Love*, Sri Ramakrishna Math .

Some of the websites consulted

http://dir.yahoo.com/Society_and_Culture/Religion_and_Spirituality/Faiths_and_Practices/Hinduism/Vaishnavism/

http://groups.yahoo.com/group/srirangasri/

http://members.aol.com/ukumbar/vsny/

http://saiva-siddhanta.ask.dyndns.dk/

http://saranagati.blogspot.com/

http://web.tiscali.it/gopala/Shad_darshana/

http://www.acharya.org

http://www.*Advaita*-vedanta.org/

http://www.*Dvaita*.org/

http://www.gurudeva.org

http://www.ibiblio.org

http://www.ibiblio.org/sripedia/ramanuja

http://www.kamat.com/indica/

http://www.koausa.org/Shaivism

http://www.parakalamatham.org

http://www.ramanuja.org

http://www.ramanujamission.org/

http://www.sacred-texts.com/hin/sbe08/

http://www.salagram.net

http://www.shaivam.org/virashaivam/index.html

http://www.shaivam.org/virashaivam/index.html

http://www.shastras.com/108upanishads

http://www.sivanandadlshq.org

http://www.srivaishnava.org/sgati/

http://www.hinduwebsite.com/

Index